ROYAL HISTORICAL SOCIETY
GUIDES AND HANDBOOKS

No. 5

GUIDE TO THE NATIONAL AND PROVINCIAL
DIRECTORIES OF ENGLAND AND WALES, EX-
CLUDING LONDON, PUBLISHED BEFORE 1856

GUIDE TO THE NATIONAL AND PROVINCIAL DIRECTORIES OF ENGLAND AND WALES, EXCLUDING LONDON, PUBLISHED BEFORE 1856

BY

JANE E. NORTON

LONDON

OFFICES OF THE ROYAL HISTORICAL SOCIETY

First published 1950
Reprinted with correction 1984

Printed in Great Britain by St Edmundsbury Press, Bury St Edmunds, Suffolk

PREFACE

A S the work on this book progressed it became clear that it would not be possible to include all the directories of all the places in the British Isles, and that some limits, both of area and of time, must be set. It was never intended to trespass on the ground covered by Mr C. W. F. Goss's *The London Directories, 1677–1855*, and it seemed that the few directories of separate London districts and suburbs not included in that book would go better, with others of a later date, in a different work, supplementary to Goss. Hence directories of places within the bounds of the present County of London have been excluded. The often very interesting Irish and Scottish directories also fall into a separate section, especially as the considerations which make the 1850's a good terminal date for the English directories do not apply in the same way to them. They too would make a convenient volume by themselves. The author's reasons for not proceeding later than the middle of the nineteenth century are given below on p. 15. The actual final date, 1855, was chosen as it is the last year covered by Mr Goss's list of London directories.

The directories included are limited to those compiled on a geographical basis, excluding directories of particular trades or professions. The entries are not confined to books which are directories in the strictest sense, but include a number of histories and guide books to which directories have been added, often by the publisher of the work and not by the author. Many guide books, however, especially those of watering-places, have short lists of doctors or lodging houses, and histories often contain the names of officials and other local intelligence. As a rule no book has been included here unless it has a substantial list of inhabitants. Moreover, in describing such books, attention has been confined mainly to their interest as directories, and statements about the reprinting or re-issuing of their contents relate, as a rule, to the directory section only. In fact, as the title implies, this is not a complete bibliography, but a guide to directories in the sense in which they are discussed in the introductory essay. As, within the field thus defined, the number of items amounts to 875, of many of which a number of copies have been examined, the author hopes to be excused for not offering a more ambitious undertaking.

The author would like specially to recommend pp. 27–28 to the attention of anyone making use of the Catalogue of Directories. It is hoped that the explanations there given will steer the reader successfully through the inevitable overlapping of certain categories in the general classification of the entries. It may also be particularly mentioned here that the outlying islands, the Channel Islands, and the Isles of Man and Wight, which could not be included under a county heading, have been grouped together under the heading ' Islands '. The author would also like to beg the indulgence of those concerned for having included the town of Berwick-on-Tweed under Northumberland.

This work was first planned when travelling about the country was both easier and cheaper than now, but, in spite of present difficulties, the author has visited many of the large public libraries and, in the end, all but a very few of the items described have been personally handled and examined. Nevertheless the work could never have been properly done without the generous help of librarians and other library officials throughout the country, with whom the author's correspondence has been so extensive that it seems only possible here to thank them compendiously as a body for their detailed replies to many inquiries, as well as for their kind welcome on personal visits and for their willingness to send volumes to London when a visit was not possible. Special thanks are due to the City of London Guildhall Library for making application for and accepting the deposit of such volumes on the author's behalf.

For permission to examine certain private or semi-private collections, the author has also to thank the Athenaeum, Liverpool, the Society of Genealogists, the Institute of Historical Research, the Chetham Library, the William Salt Library, the Rev. Charles Hutchinson and Mr A. R. Wagner, Richmond Herald. Much help has also been received from secretaries of learned societies and from private individuals, who have both written to supply information and have answered inquiries. They are again too numerous to name individually, but their assistance is most gratefully acknowledged.

It remains to apologise for the errors and omissions which in dealing with so much detail must certainly, though not excusably, have occurred, and to hope that the book may be to some extent interesting as well as useful. The author is very sensible of the responsibility which rests on anyone whose work has the privilege of being published by the Royal Historical Society.

J. E. N.

CONTENTS

INTRODUCTION

I. Origin and Development of Directories

DIRECTORIES are, by nature and origin, instruments of commerce. Like roads, railways and the telegraph, they are a means of communication, essential to extensive trade relations and a wide market and they were compiled to meet the commercial need of easy and rapid intercourse between buyer and seller. The titles of the earliest English directories, such as *The Tradesmen's True Guide, The Merchants' and Tradesmen's Useful Companion, The Merchants' Miscellany*, as well as repeated references in prefaces to the usefulness of the book to business men, show the purpose which such compilations were intended to fulfil.

The essential part of a directory is, therefore, the list or lists of names, occupations and addresses. A good deal more is generally included, such as historical information, names of officials and institutions, lists of conveyances and so on but data of this kind can be found in guide books, local histories or almanacs, which are not directories, though directories are often appended to them. On the other hand, lists of names and addresses have been compiled for a number of reasons ; there are poll books and rate books and lists of gentlemen's seats. The distinguishing characteristic of the directory is that its purpose is commercial.

The organised provision of commercial information can be traced back at least as early as the registry offices kept by nuns in the middle ages to help country girls looking for places as domestic servants, and other similar offices for many kinds of goods and services. The origin of commercial advertising in many forms, including that of the directory, can be directly connected with registry offices. They were mainly concerned with bringing together the seller and the ultimate consumer, as was also most early newspaper advertising. The first known continental directory *Les Adresses de la Ville de Paris* (1691), was a development from periodical advertisement lists and relates to retail trade. The first London directory, however, which appeared slightly earlier (1677), is concerned solely with wholesale trade and seems to have originated quite differently, arising spontaneously from the conditions of commerce in London and the fertile mind of its author, Samuel Lee.

We have thus two origins for the directory, the one, a long history of evolution from registry offices and advertisement papers, the other, an original conception arising from the needs of London's great wholesale market. Both date from the end of the seventeenth century. Subsequent development was slow at first, but with the expansion of industry and commerce in the eighteenth century the usefulness of directories became generally recognised, and they were produced in rapidly increasing numbers from about 1760. With the beginning of the nineteenth century, the development of postal services gave rise to a third type, the Post Office directory, produced by post office officials, the main object of which was to ensure the correct delivery of letters. We also find a miscellaneous group, owing its existence to a variety of motives ranging from the cultural to the purely fanciful, and including, among others, the pictorial directories of Tallis and Bisset, the police directories of Newcastle-under-Lyme and the large Histories, Directories and Topographies of the middle nineteenth century. Gradually the various kinds tended to coalesce, the eccentricities to be weeded out. The general type, the list or lists of all the inhabitants of a particular locality, emerged and became the standard.

The history of the development of the directory from registry offices comes mainly from France and is, as might be expected, a lively and entertaining affair. Registry offices, as has been said, were known in the middle ages. They were often corrupt and venal and their services suspect. Montaigne attributed to his father the idea of reformed offices where really impartial information on where to buy and sell things could be obtained. Barthélémy de Laffemas, tailor to Henri IV, developed a scheme for public offices where merchants from all over the world could get information, and his ideas were described in a book by his son, published in 1606. In 1629, Théophraste de Renaudot, the king's doctor, opened one or more 'Bureaux de Rencontre', where advice and addresses could be obtained 'de toutes les necessités et commoditez de la vie humaine'. The idea was very popular and a ballet was actually compiled on the theme, called 'Ballet du Bureau de Rencontre'. He also published a sort of 'Exchange and Mart', with lists of wants and offers, including the offer for sale of a young dromedary at a reasonable price. Similar periodicals followed, and short 'Listes d'Avis', published periodically, became common in France.[1]

It was only a step from these lists of short advertisements to making a book of the more permanent ones and in 1691 *Les Adresses de la Ville de Paris* was published. It was compiled by 'Abraham de Pradel, astrologue lyonnois', a pseudonym for Nicholas Blégny, surgeon-apothecary and a notorious quack, who had already published several pseudo-medical works and a medical journal, which was suppressed but continued surreptitiously at Amsterdam as *Le Mercure Savant*. It is said to have inspired Bayle's *Nouvelles de la République des Lettres*.

The second edition of this directory was published in 1692, under the title of *Livre Commode des Adresses de Paris*. The directory is a classified one and Blégny embellished his list with comments and freely interspersed puffs of his own books and medical wares. It includes sections on antique shops, furs, stuffs and amusements which give a remarkable picture of Paris life at the time, and details of the best places to get delicacies which make one's mouth water. Thus Le Sieur Olivet makes a speciality of Boudin blanc and Pieds

[1] *Le Livre Commode des Adresses de Paris pour 1692* (reprinted in 2 vols., ed. E. Fournier, Paris, 1878), Introduction.

à la Ste Ménéhould and Messieurs de la Rose and du Bois ' sont renommez pour les petites perruques servant aux ecclésiastiques '. The first edition only contained commercial addresses but in the second were the names of ministers, rich collectors and bibliophiles. The freedom of the author's comments gave offence and the book was suppressed.

In England, two gentlemen, Sir Arthur Gorges and Sir Walter Cope, who were probably also inspired by Montaigne, were granted a patent in 1611 for a Register for General Commerce.[1] In 1648 Samuel Hartlib applied unsuccessfully for an ordinance to establish an Office of Adresse for Accommodations. Other projects followed, and in 1650 Marchmont Needham issued a prospectus of an Office of Public Advice. He also published an advertisement paper, *The Publick Advertiser*, ' weekly communicating unto the whole nation, the several occasions of all persons that are in any way concerned in matter of Buying & Selling or in any kind of employment or dealings whatsoever '. The first number contains advertisements of various professions, lodgings and shipping. The trade entries are few. The City Mercuries, advertisement papers, were distributed free from 1667.[2]

In 1693, John Houghton began the publication of a periodical called *A Collection for Improvement of Husbandry and Trade*. This paper appeared weekly and contained an essay on some agricultural subject and two pages of advertisements. Nos. 97–172, 8 June 1694–15 November 1695, contain an embryo directory of certain classes of persons from all over the country. The first of these lists is headed

I know by experience that often patients in city and country are at a loss what Physician to choose . . . and, after resolution, where to find them ; therefore I'll continue this awhile and afterwards if desired for a small charge ; and do the like for Chyrurgeons, Attorneys, Brokers, Stage-coaches, Carriers . . . or any other that shall desire it. . . . I am sure after tryal t'will be found useful : for all people of accidental business do love it should be known where to find them and others to have choice and Persons they want.

There follows a list of 125 London doctors, with, for most of them, the street or district in which they could be found, and also a list of carriers. This was followed in later numbers by lists of counsellors and attorneys, woodmongers, schools and brokers, coaches and carriers. These four lists were repeated in rotation. Later a list of gardeners was added and a classified list of artists and some few other names in miscellaneous occupations. In No. 112, the schools include some in places as far afield as Winchester and York. After No. 129 the lists were only published sporadically and in spite of notices that all the attorneys and all the schools in England might be inserted if they pleased, the number of entries did not increase and no new classes were introduced. After No. 182 the lists ceased to appear.

Houghton's enterprise marks the branching off of the directory from other forms of advertising. His lists of names, occupations

[1] M. D. George, ' Early History of Registry Offices ' (*Economic History*, i, 1927, p. 577).
[2] J. B. Williams, *History of English Journalism* (1908), chap. ix.

and addresses, appearing among more detailed advertisements, are a first step towards reducing the bulk sufficiently to make a practicable book. The Paris directory is much too long and detailed for convenient consultation. Houghton's lists also mark off the permanent advertisement, such as those of schools and businesses, from temporary notices of houses to let, losses, offers of employment, etc., suitable for publication in a daily or weekly newspaper. His admirably conceived idea was, however, before its time. The next step, the publication of such permanent notices in book form, was not taken for many years.

The true origin of the English directory is to be found in a publication arising from different circumstances and quite disconnected from the developments described above. In 1677 there appeared *A Collection of the Names of the Merchants Living In and About the City of London. Printed for Samuel Lee.* This is simply a list of names and addresses of wholesale merchants and traders, with ' all the goldsmiths who keep running cashes ', and is dedicated to the merchants and traders of London, for whose use, together with that of their foreign correspondents, it was primarily intended. The object was purely commercial and the book is confined to the wholesale trade. The author, Samuel Lee, gives no indication that he was inspired by any example and he put ' this small Embrio ' forward with some diffidence. It may, he says, ' at the first view, seem to several persons a ridiculous and preposterous attempt '.

Private lists of correspondents and agents in distant or foreign centres of trade must have been kept by merchants in all countries from the days of the Fuggers or earlier, but no list of this kind seems to have been printed, or at any rate to have survived, of an earlier date than this.[1] London in 1677 was already the centre of an organised network of commerce. In the early part of the eighteenth century, it was thronged with foreign merchants and agents,[2] and the reason for the early appearance there of directories would seem to have been mainly their usefulness to those concerned in the import and export trades. Lee's list contains some 1,950 names and its convenience for strangers seeking business connections in the city seems obvious, though, whether because its author's diffidence was well-founded or because no copies have survived, it seems to have had no successor until 1734. From that year, however, directories of London appeared annually, all modelled on Lee's until 1763, when Mortimer's *Universal Director*, which presents some new features, was published.[3]

The needs of external trade were similarly connected with the first directory for a place in the British Isles outside London. Dublin was, by 1750, the centre of an export trade in linen and was

[1] Printed lists of tradesmen were published in Amsterdam in the eighteenth and possibly in the seventeenth centuries, but the earliest of which details have been secured is dated 1771. Other lists of inhabitants were printed there for various purposes, among them the curious lists issued by the undertakers, for their clients to mark the names of those they wished invited to funerals. The earliest of these known to the author is for 1757–8.

[2] *The Spectator*, No. 69 for 19 May 1710/11.

[3] C. W. F. Goss, *The London Directories, 1677–1855* (1932), pp. 37 ff.

regularly visited by buyers from London, Bristol and Chester.[1]
The first Dublin directory was published in 1751. Among the first
English provincial towns to have directories were Liverpool, Manchester and Bristol, which all owed their expansion at this time
mainly to the growth of foreign commerce.[2] Manchester had
foreign merchants resident there when its first directory was compiled by Mrs Raffald in 1772.[3] The author was in touch with
foreigners, for she spoke French, her cooking was French and she
owned successively, two hotels, much frequented by foreign buyers
and travellers.[4]

Another factor was, however, at work which influenced the production of directories and which connects them with Houghton
and the line of development which led to the Paris directory of
1691. From the middle of the seventeenth century, the number of
small offices providing commercial information and acting as employment agencies multiplied rapidly. In 1752 Thomas Juxon of
Birmingham, who kept an office of this kind and who had a large
number of names on his books of those who wished to borrow or
lend money, buy land or houses, or employ apprentices or domestic
servants, designed a catalogue of ' the principal inhabitants of the
town, their trades, and where they live, which may be serviceable
to strangers'.[5] It is not known whether his list was ever printed,
but James Sketchley, who also kept a registry office and had
similarly a large number of names at his disposal for various purposes, compiled and published a Birmingham directory, the first
English provincial directory, in 1763. Unfortunately no copy is
known either of his first or of his second directory, but the third
edition, published in 1767, is a classified directory of professions
and trades, modelled on Mortimer's *Universal Director*, with which
Sketchley seems to have been familiar. He hoped his directories
would be bought by strangers to Birmingham, for he advertised his
first edition in a London newspaper.[6] Mrs Raffald also kept a
registry office, and when Joseph Reed's play, *The Register Office*,
was performed in Manchester about 1772, she wrote to the press
to defend the character of her office, which was not at all like the
one depicted in the play.[7] Charles Wosencroft, who published a
directory of Liverpool in 1790, was another registry office keeper,
but by this time the compilation of directories had passed beyond
the stage where it required exceptional facilities or initiative.

It is evident, unfortunately, that the history of the development
of directories, and the reciprocal influence on and by them of
expanding trade, is obscured by the numbers of them which have
failed to survive. For the years 1763 to 1790, at most fifty provincial English directories are certainly recorded, covering ten towns,
three counties and six larger areas. Shrewsbury was neither a port

[1] C. Gill, *Rise of the Irish Linen Industry* (1925), p. 57.
[2] A. Anderson, *Origin of Commerce* (1787), iii. 324–5.
[3] J. Aikin, *Description of the Country Round Manchester* (1795), p. 184.
[4] J. Harland, ' Collectanea Relating to Manchester ', *Chetham Soc. Pubs.*,
lxxii (1867), 149.
[5] B. Walker, ' Birmingham Directories ', *Birm. Arch. Soc. Trans.*, lviii
(1937 for 1934).
[6] *London Chronicle*, 14–16 July 1763.   [7] Harland, *loc. cit.*

nor an industrial centre, but already in 1784 Thomas Minshull
' almost blushed' to find that it was without a directory, and he
refers (in 1786) to ' the numerous editions works of this kind run
through in almost every trading town in the kingdom '.[1] William
Bailey, in the preface to his *British Directory* (1784), said ' there
have been many attempts of a similar nature ', and the compiler
of the Bristol directory for 1785 said ' the public have long been
acquainted with the utility of publications of this sort. In most
populous places they are now become not only useful but extremely
convenient in facilitating business and the various intercourses of
mankind.' Something must no doubt be allowed for the obvious
advertising value of such remarks, but it is at any rate clear that
since 1763 directories had become commonly recognised as useful
and necessary instruments of communication.

It seems, then, that when the directory first appeared at the end
of the seventeenth century, the need for it was not, except in London, great enough for the idea to be generally adopted. After
1763, however, there was a rapid increase in the numbers produced
and their usefulness was generally recognised. The reason lies in
changes in the conditions of trade. Already before this date London
was a centre of trade for the whole country. Goods for export
were collected there and imported goods were distributed. Manufactures were also collected there for resale to other parts of the
country. This distributive trade was already highly specialised.
Defoe distinguished two classes : merchants, concerned with imports
and exports, and tradesmen, including wholesalers, retailers and
warehouse keepers, concerned with internal trade. He describes the
passage of goods from the country through warehouse keepers to
merchants, and of imported and home-produced goods, through
wholesalers ' to country tradesmen in every corner of the kingdom ',
who supplied them to chapmen and shopkeepers, who bought ' in
parcels ' to sell again. Goods were often ordered by letter, or
country manufacturers made visits to London, perhaps once a year,
' as is the custom ', to do business with warehousemen.[2]

Though Defoe emphasised the great importance of London, it was
not the only distributing centre. Foreign trade was carried on from
other ports such as Bristol and Hull, and internal trade also went
by ship from port to port. Chester and Norwich were centres of
inland trade. Liverpool rapidly increased in importance during the
first half of the century. Cross posts were extended under the
management of Ralph Allen from 1720 and saved business correspondence from having to go through London. Goods were distributed from ports and inland centres to smaller towns and even to
villages and, as in London, there were wholesalers and retailers everywhere occupied in circulating them.[3]

For this trade, however, extensive as it was, directories were
as yet hardly needed. Some of it still took place at periodical fairs.

[1] Preface to *The Shrewsbury Guide for 1786.*(No. 616 below).
[2] Defoe, *The Complete English Tradesman* (2nd ed. 1727), pp. 1 ff. See
M. Clare, *Youth's Introduction to Trade & Business* (1764), pp. 92–3, for a
model order for groceries from a young man setting up a shop in Chester
to an importer in London.
[3] Defoe, *A Tour through Great Britain* (1724–7).

In the north it was largely carried on in great central markets like the Leeds cloth halls, to which came buyers and sellers from the country round, from London and from abroad. The Manchester manufacturers, who themselves took their goods on packhorses all over the country, had been famous since the seventeenth century,[1] and this method of trading spread all over the manufacturing districts of the north.[2] It was imitated by a host of small travelling dealers, whose competition was disliked and feared by the established tradesmen. On arrival in any town, they set up their headquarters at the local inn and the population from all around came to them to buy their wares.[3] Where more up-to-date methods prevailed and there were tradesmen with permanent warehouses or retail shops, relations between buyer and seller were close and personal. Defoe urged on the young apprentice the importance of getting to know his master's customers individually, especially the country shopkeepers.[4]

It is evident that, under a system of trade which in the main was carried on at well-recognised centres, to which the customer came in search of his supplier rather than the other way round, and at a time when the number of persons concerned was still relatively small, an extensive knowledge of individual addresses was not very urgently needed. It is significant that the first provincial directories not for ports are for Birmingham and Sheffield, places where a multiplicity of small trades prevailed. From the middle of the eighteenth century, however, the changes of the Industrial Revolution affected methods of trade. The old system continued in many places, but new ideas spread. The growth of large-scale industry forced the manufacturer to look for customers beyond his local knowledge, and buyers came from greater distances to seek out producers. Better means of communication, such as improved roads and conveyances, greatly extended the range of commercial travelling. Riders carrying samples largely replaced the old cumbrous method of travelling the goods themselves and they went farther and faster.[5] More rapid carriage of letters and goods increased the number of mail orders direct from merchants to manufacturers.[6] Local agents were employed to collect large orders from separate small producers, and direct trade between manufacturers and retailers increased.[7] Increased competition broke up old connections between traders personally known to each other, as new men came pushing in to manufacture and trade.

The wider area covered, the growth of old towns and the rise of new centres of industry made it more difficult for traders to establish contact with one another. Already in 1767 Sketchley described the situation in the preface to his Birmingham directory for that year. ' Let us suppose,' he says, ' a merchant at Birmingham, Walsall or Wolverhampton, who wants to purchase a parcel of Buckels and

---

[1] D. Newman, *Trade of England Revived* (1685).
[2] *The Complete English Tradesman* (2nd ed. 1727), p. 326.
[3] *The Case of the Fair Trader* (c. 1709).
[4] *The Complete English Tradesman* (2nd ed. 1727), p. 12.
[5] J. Aikin, *op. cit.*, pp. 183-4.
[6] H. Heaton, *Yorkshire Woollen & Worsted Industries* (1920), chap. v.
[7] C. Gill, *op. cit.*, pp. 252-3.

Spurs and is not particularly acquainted with any maker ', he can refer to Sketchley's classified list of manufacturers and find what he wants.[1] The author hopes that his directory will be a guide to natives or foreigners at a loss for any of the manufactures carried on in the town. In 1794 the author of the Leicester directory of that year remarked that the increase in manufactures and trade had made a directory of bankers, manufacturers and tradesmen very desirable, not only to the inhabitants but particularly to those who came either to give or take orders. Sketchley's Sheffield directory for 1774 is a model of the kind of information which a directory of this date could usefully provide. It contains a classified list of manufacturers, an alphabetical list of merchants, manufacturers, etc., lists of posts to and from the town with cost of postage, of coaches with the inns where they set down and the places they conveyed goods to, and a list of London merchants ' who have any trade with Sheffield, Birmingham and their neighbouring towns '.

The increasing size of the market is shown by the appearance of directories covering a larger area than a single town. The first known county directory is Sadler's directory of Hampshire (1784). In 1785, J. F. Henington published a directory of Bedfordshire. He also projected directories of five other counties and though none of these has survived, it is by no means certain that he did not publish them. William Bailey's first directories covered still larger areas, including the chief towns in a number of counties, and in 1784 he published four volumes covering the principal places over the whole of the country. *The Universal British Directory*, which appeared in parts between the end of 1790 and 1798, was still more ambitious, and included many medium-sized and small towns, as well as the large industrial and trade centres. This directory was not aimed only at the home market. ' It will convey to distant realms ', the author said in the preface, ' the most august idea of the resources of the British Empire '.

Thus the use of directories was well established by the early part of the nineteenth century.

The experience of the mercantile world [to quote the rather wordy Mr R. J. Battle of Hull] affords ample and decisive evidence that the provision of local and personal reference, in a printed form, materially tends to enlarge the sphere and improve the facilities of commercial intercourse ; and by promoting the economy of time and employment, in the prevention of tedious and troublesome enquiry, supplies the most advantageous means of promptitude in the transaction of business.[2]

The long list of subscribers to Holden's *Annual London & Country Directory* for 1811 [3] shows how widespread was its use. Among the large number of merchants and manufacturers are such well-known names as Barclay & Perkins, Boulton & Watt, and Wedgwood ; there are banks (including the Banks of England, Ireland and Scotland), insurance companies, schools (including Christ's Hospital), doctors (including Dr Lettsome), coffee-rooms, three police offices, the Stock Exchange, Somerset House Tax Office and

[1] Sketchley copied these remarks almost verbatim from the preface to Mortimer's *Universal Director*, where they are applied to London.
[2] From the preface to his directory of Hull (1803).
[3] Printed in vol. i of the work.

the Exchequer Bill Pay Office, the Twopenny Post-Office in Gerrard Street (four copies) and several booksellers, including Johnson Gore, publisher of the famous series of Liverpool directories.

All the conditions which had made directories generally acceptable —improved communications, development of industry, spread of home and foreign trade, growing size of the population and its increasing concentration in towns—continued with redoubled force as the century went on. Fast goods wagons and coaches halved the time taken between London and the north and speeded up travel between the principal towns. Producers sought for markets over ever-wider areas, and at the same time trade sprang up in remote places which had hardly known it before. Linen manufacturers in Belfast were selling direct to retail shops in English provincial towns before the end of the Napoleonic wars.[1] Commercial travelling spread over the country. In 1830 a representative of A. & C. Black, the Edinburgh publishers, travelled over 1,400 miles, by coach, by gig and on foot, in under three months, collecting orders for the seventh edition of the *Encyclopedia Britannica*.[2] In 1840 a traveller for a London business house turned up at the isolated village of Haworth, where he was entertained by Patrick Brontë.[3] A pamphlet published in 1857, called *Advice to a Young Commercial Traveller*, draws a contrast between the new system by which the traveller had to search out his customers and that prevailing fifty years earlier, when they came to find him at his inn. The use such travellers made of directories is shown by a copy of W. White's *Directory of Leeds and the Yorkshire Woollen Districts* (1857), which once belonged to one of them.[4] It has a note in ink at the end, ' Reference to parties visited for cloth measures. 1. does not like or require them. 2. supplied with them. 3. favorable to the principle but not buying now.' Certain names in the book are numbered accordingly.

The old conditions lingered on, especially in the north, where the cloth halls and the system of scattered domestic manufacture were still in existence until after the middle of the century.[5] Though the chief roads were good, the small crossroads were still very bad and often impassable in winter. Between some towns there was still, in the late 1820's, nothing but the old pack-horse tracks, and some villages had almost no means of communication with the outside world at all.[6] A national market did not really exist until the railway system was well established.

By that time directories had extended far and wide. The prospect of revived foreign trade stimulated the production of the first of Pigot's general directories in 1814, and from the 1820's his great surveys covered the whole of the country, including the villages.

[1] Gill, *op. cit.*, p. 252.
[2] ' On the Road a Hundred Years Ago ', ed. by James Cannon in *The Publishers' Circular*, 9 February 1935 and following numbers.
[3] E. C. Gaskell, *Life of Charlotte Brontë*, i (1857), 205.
[4] Now in the Institute of Historical Research (London).
[5] E. Baines, ' Woollen Trade of Yorkshire ', in T. Baines, *Yorkshire Past & Present* (1870), i.
[6] E. C. Gaskell, *op. cit.*, i. 18, gives a vivid account of the conveyance of a wagon-load of goods to Bradford in winter-time.

A class of professional directory publishers, employing skilled agents to collect information, came into existence. Competition between rival publishers made its appearance.[1] Annual directories began to be asked for [2] and the idea of including most of the inhabitants and not merely the more important commercial names began to spread.[3] By 1839 it could be said, though with some exaggeration, that ' every town of the least pretension in England has published for the use of its inhabitants and visitors that information which the pursuit of trade or the tour for pleasure requires '.[4]

This last quotation refers to two types of directory. The latter, connected more with retail than with wholesale trade, has a rather different history from that which has hitherto been described. Mortimer's *Universal Director*,[5] which in some ways forms a landmark in the history of directories, included besides the usual list of merchants and bankers, the names of artists, musicians, doctors and other professional men, and lists of booksellers and other shopkeepers. It is addressed to ' Noblemen and Gentlemen ' and not, as more usually, to ' Merchants and Tradesmen '. Directories of watering places and spas are of this type and they evidently sprang from the fact that such towns were full of visitors, unfamiliar with the place. They are generally attached as appendices to guide books, and in the embryo form of lists of medical men and lodging houses appeared in guides long before any directory proper of the town was published. As the habit of spending holidays at the seaside spread from the upper to the middle classes, the number of such directories increased. In 1816 the lack of a directory for Aberystwith was said to have long been a subject of complaint and ' this is not to be wondered at when the number of holiday makers from every part of England and Wales is considered '.[6]

In such places, the production of directories seems to have depended as much on local initiative as on favourable local conditions. Bath had a directory proper as early as 1792 and lists of medical men as much as twenty years earlier. Brighton had a directory before 1799, but no directory of Scarborough is known until the 1840's and Margate, which was a popular resort in 1766 (Gray called it ' Bartholomew Fair by the sea-side ' in that year [7]), has no known directory till late in the nineteenth century.

The information in directories of this kind tends to be selective, covering mainly the professions and better-class retail shops and private inhabitants. The Worthing guide of 1811 [8] contains only a street directory of the principal tradesmen. Powell's *Hastings Guide*, published about 1820, includes, besides lodging houses, only the shops in the High Street. *The Watering Places of Great Britain* (1831–33),[9] which calls itself ' emphatically a fashion-

---

[1] *Cf.* below, Hull, 1803 (Nos. 818, 819) ; Bristol, 1816 (No. 313) ; Lancs, 1818 (No. 421), and see p. 65.
[2] *Cf.* Liverpool, 1827 (No. 481), and see p. 21.
[3] *E.g.* Sheffield, 1817 (No. 851).
[4] Isle of Wight directory, 1839 (No. 395).
[5] T. Mortimer, *Universal Director* (London), 1763.
[6] *The Aberystwith Guide*, 1816 (No. 868 below).
[7] *Letters of Thomas Gray*, ed. D. C. Tovey (1900–12), iii. 113.
[8] No. 690 below.   [9] No. 400 below.

able directory ', has a special note to say that it does not include all tradesmen and lodging houses. Sometimes lists specially useful to visitors were included. The first Cheltenham directory (1800) has a separate list of laundresses and clear-starchers. Long lists of private residents, under streets or houses and villas let for the season are a feature suited to the convenience of visitors and useful to local shops catering for a shifting population.

The pure court directory, consisting only of the names of private residents, is a late development except in London, where the first edition of Boyle's *Court Guide* was published in 1792. Separate lists of private addresses were included in *The Universal British Directory*, but they are rare in provincial directories before the middle of the nineteenth century, though the general alphabetical lists often included names unconnected with trade. An extreme example of the court list would seem to be a directory of Kensington, published in 1863,[1] which was limited to those ' whose vocation in life does not debar them from admission to our West End Clubs '.

Another type of directory derives from the needs and the opportunities of post office officials. Outside London the Post Office did not undertake any delivery of letters to houses until 1764. In that year the Postmaster General was given authority to set up penny deliveries in other towns or cities. From 1774 free deliveries within post towns were instituted. Penny deliveries in rural districts were now gradually extended, and postmasters sometimes undertook the delivery of letters privately for a fee. After 1801 it became the policy of the Post Office to extend penny deliveries as a means of encouraging the use of postal services, and the general free delivery of letters was established in 1843, though it was still not available everywhere even as late as 1897. The Dead Letter Office was established in London in 1784, but any postmaster might find himself required to deal with lost letters.[2] These increasing demands on post office officials created a new use for directories, and a number of them were compiled by or with the assistance of postmen, the profits being divided between the editor and his helpers.

The first directory with a post office connection seems to have been Williamson's directory of Edinburgh (1773). Peter Williamson, an odd character with a picaresque past, kept a coffee shop in Edinburgh and was employed by gentlemen frequenting it to forward letters. He opened an office and established a regular penny post, with hourly deliveries and four men in uniform who delivered and collected letters, ringing a bell on their rounds to announce their approach. The General Post Office soon took over the business, compensating Williamson with a small pension.[3]

The first directory compiled and owned by post office officials themselves was the London Post Office directory, which was first published in 1800, under the title of *New Annual Directory*.[4] It

---

[1] *The Aristocracy of London*, pt. i (O'Byrne Bros.), 1863.
[2] *The Post Office* (H.M. Stationery Office, 1911), pp. 36 ff.
[3] T. B. Lang, *Historical Summary of the P.O. in Scotland* (1856), pp. 15–16.
[4] The reference in H. Joyce, *History of the Post Office* (1893), p. 309, to ' what is virtually the first county directory ' compiled by three post office

was edited by two inspectors of the inland letter-carriers, called Ferguson and Sparke. A third inspector, called Critchett, joined them in 1803, and when he died in 1835 the copyright appears to have been his sole property. In 1836 Frederic Kelly, the chief inspector of the inland letter-carriers, purchased the copyright from Critchett's widow and carried on the directory with the assistance of the clerks in the Post Office, the profits being unequally divided between him and the assistant inspectors, the letter-carriers themselves collecting a small commission on sales. In Kelly's hands the work rapidly expanded and soon the desirability of using public servants to promote an enterprise in private hands was called in question. In 1847 Kelly was prohibited from employing any person connected with the Post Office to serve him in his private character as the publisher of the *Post Office Directory*. However, by this time he had set up a separate organisation at Boswell Court, under the management of his brother, where he employed a staff of his own.[1] The title, *Post Office Directory*, was retained for all Kelly's publications and at a later date Kelly & Co. tried, though unsuccessfully, to establish an exclusive claim to it.[2]

A directory of Edinburgh, compiled and owned by the letter carriers of the Edinburgh Post Office, was started in 1805 and continued to be published under the patronage of the Secretary to the Post Office for Scotland and for the Edinburgh Postmen until 1917, after which it appeared under a different imprint. In Ireland a list of noted houses, giving the post town for each, was compiled by Ambrose Leet, vice-president of the Inland Office of the Dublin Post Office, and printed with the sanction of the Postmaster General for the use of the Post Office in 1813. An edition for general circulation was published in 1814.[3] A Dublin Post Office Directory was started by officials of the Post Office there in 1832, much to the disgust of the owner of the eighty-year-old *Wilson's Dublin Directory*.[4] A Post Office Directory of Glasgow, by Glasgow post office officials, was begun in 1828. James Findlay's *Directory to Gentlemen's Seats in Scotland*, first issued in 1843, was another semi-official publication, the information for it being obtained from Scottish postmasters.

Among English and Welsh directory compilers, James Butterworth was postmaster at Oldham, William L. Kelly kept a branch post office at Newport, Mon., and J. L. Bird was postmaster at Cardiff from 1802. There are no known directories by him at this date, but his nephew, William Bird, who published one in 1829, was an assistant in his post office. Snare's Reading directory (1842), the first English directory outside London to be called a Post Office Directory, was revised through the Post Office by permission of

officials about 1793, seems to be due to a confusion of *The Universal British Directory* with Ferguson and Sparke's directory. Joyce gives no references and no trace of such a directory as he describes has been found.

[1] The story of Kelly's management of the *London Post Directory*, which is an entertaining one, may be followed in Parliamentary Reports and in *Hansard* between 1837 and 1847.

[2] *The Post Office Bradford Directory* (1879), preface.

[3] A. Leet, *Directory to the . . . Noted Places in Ireland* (2 vols., 1813; 2nd ed., 1814).

[4] *Wilson's Dublin Directory for 1832*, p. iii.

the postmaster. The *Post Office Directory of Southampton*, first published in 1843, was compiled by a clerk in the Post Office and was specially designed to ensure the correct addressing of letters. The *Post Office Bath Directory* (1st edn. 1858) was produced by two officials of the Bath post office, with permission of the Postmaster General. In the 70's and 80's of the century, a number of so-called Post Office directories were started, some with and some without acknowledgement of the assistance of post office officials. The popularity of the title was no doubt in part due to the great success of Kelly's Post Office directories and in part evidence of the general use now made of directories for addressing letters.

Finally we may notice a number of directories showing interesting variations from the usual type or arising from unusual motives or special opportunities of securing information.

One variant on the ordinary type is the illustrated directory. Of these the most fascinating is *Tallis's London Street Views*, published in numbers, 1838–40. Each number contains an engraving of a street, the front elevation of each house being depicted as it stood, often with the name of the occupier above it, thus forming a novel street directory. Each has also an inset view and an alphabetical list of names.[1]

Bisset's illustrated directories of Birmingham [2] are rather indexed collections of engraved advertisements than formal directories. They consist of plates containing lists of trade names and addresses engraved against a symbolical background or sometimes against a view of some part of Birmingham. Some of the plates are engraved trade cards of single firms. Bisset planned a similar directory for the whole of the country, but it was never completed. He seems to have intended to supply the plates singly to individuals for use as cards or advertisements, but no applications for them were made and the whole enterprise was a costly failure.[3] However, he had started a process through which the engraved trade cards of the eighteenth century evolved into printed advertisements in books and which provided a fruitful field of employment for local schools of engravers. Many directories from this date, and especially in the 1820's, include a number of engraved advertisements, sometimes very pretty and often, when they depict scenes in streets, shops or factories, of no little historical interest.

Other compilers were inspired by cultural motives. One of the most far-sighted of these was John Ferrar, who compiled a directory of Limerick for 1769.[4] 'This Pamphlet', he says, 'will appear at first view trifling to some but . . . it will shew the present state and constitution of this City better perhaps than a voluminous history.'

Short historical notes were an interesting feature of the directory proper from an early date, and lists of important events in the history of the town, like the *Annals of Liverpool* in Gore's directories, are often a most valuable part of the book. Later these were

---

[1] *See also* Goss, *op. cit.*, p. 131. There is a nearly complete set of the *Views* in the British Museum.
[2] Nos. 716, 722 below. *See also* No. 20.   [3] B. Walker, *op. cit.*
[4] *The Limerick Directory*, John Ferrar. Limerick (1769).

sometimes supplemented by articles on the geology, fauna and flora of the district. Edward Baines and William Parson published a combined history, directory and gazetteer of Yorkshire in 1822, and this type of volume was commonly followed by them and by their successor, William White. White made a feature of the learned character of his directories, always acknowledging in his prefaces the help of numerous literary or scientific gentlemen and referring to Parliamentary Reports and other sources consulted. The titles of his later editions generally mention the learned societies of which he was a member, and the ' great variety of archaeological, architectural, agricultural, biographical, botanical, geological and statistical information ' contained in the book. His title and style of directory became popular and were copied from about 1845 by a number of imitators, who often did not scruple to pirate their text from him and from each other. Attempts at research were sometimes somewhat naïve. In the *General Directory for Somerset* (1840), ' the statistical details ', to quote from the preface,

have been taken in every instance from Parliamentary returns or other offical documents ; these we have rigidly followed even when informed that they were erroneous, because authorities cannot be safely departed from and the fault, if any, in such case becomes that of our authority and not our own.

An even more ambitious attempt to combine information and culture was *The Cheltenham Annuaire* (1837), which was dedicated to the President and Vice-Presidents of the Cheltenham Literary and Philosophical Institute. The directory was said by the compiler to have been his main object, but only private and professional names are included and a large part of the book is taken up with learned essays on a variety of subjects. According to a review in the *Gloucester Chronicle*,[1] it was not to be ' confounded with the mere directory ; for whilst it admirably supplies the place of such a publication, it aims at intellectual objects '. The admission of a list of trade names and the altered position and restricted extent of the essays in the second edition, however, mark the beginning of a progressive commercialisation of the work, which soon ceased to differ from the ordinary watering-place directory.

Yet another type of directory is to be found in the police directories of Newcastle-under-Lyme. The author of these, Isaac Cottrill, was police officer for the borough, where a police office was established in 1834. He seems to have been an active and zealous follower of his profession and he gave the population fair warning that he had his eye on them. The list of householders with their trades and residences, which he published as a directory in 1836, he had compiled for his own use as a police officer. Such information, he said, could not, for police purposes, be too distinctly noticed. Thomas Pearce, who published a directory of Walsall in 1813, was constable there from 1804 to 1812. He gives some interesting particulars about the arrangements for a police force in Walsall at this time.

Lastly we may notice a few directories of places of little commercial importance, that seem to have originated from fashion or from some fancy on the part of the author. ' As other towns have their

[1] Quoted in the 1838 edition of *The Annuaire*.

directories or guides, why not Berwick-on-Tweed ? ' as was said
by the author of the directory of that place published in 1806,
though he ruefully confessed that the undertaking had been too
much for him.   A description of Bromley,[1] a very small place in
1797 when the book was published, has a directory abruptly inserted
in the middle, ' as directories have been found of the greatest utility
in large towns '.   Short directories are sometimes appended to local
histories.   Thus James Mountain's *History of Selby* (1800), has a
directory at the end.   *The History of Newton-Abbott*, by the Rev.
D. M. Stirling (1830), has one too.   The local printer or publisher
rather than the author, was often responsible for compiling these.[2]

The terminal date to a list such as is contained in this book is
necessarily somewhat arbitrary, but as directories had become
fairly common and fairly uniform by the 1850's, that would seem
a convenient period at which to stop.   The new facilities for personal
intercourse dating from the 1840's—the penny post, the telegraph
and the development of railways—all contributed to make the production of directories a profitable undertaking.   Frederic Kelly,
that astute business man, began the extension of his activities from
London to the provinces by remarking that ' the increased and
rapidly increasing facilities of communication seemed to indicate a
necessity for more extended and elaborate works of the present
description than had before been attempted.'[3]   Between them, he,
Pigot and William White provided a system of directories which
covered the country at reasonably frequent intervals.   Attempts
by other publishers to produce similar series were most of them
ephemeral and often not very reliable, and for some time there was
no great increase in new town directories, but from 1850 it should
not be difficult for an inquirer to find a good directory of any fair-
sized place in England, either by itself or in one of the county
directories.

The contents also have become pretty generally, though not
universally, stereotyped.   A town directory may be expected to
contain alphabetical, classified and street lists.   County directories
generally have alphabetical lists for villages and alphabetical and
classified lists for larger places, with street directories added for
the biggest towns.[4]   Very few of them pretend to include all the
inhabitants.

[1] No. 406 below.
[2] This kind of directory is particularly difficult to trace, as the directory
is commonly not mentioned on the title and such books are, as a rule, not
classified under directories in library catalogues.   As it has hardly been possible to examine all local histories, though a great many have been examined,
the author thinks some directories may have been missed for this reason.
[3] *Post Office Directory. Birmingham, etc.*, W. Kelly & Co., 1845 : Preface.
[4] About 1840 some attempt was made to include railway time tables in
directories, but they soon became too bulky.   Pigot's *Directory of Yorks, etc.*
(Aug. 1841) has a time-table of fifteen pages, prefixed by the following note :
' Although variations in time will occasionally be detected, yet the information
these tables convey will be found sufficiently accurate for all purposes of the
traveller.'

II. Authorship, Methods of Compilation and Tests of Reliability

The historical origin and development of directories having been described, we may now turn to some points about their authorship and compilation which affect their reliability as sources of information. It would be misleading to regard them as either precise or accurate. A glance at any two directories of the same place for the same year will reveal disconcerting differences. It is easy to scramble together a list of names and sell the result as a directory, and there are plenty of examples of dishonesty among directory compilers ; but even when a directory may be assumed to be an honest and independent effort, a number of factors have still to be taken into account in estimating its reliability.

In general, when a directory is printed and published in its own locality, and forms, or is intended to form, part of a series appearing regularly over a number of years, it can be expected, *prima facie*, to be reasonably reliable. The compiler and publisher would have had a reputation to maintain, and if their directory was seriously inaccurate it would not have continued to be favourably received. Further, a directory produced by an inhabitant of the locality has a certain advantage over a directory produced by a stranger or covering large areas. A man compiling a directory of his own town will presumably start with greater local knowledge than someone from outside. Against this, however, may be set the fact that the publishers of big national directories in the nineteenth century made use of trained experts for collecting information. Methods of collecting entries are an important factor in the reliability of a directory and, as they were very various, they must be considered in some detail.

The best way of compiling a list of names, occupations and addresses is obviously to visit each house and ask for information, and it is frequently claimed in early directories that this method has been used. William Bailey, for his 1784 directory, ' visited every town and personally waited on every house in the kingdom to acquire a proper information '. Charles Pye stated on the title of his Birmingham directory for 1785 that it was ' taken from personal application '. Later on he said that this method did not pay him and gave it up. Joseph Mathews said in 1812 that he had called personally at every house ' of trade and respectability '.[1]

These inquiries were, in the early days, generally made by the compiler himself, though sometimes local agents were employed. Bailey, in his 1787 directory of Bristol and Bath, specially mentions that ' the executive part ' had to be entrusted to others. Wilkes, besides using other methods of compiling *The Universal British Directory*, employed local printers or booksellers, recompensing them apparently by supplying them with offprints for local sale. Holden, in his 1811 directory, refers to the assistance of ' a gentleman of the first respectability ' in most of the towns included. In 1814 Samuel Rowe employed ' an intelligent person ' to collect names from door to door for his Plymouth directory.

---

[1] *Mathews's Bristol Directory for 1812.*

This led, as the number of places and persons concerned increased, to the rise of a class of professional directory agents, who sometimes set up later as directory publishers themselves, claiming as an advantage that they had worked for Pigot or White.[1] William White himself started his connection with directories as a compiler for Edward Baines. Frederic Kelly, though he began by using letter-carriers to collect his information, was already employing some paid agents in 1845 and in 1847, when he was prohibited from making use of post office officials, recommended his directories as being compiled by ' selected whole-time agents '. Agents paid for the job were said to be more reliable than those paid a commission on sales, as the commission tempted them to make inquiries only from people from whom they expected to get orders.[2]

The assistance of persons with other qualifications was also made use of. The number of directories compiled by postmen has already been described. Archdeacon's Greenwich directory for 1852 refers to ' information being usually obtained from Tax Collectors and others '. At a considerably later date the services of Poor Law overseers seem to have been utilised.[3] Spalding's directory of Cambridge for 1895 was revised ' in several instances, most kindly, by the clergy '.

Sometimes directories were compiled from other sources and checked locally. Thus for the Somerset directory of 1840, ' a copy of the directory for each town was forwarded to some inhabitant well-acquainted with the place, where it was inspected and corrected by a great number of persons '.

A variant on the method of making personal inquiries was to send or leave circulars, with a request for them to be filled up. Pye published a guide to Birmingham [4] for the inadequacy of which he excused himself by saying that he had distributed cards to all the public institutions, asking them to communicate any information they thought fit, but in spite of this ' genteel way of soliciting assistance in a private manner ', several of them had failed to respond. This book is not a directory, but its fate illustrates the inadequacy of the method. For the Leicester directory of 1843 more than 3,000 blank forms were distributed, with no very successful result.

Other untrustworthy devices were employed. One was to advertise, in the press or by handbills, for entries. The Newcastle-on-Tyne directory for 1795 was compiled in this way. Charles Pye's handbill for his Birmingham directory (1800), of which he says he circulated several thousand copies, besides putting notices in the press, is reprinted in that directory. It runs as follows :

C. Pye respectfully informs the inhabitants at large that at the request of several individuals, he has opened an office in Colmore Row, late the Soup Shop, where all Merchants, Factors, Manufacturers, Professional and other persons who conduct any Business on his, her or their own account, are

---

[1] *E.g.* Joseph Bentley ; *see* 775 below. W. Parson, R. Gell and T. Bradshaw were also professional compilers.

[2] *Ward's North of England Directory*, 1852.

[3] *Directory of Herefordshire* (Jakeman & Carver), 1890. *Grantham Directory* (W. J. Cook & Co.), 1892. *York & District Directory* (W. J. Cook), 1893.

[4] C. Pye, *A Description of Modern Birmingham* (1820).

requested to send their proper address, in writing with Sixpence for the insertion thereof before Saturday the 22nd inst which will entitle the Persons whose names are registered to receive a printed Directory for *One Shilling and Sixpence*, provided they send for the same to the Directory Office within fourteen days after they are published . . . N.B. . . . if this Directory be incomplete the fault must remain with the inhabitants, as it cannot be rendered cheaper except by Piracy.

The resultant entries cover only sixteen pages, perhaps because of the 6d. charge and perhaps also because a rival directory, compiled by house-to-house visit and with no charge for insertion (which resulted in a list of 96 pages), was in preparation at the same time. The names for the first edition of *The Cheltenham Annuaire* were obtained by advertising, but the result was not considered satisfactory. Sometimes advertisements were used in addition to a house-to-house canvass, for instance for Pigot's directory of Manchester and places round (1838). It was common in early directories to trust to the initiative of the public to supply additions and alterations, which were then issued free to purchasers of the directory. For instance Gales and Martin announced in their directory of Sheffield (1787) that a register would be kept open at Gales' shop for entering additions and corrections.

Another likewise unsatisfactory method was to make use of lists already compiled for other purposes. The Bath directory for 1826 contains a notice that the previous edition had been compiled from rate books but the publishers had found that these omitted permanent lodgers, including ' gentlemen, professional gentlemen and others of great importance to Society, who never pay poor rate ', and also contained many errors, and that the only reliable method was personal application at every house. The Ryde directory for 1846 was ' copied from official lists of the occupiers of houses, corrected by personal knowledge and inquiry '. The preface to the Sheffield directory for 1817 expressly states that ' the list is not a copy of any other that the town regulations may require '.

Another obvious, if illegitimate, source was somebody else's directory, used with or without the owner's permission. Wilkes often made use of existing publications, without too particular a regard for their date. Thus the directory of Hull, contained in a number of *The Universal British Directory* published in 1793, is taken from Battle's Hull directory for 1791, even the name of the mayor being unchanged. Charles Pye complained that the Birmingham section of *The Universal British* was pirated from his 1791 directory. Holden, though the descriptive text of his country directories is freely taken from *The Universal British*, asserted in his London directory (1799) that he had sought no assistance from any other work but had had every name collated by personal application. The whole question of piracy and violations of copyright in directories will be discussed in more detail later.

Even when the house-to-house method was adopted, investigators in the early days met with difficulties, not all of which would suggest themselves readily to us. The weather was often an adverse factor. ' The severity of the late season . . . by destroying or impeding the usual facilities of intercourse and information ' had, Pigot said, been a powerful obstacle in the way of his *Commercial*

Directory for 1814. To compile his *Directory of Scotland, Ireland & the four Northern Counties for 1820*, the publishers and their agents toiled ' through a winter of unusual severity '. For Parson and White's directory of the clothing district of Yorkshire (1830) ' some of the remote districts ', they pointed out, ' had to be surveyed when little but snow and ice met the view '. Even as late as 1867, the publisher of a Huddersfield directory apologised because the long continuance of wet weather ' rendered it at times impossible to collect information '.[1]

Another difficulty was the frequent unwillingness of the public to supply information. Some of the inhabitants of Birmingham would not help Charles Pye, ' being prepossessed in their own opinion that I was taking down names for the Militia '.[2] In Newcastle in 1801, ' the ignorance of some and the petulance of others ' hindered inquiries. There were even some who asked not to have their names inserted. In Leicester in 1843 not a few of the parties applied to ' would neither give their names verbally nor in writing '. Matters do not seem, in this respect, to have improved in later times. In 1880 the people of Plymouth having been ' pestered beyond enduring in the matter of directories ', were ' naturally short in their replies to our agents' inquiries '.[3] Pigot's agents encountered a slightly different obstacle when investigating in the north, where ' imperfect or mistaken answers . . . and even provincial pronunciation ' led to errors.[4] An unexpected difficulty is revealed in the preface to Pigot's Manchester directory for 1840, where it is explained that ' a few discrepancies may perhaps be noticed . . . arising from the information being collected, in the outside of the town and its suburbs, mostly from domestics '.

In all these cases the difficulty, when it did not lead to actual omissions, is likely to have affected the entries for occupations the most seriously. Trades were, in any case, not always very clearly defined in early days and the description of them in the brief space of a directory entry must often have been difficult. It was not made easier if people refused to give information themselves. John Gray of Croydon felt obliged to explain with apologies that he had been in some instances

compelled to use his own discretion in the description of occupations or qualities of the residents ; and if in any instance he may have employed a term which is not such as the individual himself would have preferred, he can only assert his innocence of any intentional offence, it having been his anxious endeavour to avoid rudeness on the one hand and mere compliment on the other.[5]

The character and occupation of the compilers may also be taken into account in estimating the reliability of directories. Some authors, like William Gye of Bath and J. G. Rusher of Banbury, to name only two, were men of distinction, well known in their

[1] *Huddersfield Directory & Year Book* (Huddersfield, G. Harper), 1867.
[2] *Pye's Birmingham Directory for 1797*, preface.
[3] *Eyre Bros. Post Office Plymouth Directory*, 1880.
[4] *The Commercial Directory for 1814–15*, preface. *See also* preface to *The Commercial Directory of Scotland, Ireland, etc.* 1820.
[5] *A New Commercial & General Directory of Croydon*, 1851.

own cities or towns, and their publications are to be treated with
respect. At the other extreme we have a plain rogue, like John
Mackoull of Worthing.[1] The great majority of directory compilers
have been local printers or publishers of whom there is little to say.
Some others pursued occupations which must have made it easy
for them to collect their material. Registry office keepers, post
office officials and policemen have already been mentioned.[2] Common professions among directory compilers are those of land and
house agents and auctioneers. In these employments they would
have been in close touch with changes in addresses and in the owner-
ship of businesses. Frequently they were agents to some insurance
company, an occupation involving house-to-house canvassing.
Some of them were accountants, again a profession which would have
kept them in touch with the business community. One of them at
least was a debt collector. Compilers of directories of watering-
places often ran lending libraries, which would have furnished them
with the names and addresses of most of the visitors. Thomas
Pearce of Walsall was unusually highly qualified for, besides being
parish clerk, constable and insurance agent, he had twice acted as
an officer under the Census Act.

Besides these sober occupations, we find a variety of others,
which are perhaps only relevant in so far as they may throw some
light on the personalities of the compilers concerned. Thomas
Haigh of Leeds was a schoolmaster, Richard Weston of Leicester
was a writer on agriculture, Peter Whittle of Preston was an antiquarian of uncertain qualifications, William Hilton of Newcastle-on-
Tyne was a poet, R. G. Battle of Hull was an ink and blacking
manufacturer. The number of occupations followed unsuccessfully
by Charles Pye of Birmingham is enough to cause one to distrust
him as an expert in any.[3]

Another point which requires elaboration is the question of the
period to which the information in a directory may be taken to
apply. In this book directories are entered under the date of their
publication. Where possible this is made more precise by the date
of the preface or by any other available information. But the date
of publication may be misleading, as may also be a statement on
the title that a directory is ' for ' a given year. It is obvious that
such dates are not exactly applicable to the data in the directory,
which will have taken a period of time to collect and print. The
margin of error will vary with the time taken in the process of
production and with the degree of mobility of the population in the
area concerned.

There is not much information about the time taken in actually
collecting the names. The material for the Newcastle-on-Tyne
directory of 1795 was apparently collected within just over two
months before the date of publication. For Kelly's *Post Office
London Directory* (1840), the preface of which is dated 25 November

---

[1] See No. 690 below.
[2] Professional whole-time compilers have also been described above. The
notes appended to the items in the general list include any information
available about the characters and occupations of the compilers.
[3] See No. 708 below.

1839, the information was collected during September and revised later. The interval between finishing the investigation and publishing seems usually to have been from two to three months.[1] The publisher of the *Post Office Bath Directory* (1858) guaranteed delivery nine weeks from the time he received the material. On the other hand Holden asked for alterations to be sent in by 10 September and the directory was to be published on 1 March, an interval of nearly seven months.[2] *Mathews's Directory for Bristol* (1864) refers to a rival publication, issued about midsummer, which had been compiled the previous summer and autumn. There are cases of directories being published one year and re-issued without alteration or comment a year or even several years later.

In most directories the lists are brought more nearly up to date by a list of additions and alterations added at the last moment. In the eighteenth century such information was often asked for in .the directory and the list published and supplied free to purchasers some months later. Not unnaturally a few separate pages of this kind were liable to be mislaid and they are unfortunately often rare or missing altogether. Some publishers had a most misleading habit of issuing different lists of addenda with different copies of the same edition. From a bibliographical point of view, these constitute different issues of the edition, but it is often not possible to tell in what order they came out. Sometimes the addenda from one issue are incorporated in the next, which then becomes, strictly speaking, a new edition, but very frequently they are not. William White's directories are particularly confusing in this way, and the same difficulty occurs in some of Pigot's.[3]

The general mobility of the population was of course very high during the period under discussion. Not only were numbers increasing but people were moving from south to north and from country to town.[4] These big changes affect the rate at which a directory may be considered to go out of date as well as its accuracy at the time of publication. There were few towns, Bristol being the most important, which had an annual series of directories before 1855. Gore's series for Liverpool was nearly biennial from 1805, though it was said in 1827 that an annual directory was much needed.[5] Pigot's and Slater's Manchester series was more nearly triennial. Kelly's county directories were issued at very varying intervals, the most frequent being about four years. It is evident that none of these can be very trustworthy beyond the year of publication. The editor of the Hull directory for 1835 says that by

[1] See Bristol, 1814 and 1830.　　[2] In 1811 (No. 24 below).
[3] Every effort has been made to note the various addenda lists, but anyone requiring very special or accurate information from these directories will do well to consult as many copies as possible.
[4] The maximum rate of increase in big cities took place between 1821 and 1831 ; in medium-sized towns it was greatest between 1841 and 1851. The Census of 1851 listed six types of cities in the order of their rate of growth between 1801 and 1851. The order is as follows, beginning with the most rapid : watering places, manufacturing places, mining and hardware places, seaports, London, county towns (A. F. Weber, *The Growth of Cities* (1899), pp. 56-7, n. 4).
[5] In *Picken's Directory of Liverpool for 1827.*

the time his survey had been concluded, there had been so many changes that another survey had to be made before publication.

On the other hand for small non-industrial places like Banbury, which in fact can boast of an annual series from 1832, the changes cannot have been nearly so great. Watering places had, of course, a rapidly shifting private population. *Baxter's Stranger in Brighton*, which included a directory in 1822 and 1824, had none in 1826 because the town was changing too fast to make it worth while. Special local conditions affected other places. Thus Harriet Martineau observed of the Lake District :

There is a perpetual change going on in such neighbourhoods . . . as that of Ambleside. Retired merchants and professional men fall in love with the region, buy or build a house, are in transport with what they have done and after a time go away. In five or six years, six houses of friends or acquaintances of mine became inhabited by strangers.[1]

A point of some importance which should be noted when possible, is the time of year at which the collection of names was made. The bulk of removals take place at the quarter-days, especially in June and December. As Bailey explained, ' the survey of London . . . is never taken till after Christmas in each year on account of the continual fluctuations . . . at that season more than any other '.[2] The best time therefore for the investigation to have been made is immediately after one of these dates, which usually meant publication about the beginning of September or March.

The possibilities of checking the information in one directory by comparison with others of the same date are limited. Competition between rival directory compilers was spasmodic and generally ended in the triumph of the older-established directory, as for instance in the attempts to oust Mathews of Bristol and Gore of Liverpool. It was, however, very bitter and often accompanied by assertions that unfair allegations had been made by one of the competitors or by accusations of piracy. Thus the preface to Stapleton's East Kent directory of 1838 refers to ' the narrow-minded and unprincipled conduct of certain individuals in the trade ' who use local journals ' to propagate the grossest misstatements and cowardly innuendoes ' to prevent its publication. Sometimes the personal remarks verge on the ludicrous, as in Clayton's attack on Battle on 1803.[3] In the late 40's and 50's a number of county directories, often of an obviously inferior kind, sprang up, but they mostly ceased after a short time from sheer inefficiency. The great rivals of these later days in the field of county directories, Pigot & Slater and Kelly, were content to divide the country between them, while William White remained successful in his own area owing to the rarer appearance and the distinctive character of his publications. Within his own section Kelly laid about him with a bludgeon whenever competition raised its head. He succeeded in suppressing Robson and Watkins in London, to the accompaniment of much

[1] H. Martineau, *Autobiography* (1877), ii. 221. The period referred to is the 1850's.
[2] In his directory of Liverpool (1787).
[3] See No. 819 below.

abuse,[1] and freely threatened, and sometimes brought, action in the courts against those whom he believed infringed his copyright. At a later date Kelly & Co. successfully invaded the north and absorbed some of the most famous directories like Gore's and Slater's, but this was done by different methods and is anyway outside our present scope.

Legitimate methods of competition were tried, such as the use of better type and paper, more convenient arrangement of the contents and more accurate methods of compilation, but complaints of piracy are remarkably common and this matter requires some comment. Actual copying of lists of names from one directory to another, though it would appear easy to do and difficult to detect when done, seems to have been rare. In fact no instance of it, except in the case of Wilkes,[2] has been established within our period. Indeed, as has been observed, the differences between contemporary lists are disconcerting. Copying of the descriptive text, however, is positively blatant, and imitation of the general appearance, binding or arrangement of a well-known directory, with the evident intention of being mistaken for it, is not uncommon.

Piracy of the text varies from what may charitably be regarded as a crude use of an authority to mere copying. The notes to Holden's directories are recognisably adapted in an abbreviated form from *The Universal British Directory*. F. & J. White, later Francis White & Co., both imitated and directly copied from William White in all their directories. Their first directory (of Nottinghamshire in 1844) contains many phrases, sentences and, as the book goes on, whole sections copied verbatim from William White's Nottinghamshire directory of 1834. The device of disguising borrowings in the first few pages by adaptation or additional matter, while the rest of the book is simply a copy, was very common. It was also used to hide the re-issue of an old edition in a subsequent year. F. & J. White's directory was itself pirated by E. S. Drake, all of whose directories seem to have been piracies, in 1861.

Similarly the text of Hagar's directory of Leicestershire (1849) is taken, though slightly altered and brought up to date, from W. White's directory of 1846 and Drake copied Hagar word for word in a directory of Leicestershire for 1861. White ignored Hagar but he proceeded against Drake and obtained a legal injunction against him.[3] Drake had worked for White for several years. His prospectus was said to have been headed ' Drake & Co.' in large letters, ' formerly with ' in very small type and ' William White ' in letters the same size as ' Drake & Co.', with the intention of conveying the impression that White was concerned in the publication. The arrangement and text of Drake's directory were shown to have

---

[1] See Kelly's Post Office London directories for 1850–5 and Watkins' *Commercial & General London Directory*, 1852 to 1855. Both sides freely issued pamphlets, Warnings and Cautions against each other. Watkins' directory was really in some ways the better of the two but he was no match for Kelly.

[2] See p. 18 above. Kelly in his *Post Office Directory of Birmingham* (1860) stated that *Cassey's Directory of Worcestershire* (1860) contained names and addresses from Kelly's directory of 1854, which had become quite out of date.

[3] Preface to W. White's directory of Norfolk, 1864.

been copied from White's and information from White's to have
been included without alteration, though out of date.

William White was in danger, at least once, of being convicted
of piracy himself. When his directory of Sheffield for 1833 was in
the hands of the binders, he received a notice from the attorneys of
a Mr. Thomas, threatening him with legal proceedings if it included
any part of Thomas's *Local Register*, and he found himself obliged
to insert a disclaimer, which, after giving a list of authorities consulted for the work, he gracefully did in the following terms :

and he owes some little to Mr Thomas's *Local Register*, but happily for W. W.
the detached and tautological notices in the lean pages of that work are so
ill-suited to his ideas of historical narration, that he has not adopted any of
them, and having observed amongst them several glaring anachronisms, he
trusted not to their authority, but preferred searching the books and newspapers from which they had been extracted . . .   W. W. hopes that the
following pages bear not the slightest resemblance to those of Mr T.'s
Register . . .

Considered from the point of view of the primary purpose of a
directory in supplying information about names, occupations and
addresses, the importance of these textual piracies is that they throw
in varying degrees, a general doubt on the honesty of the compiler.
They must be taken in conjunction with other evidence in estimating
the reliability of the publication in which they occur.

The use of directories as historical sources is being increasingly
appreciated. Attention here has been mainly confined to the lists
of names, but other parts are often of value. The *Annals of Liverpool* in Gore's Liverpool directories are a notable example. A great
deal of general history is also to be gathered from a study of the
names and occupations themselves. Eighteenth and early nineteenth century directories are often attractive little books to read
and to handle, very different from the monster volumes into which
they have evolved to-day. It is a pity that so many of them have
vanished, but it is more remarkable that so many of such essentially
ephemeral productions have survived at all, and it is encouraging
to find that some very early ones, for instance the 1798 Birmingham
directory, have come into public collections in quite recent years.
There seems ground for hope that more of them may be discovered
in the future.

CATALOGUE OF DIRECTORIES OF
PLACES IN ENGLAND AND WALES,
excluding London,
PUBLISHED BEFORE 1856

PREFATORY NOTE

THE books included in the following catalogue are, with very few exceptions, only such as contain substantial lists of names and addresses. This accounts for the omission of some books which have the word 'directory' on the title but are, in fact, no more than guide books, for instance, Rusher's *Reading Guide or Berkshire Directory*, which contains a variety of local intelligence but not any proper list of inhabitants.

CLASSIFICATION

The catalogue is divided into three parts:

I. *National Directories.*—This includes directories of more than two counties or of a number of towns all over the country, including Wales. They are listed under publishers, an arrangement which does not differ much from a chronological one except in 1839–40, when Robson is contemporary with Pigot, and after 1845, when Kelly and Slater coincide. William White, who, from the area he covered, may be regarded as a national directory publisher, never published a directory of more than two counties at once and his directories are listed under their respective counties. A descriptive note about him and some of his associates is, however, appended to the list of national directories.

II. *Local Directories.*—These are arranged chronologically under counties in alphabetical order, the towns in each county in alphabetical order after the relevant county directories. Besides directories of single counties and towns, they include directories of not more than two counties. Directories of a number of towns, nearly all within one county, are entered under the main county and not under the National division. There are one or two cases of a few towns in one directory which are entered under the main town and not under the county, *e.g.* Liverpool, 1787. Some directories, though mainly of one town, include surrounding areas of various sizes and not always in the same county. These are generally entered under the main town but if the surrounding area is large, they will be found in the County section. Cross-references (see below) are given where necessary.

III. *Welsh Directories.*—There are no separate county directories for Wales. Directories of Welsh towns are listed under the towns, in alphabetical order, in the section 'Wales' on pp. 222–5.

CROSS-REFERENCES

Cross-references are given whenever the overlapping of the main sections of the classification seems to make the finding of a particular directory difficult. No cross-references are given to the National section, the directories in which may include any county or town in the country, but in all cases in the Local section, where a county or part of a county is included with another county, or a town is included in a directory of a county not its own, there is either a general reference at the beginning of the section or a special reference at the relevant date under the county or town. There are also a few cross-references from towns to their own counties and vice versa, when these seem specially necessary, but such references are not given as a general rule, and in looking for directories of towns or parts of counties, both the county and the town section should always be consulted.

ABBREVIATIONS

The following abbreviations are used in each entry to indicate the kind of directory involved.

Ct. . Court. Alphabetical list of private persons, with their addresses.

Cm. . Commercial. Alphabetical list of persons engaged in trades and professions, with their occupations and addresses.

Gen. General. Alphabetical list of inhabitants, including both court and commercial.

Pr. . Professions. Classified list of professions, with names and addresses of persons engaged in them.

Tr. . Trades. Classified list of trades, with names and addresses. These often include professions as well.

Misc. Miscellaneous. Alphabetical list of inhabitants not included in a succeeding classified list.

St. . Streets. List of streets, with names and occupations of persons residing in them. Lists of streets with no names of occupants are referred to as ‘ street lists ’.

Adds. List of additions and alterations.

LOCATION OF COPIES

The lists of copies are not exhaustive. When a number of copies are known to exist in most public libraries, only a few in representative public collections have been mentioned, and when there is a choice, public collections have been referred to, in preference to private collections. When the name of a town is mentioned without qualification, the Public Library of that town is to be understood. The British Museum Catalogue has a section headed ‘ Directories ’ but the books themselves are so diversely classified, under this section, under the names of authors, under the names of places and elsewhere, that it has been thought useful to quote the shelf number for all copies which do not appear under the heading ‘ Directories ’. The following abbreviations are used for collections other than those in municipal public libraries.

A.R.W.   .   Collection formed by the late Mr A. T. Butler, now belonging to Mr A. R. Wagner, Richmond Herald, College of Arms, London.

Bangor   .   Univ. Coll. of N. Wales, Bangor.

Bishopsgate   Bishopsgate Institute, London, E.C.

B.M. . . British Museum.

Bod. . . Bodleian Library, Oxford.

C.U.L. . . Cambridge Univ. Library.

Chetham . Chetham Library, Manchester.

Gen. Soc. . Society of Genealogists, Malet Place, London.

Guildhall . City of London Guildhall Library.

I.H.R.   . Institute of Historical Research, Univ. of London.

L.L.   . . London Library, St. James's Sq., London.

Liv. Ath. . The Athenaeum, Liverpool.

M.M.   . . Manx Museum, Douglas, Isle of Man.

Maidstone . Kent County Library, Maidstone.

Morrab   . Morrab Library, Penzance.

N.L.W. . . National Library of Wales, Aberystwith.

P.L.   . . Public Library.

Salt .   . . William Salt Library, Stafford.

U.L.   . . University Library.

W.S.L. . . Women's Service Library (London & National Soc. for Women's Service, London).

NATIONAL DIRECTORIES

BAILEY'S DIRECTORIES, 1781–1787

The first person to attempt a directory covering a larger area than a single town and its environs was William Bailey. His first directory, which includes London and the principal English towns north of the Trent, was published in 1781, under the patronage of John Stephenson, a merchant of Hull, to whom it is dedicated. His own name does not appear in any of the towns in it, but in 1783 he was apparently living in Birmingham, where his *Western and Midland Directory* was printed by Pearson & Rollason. He was perhaps the William Bailey who went bankrupt in that town in 1784.[1] At any rate he had moved to London, to 53 Basinghall St. when his *British Directory* was published in four volumes between June and September of that year. By the time the fourth volume was published he had set up a printing works as William Bailey & Co., at Featherstone St., Moorfields. This enterprise seems to have been a failure, for in 1785 the second edition of the first volume was published by William Richardson. According to the title this was part of a new edition of all four volumes, but no copies of the other volumes seem to have survived.

He appeared to have projected a general directory of England in parts in 1787. Of this the only survival is Part 3, Bristol. He published a directory of Liverpool in the same year, but the only surviving copy of this does not appear to be part of his general directory. In 1790 he was living at 46 Tottenham Court Road, where he published the fifth edition of his directory of London.

Bailey claims in his 1784 directory that he obtained his information by himself personally visiting every house.[2] The directories in every edition are alphabetical commercial lists for a number of towns.

1781

1. BAILEY'S NORTHERN DIRECTORY . . . FOR . . . 1781. CONTAINING . . . EVERY PRINCIPAL TOWN FROM THE RIVER TRENT TO BERWICK-UPON-TWEED; WITH LONDON & WESTMINSTER, EDINBURGH & GLASGOW. . . . WARRINGTON; PRINTED BY WILLIAM ASHTON . . .

    xii + 7–318. [Cm.]

    $6\frac{3}{8} \times 3\frac{7}{8}''$. Price 4s.

    Guildhall. Rochdale.

---

[1] B. Walker, 'Birmingham Directories' (*Birm. Arch. Soc. Trans.*, lviii, 1934, [pub. 1937]).
[2] *Cf.* p. 16 above.

1783

2. BAILEY'S WESTERN & MIDLAND DIRECTORY FOR . . . 1783
CONTAINING [towns in Berks, Hants, Wilts, Dorset, Som,
Devon, Cornwall, Glos, Worcs, Heref, Shrops, Oxon, Derby,
Chesh, Staffs, Notts, Warw, Lancs] WITH . . . LONDON & WEST-
MINSTER . . . BIRMINGHAM; PRINTED BY PEARSON & ROLLA-
SON. MDCCLXXXIII.
   xii + 9-368 (including *145-*152). [Cm.]
   $8\frac{3}{8} \times 4\frac{7}{8}''$.
Guildhall.

2a. [Another issue.] With additional pages in the London section,
   as follows : *129-*136 ; *137-*144.
   Birmingham (2 copies).

1784

3. BAILEY'S BRITISH DIRECTORY . . . FOR . . . 1784. IN FOUR
VOLUMES . . . VOLUME THE FIRST . . . CONTAINING . . . LON-
DON & WESTMINSTER & . . . SOUTHWARK . . . LONDON :
PRINTED BY J. ANDREWS, LITTLE EASTCHEAP ; & TO BE HAD
OF THE AUTHOR, 53 BASINGHALL STREET . . . MDCCLXXXIV.
   vi + 306. [Cm.]
   Preface dated 4 June, 1784.
[Vol. II] . . . VOLUME THE SECOND. THE WESTERN DIREC-
TORY . . . CONTAINING [towns in Berks, Wilts, Dorset, Som,
Devon, Cornwall, Glos, Worcs, Bucks, Oxon, Nhants, Leics,
Notts, Staffs]. [Imprint & date as Vol. I.]
   xii + 315-494. [Cm.]
   Publication announced for July 1784.
[Vol. III] . . . VOLUME THE THIRD. THE NORTHERN DIREC-
TORY . . . CONTAINING [towns in Chesh, Derby, Lancs, Lincs,
Dur, Yorks, Nthumb, Westm, Cumb, Hants, Shrops, Heref,
Rutl]. [Imprint and date as Vol. I.]
   viii + 495-746. [Cm.]
   Publication announced for August 1784.
[Vol. IV] . . . VOLUME THE FOURTH. THE EASTERN DIREC-
TORY. CONTAINING [towns in Beds, Cambs, Essex, Herts,
Hunts, Kent, Mdsx, Norfolk, Suffolk, Sussex, Surrey, Warw]
. . . LONDON : PRINTED BY W. BAILEY & CO., 7 FEATHERSTONE-
STREET, MOORFIELDS. TO BE HAD AT THEIR OFFICE, 53 BASING-
HALL STREET . . . MDCCLXXXIV.
   viii + 747-970 (pagination 929/30 repeated). [Cm.]
   Publication announced for September 1784.
   $8\frac{3}{8} \times 5''$. Price 3s. per vol.
B.M. (impf.). Guildhall. I.H.R. (Vol. IV only).

1785

4. BAILEY'S BRITISH DIRECTORY . . . FOR . . . 1785. IN FOUR
VOLUMES . . . THE SECOND EDITION. LONDON ; PRINTED FOR
WILLIAM RICHARDSON, 91 CORNHILL . . . MDCCLXXXV,

Only the first volume, covering London, for which see Goss, *op. cit.*, p. 66, seems to have survived.

1787

5. BAILEY'S GENERAL DIRECTORY OF ENGLAND, WALES, &c. *See* BRISTOL, 1787 (No. 253).

WILLIAM TUNNICLIFF, 1787–1789

Tunnicliff was a land surveyor. The lists of names in his books are short and include only the principal inhabitants in each of a few towns, but the entries of occupations are interesting, especially in the part on the Potteries. His *Topographical Survey of Hants, Wilts, etc.* (1791), contains only lists of the owners of large country seats and is not worth including as a directory.

1787

6. A TOPOGRAPHICAL SURVEY OF THE COUNTIES OF STAFFORD, CHESTER & LANCASTER . . . BY WILLIAM TUNNICLIFF . . . NANTWICH : PRINTED & SOLD BY E. SNELSON . . . MDCCLXXXVII.
     xiv + 118 + 2 ; fly-title, map and 8 plates for each county. [Ct. Cm.]
          $8\frac{5}{8} \times 5\frac{1}{4}''$. Boards, label.
   Bod. B.M. (1303.b.19). Guildhall. Rochdale. Salt.

1789

7. A TOPOGRAPHICAL SURVEY OF THE COUNTIES OF SOMERSET, GLOUCESTER, WORCESTER, STAFFORD, CHESTER & LANCASTER . . . BY WILLIAM TUNNICLIFF . . . BATH, PRINTED & SOLD BY R. CRUTTWELL . . . MDCCLXXXIX.
     vi + 88 + 118 + 2 ; fly-title, map and 8 plates for each county. [Ct. Cm.]
          $8\frac{5}{8} \times 5\frac{1}{4}''$.
     Dedication dated December 1788. The second part is only a re-issue of the 1787 directory.
   Guildhall. I.H.R. L.L.

THE UNIVERSAL BRITISH DIRECTORY, 1790–1798

The promoters of the next attempt at a national directory were Peter Barfoot and John Wilkes. Barfoot was a country gentleman, living at Midlington Place, Droxford, near Southampton. In 1786 he published *Two Letters addressed to . . . William Pitt*, signed ' Veritas ', in which he made proposals for an equal system of taxation and for reducing the National Debt. Later he became involved in a dispute with the turnpike commissioners and the bishop of Winchester, in which he seems to have behaved with considerable arbitrariness and lack of courtesy. Wilkes acted as his agent in this affair and was probably the author of the account of it which was subsequently published.[1]

John Wilkes seems thus to have been in close connection with this wealthy patron, whom, no doubt, he persuaded to finance *The Universal British Directory*. He was born in 1750 and was established as a printer at Winchester by 1772. He became proprietor of the *Hampshire Chronicle* and was made a freeman of the city. In spite of this respectable position, he seems to have been something of a rogue. As will be seen, there are some shady features about *The Universal British* and he was fined for piracy in connection with a later enterprise, the *Encyclopedia Londonensis*.[2] Nevertheless he seems to have prospered, and when he died in 1810 he had become John Wilkes, of Milland House, in the County of Sussex, Esq.[3] It is tempting to connect him with his famous namesake, especially in view of the long accounts of irregularities in Parliamentary elections which are a feature of the historical parts of *The Universal British Directory*, but there seems no evidence of any relationship.

The directory was published under a Royal Patent dated 28 August 1789, conferring on Peter Barfoot and John Wilkes the sole right of printing and publishing it, and forbidding any other British subject to reprint, abridge or import copies of it without their consent. Wilkes, inspired perhaps by his own habit of piracy, seems to have liked this way of protecting his copyright, for the *Encyclopedia Londonensis* was published under a similar patent.

The directory was issued in parts at irregular intervals. The parts were printed by Wilkes and the London agents were, at first, C. Stalker, a bookseller, and Messrs Brideoake & Fell, described as agents. These were, however, soon replaced by a firm called Champante & Whitrow, of Jewry St., Aldgate. This firm is described in contemporary directories as wholesale stationers and wax chandlers and they also acted as commission agents for a wide range of articles such as Hampshire Tiller's Rat Powder and Berkenhout's dyes, which were advertised for sale by agents of *The Universal British Directory* in various towns.[4] The directory seems to have been hawked from door to door in company with such articles. Wilkes, who sold his business in Winchester in 1784, set up a printing office in 1792 in Ave Maria Lane, where he carried on business until his death. Later numbers of the directory were issued from this office.

Other, sometimes rather peculiar, publications were also sponsored by Champante & Whitrow and sold from the Universal British Office.[5] These included an edition of Culpeper's *British Herbal*, with additions (of a doubtful nature) by E. Sibly, Fellow of the Harmonic Philosophical Society in Paris ; a book called *Laws for Regulating*

---

[1] *A Candid Review of the Facts in the Litigation between Peter Barfoot, Esq. and Richard Bargus and others* . . . (London : Green & Co. [1788]). There is a copy in the Bodleian.

[2] Timperley, *Dictionary of Printers* (1839), p. 832.

[3] 'Early Printers & Booksellers of Winchester', *The Library*, 4th ser., i. (1920), pp. 106–7.

[4] *See* adverts. in *The New Bath Directory for 1792* (No. 624).

[5] *See* adverts. in *The New Birmingham Directory for 1798* (No. 714).

Bills of Exchange, by J. Blagrove, which seems calculated to assist fraudulent billbrokers ; a *Grand Imperial Bible* in one hundred and six weekly parts ; and an edition of the *Prayer Book*, with notes by the Rev. J. Cookson, Master of Churcher's College, Petersfield. Champante & Whitrow were agents for Chapman's Birmingham directory, 1801.

The Universal British Directory contains directories of London and of a large number of places, great and small, throughout England and Wales. The provincial directories consist of an historical and descriptive introduction, alphabetical lists of names, court, professional and commercial, and information about conveyances, fairs, etc. The method of compilation was varied and sometimes dubious. An agent was said to have been appointed in every town to enrol names and collect subscriptions.[1] Some of these agents can be identified. Thus W. Gye of Bath, John Reed of Bristol and J. Poole of Chester, besides others, who published offprints from *The Universal British*, with special title pages, must have been employed by Wilkes and have been supplied by him with the offprints for separate sale. Another local printer, John Bird of Cardiff, recorded in his diary that Wilkes applied to him for the names of the inhabitants and other particulars of Cardiff and Caerphilly and that he had sent such an account as he was able to collect.[2] Perhaps he too was supplied with an offprint, though no copy has survived. His 1796 Cardiff directory was used for the revised edition of the second volume of *The Universal British*.

Sometimes Wilkes adopted a simpler method. He took an existing directory and copied it, re-arranging the contents where necessary to fit his classifications, and disregarding recklessly their applicability to the date at which he was publishing. His use of Battle's Hull directory for 1791 has already been mentioned.[3] The directory of Birmingham, which was compiled for Wilkes by a local bookseller called John Ward, produced an indignant protest in *Aris's Birmingham Gazette* for 20 February 1792 which sheds some light on the methods of Wilkes and of some of his agents. The writer was Charles Pye, author of a number of Birmingham directories. The notice runs as follows :

The Public are herebye informed that the compilers of what is called *The British Directory* have, with a very few Additions, copied my Directory for 1791, and to shew their Ignorance of the Business have introduced as Resident Gentry, a number of Persons who either carry on their Business in one place and reside in another, or are second Partners in their respective Houses ; one Person, whose Name was omitted in 1791, being asked (for they are hawked about) to purchase the Book, enquired if his Name was inserted, but it not being there, he demanded the Reason, and received for Answer that it must be omitted in the last ;—in Fact, it is now so long since the Survey was taken that every Page is full of false Information . . .

Other directories and guide books may, in some cases, have been used by arrangement with the local publishers. Thus the Worcester section is adapted from Grundy's *Worcester Royal Directory* for 1797, one of a succession of directories by this publisher, but it has

---

[1] *See* advert. of *The Universal British Directory* in Bath directory cited above.
[2] I. Jones, *History of Printing & Printers in Wales* (1925), pp. 95–6.
[3] p. 18 above.

an additional note, evidently supplied by a correspondent on the spot, who is very likely to have been Grundy himself. The numbers containing the Manchester directory seem to have been published almost at the same time as Scholes' Manchester directory from which the information is taken, and the Sheffield section was actually published before the local directory in which the historical introduction is almost verbatim the same.

Similar connections can be traced with a number of contemporary directories. Further details will be found in the list of volumes of *The Universal British Directory* below. No doubt other directories, of which no copies now exist, were also used.

The Parts in which the directory was issued are of about sixty pages each, and the part number is generally printed at the bottom of the first page of each gathering. It was advertised to be complete in forty-two parts at 1s. each, but there are sixty-nine numbered parts (1–71, there being for some reason no parts numbered 19 or 33), besides several supplements. At intervals the parts already published were re-issued in volume form and the whole makes up five volumes. These volumes were themselves re-issued, Vols. I and III three times and Vol. II, so far as can be traced, only twice. The contents were partially, but only partially, revised for the later editions.

Considerable difficulty arises in ascertaining the dates to which the information in *The Universal British Directory* applies. The editor's habit of lifting information from earlier directories has been mentioned. Besides this, the parts themselves are undated and the title-pages of the volumes into which they were collected are misleading. There was more than one issue of some, but not of all, of the parts, and existing copies of the volumes are sometimes made up, either at the time of publication or by the supplying of missing parts at a later date, of different issues of the parts. As many of the directories never were revised, the later editions of the volumes are particularly out of date. The safest way of finding the date of compilation of a corporate town is to note the name of the mayor, though the name of the mayor is often omitted in revised issues, no doubt just because it gives too exact an indication of the year to which the directory really refers. Some of the parts mention dates evidently nearly contemporary with the time of compilation, and from these a guess at the date of publication can be made. Existing collections of the volumes into sets by the number of the edition are misleading, as the republication of different volumes took place at different times.

Vol. I, 1790

8. The Universal British Directory of Trade & Commerce, comprehending . . . London, Westminster & . . . Southwark ; & . . . all the Cities, Towns & Principal Villages in England & Wales . . . London : Printed for the Patentees & Sold by C. Stalker . . . Stationers' Court, Ludgate Street & Messrs Brideoake & Fell . . . MDCCXC.
 cxx + 773 + 3 ; plan of London, 1791.

This volume contains Pts. 1–14, covering London. The first part was published in 1790 and a date, 10 May 1791, is mentioned in Pt. 14. The title page was issued with the first number. Many copies of the volume must have come into existence by subscribers having their parts bound up, but Wilkes may have issued copies as well. Existing copies are located below in accordance with their title page but they will be found to be made up of very varying issues of the parts.[1]

Bod.   B.M.   Guildhall.   Manchester.

1791

9. THE UNIVERSAL BRITISH DIRECTORY OF TRADE, COMMERCE & MANUFACTURE . . . LONDON : PRINTED FOR THE PATENTEES & SOLD BY CHAMPANTE & WHITROW, JEWRY STREET, ALDGATE. MDCCXCI.

Pagination as above. Most of this is the same sheets as 1790 with a cancel title and slight revision of some of the parts, notably of the addenda on pp. 345–7. It was advertised as 'this day published' in *Aris's Birmingham Gazette* on 12 September 1791.

B.M.   Guildhall.   I.H.R.

1793

10. [Title as above but] SECOND EDITION. VOLUME THE FIRST. LONDON ; PRINTED FOR THE PATENTEES AT THE BRITISH DIRECTORY OFFICE, AVE MARIA LANE & SOLD [as 1791].

Pagination as 1790 ; plan dated 1792.

The dedication is dated 10 June 1793. With the exception of a few alterations and additions, this is another re-issue, or a reprinting from the same setting of type, of the first edition. This is the first time the volume number appears on the title and the volume was probably published together with the first edition of Vol. II.

Bishopsgate.   B.M.   Guildhall.

1798

11. [Title as 1793 but] THIRD EDITION.

cxxviii + 773 + 3 ; plan dated 1798.

Dedication dated 1790 but some of the sections are headed 1797. It was perhaps published with Vol. V. The contents are again partly revised but mostly a reprint of the first edition.

Bishopsgate Inst.   Gen. Soc.   Guildhall (2 copies with different mixtures of issues of the parts).

[1] Details of this volume are given, in spite of its being a London directory, because Goss's description of the various editions is confusing and not always correct.

12. Annual supplements, bringing the directories up to date, were promised in the preface to Vol. I but only three supplements were issued, all confined to London. These were *List of the Liverymen of London*, 1792, 156 pp., with Appendix, 12 pp., also issued separately ; *A Supplement to the British Directory*, 1792, 74 pp., containing additions to the London directory and the Law directory in Vol. I ; and *Directory to the Nobility & Gentry*, n.d. but after 1793, 56 pp., containing a court directory and six pages of additions to Vol. I.[1] These supplements were also issued in Vol. V, *q.v.*
Bod. (2 copies of the three supplements bound in 2 vols.).
B.M. Guildhall (first two supplements only).

Vol. II. 1793

13. THE UNIVERSAL BRITISH DIRECTORY OF TRADE, COMMERCE & MANUFACTURE . . . VOLUME THE SECOND. [Imprint as Vol. I, 1793.]
916 + 4. [Ct. Pr. Cm.]
This contains Parts 15–32, Abbotsbury–Dudley. There is no hiatus between Pts. 18 and 20, so there seems for some reason, to have been no Pt. 19. Pts. 15–18 were published by 20 February 1792, when Pye denounced the Birmingham directory in Pt. 18 as a piracy. In Pt. 30 is an entry, ' at this time, 1792 ' and the latest date mentioned is September 1792 in Pt. 32. It appears, therefore, that the parts were compiled between 1791 and the end of 1792.[2] It seems likely that the volume was issued in 1793 with the ' second edition ' of Vol. I.
The following directories were used in compiling this volume. Further details of the use made of them will be found in the entries for them in the Local Directories section. BATH, 1792 ; BIRMINGHAM, 1792 ; BRISTOL, 1792 ; CARLISLE, 1792 ; CHESTER, 1792 ; DOVER, 1792. The descriptive part of the Chichester directory is taken from Alexander Hay's *Guide to Chichester*, of which several editions were published from 1784 onwards. There was no directory attached to this guide until 1804, so Wilkes must have got the list of names from another source. *See also* CARDIFF, 1796.
Bod. B.M. Guildhall. I.H.R. Manchester.

1797 *or* 1798

14. [Title & imprint as first edition.]
Pagination as first edition. The principal clue to the date of publication is in the Chelsea directory (Pt. 30, p. 749), where the list of Officers of the Royal Hospital is dated 1797. From Pt. 20 onwards some of the directories have been revised

---

[1] Goss's account of these supplements is very confused.
[2] Apart from any that Wilkes may have taken from earlier publications. *Cf.* p. 18 above.

but the revision is often superficial and many directories are the same as in the first edition.
Guildhall.

VOL. III.   1794

15. [Title as Vol. II but] VOLUME THE THIRD.
396 + 4. [Ct. Pr. Cm.]
Contains Pts. 34–48, Exeter–Morton. There seems to have been no Pt. 33. Perhaps the supplements to Vol. I were issued instead of Pts. 19 and 33. The most significant dates are in Pt. 37, ' at the time of printing this article, July 20, 1793 ', and in Pt. 45, '. . . . just finished (June 1794) . . . a most complete set of baths '. The latest date mentioned is 25 August 1794 in Pt. 46. It seems therefore that the parts were compiled during 1793 and 1794 and the volume published about the end of 1794.
The following directories are connected with this volume ; HULL, 1791 ; LIVERPOOL, 1794 ; MANCHESTER, 1794 ; see the relevant entries in the Local Directories section.
Bod.   Bristol (the title is of this edition but Pts. 35–40 are 3rd ed.).   B.M.   Guildhall.   I.H.R.   Manchester.

1795

16. [Title as 1794 but] SECOND EDITION.
Pagination as 1794. The date of this edition is indicated by an interesting addition on p. 234 in Pt. 37, where it is said that about 4,000 prisoners of war were confined at Portchester in 1761. In this edition a remark is added, ' There are about the same number at this time (Feb. 1795) '. Only the first four parts, 34–37, are revised.
B.M. (2 copies, one with 1st eds of Pts. 35–37).

1799

17 [Title as 1794 but] THIRD EDITION.
Pagination as 1794. Pts. 34–41 were revised for this edition. The remainder are the same as when first published in 1794. The approximate date of publication is shown by the date, 1799, given for the members of Parliament for Ipswich (Pt. 40, p. 423).
Guildhall.

VOL. IV.   1798

18. [Title as Vol. II but] VOLUME THE FOURTH.
984. [Ct. Pr. Cm.]
This volume contains Pts. 49–part of 66 + part of 67, Norwich–Yoxford. Significant dates range from 1 May 1795 (Pt. 55, p. 196), through April 1796 (Pt. 56, p. 400) and 25 June 1797 (Pt. 62, p. 755) to 13 January 1798 (Pt. 65, p. 915).

The following directories are connected with this volume : SHEFFIELD, 1797 ; SHREWSBURY, 1797 ; WORCESTER, 1797 ; *see* the relevant entries in the Local Directories section. Bod. B.M. Guildhall. I.H.R.

VOL. V. 1798

19. [Title as Vol. II but] VOLUME THE FIFTH.
296 + 72 + 156 + 12 + 3–50 + 6 + 3–38 ; map dated 1798. [Ct. Pr. Cm.]
This contains the rest of Pts. 66 and 67 and Pts. 68–71, with the three supplements to Vol. I as described above (No. 12) and a street directory of the Nobility & Gentry of London. On the last page are directions to the binder on the order in which to bind up the various sections. These directions were not always followed and, in particular, the leaf containing bankers, etc. in the 1792 supplement, which should have been cut out, was sometimes retained instead of the later edition of the same leaf in the 1793 supplement. There is a reference to April 1798 in Pt. 67. The binder is directed to bind the plan of London and the *Anecdotes of London* with the first volume, which perhaps indicates that the third edition of Vol. I was published at the same time as this volume.
Bod. B.M. Guildhall. I.H.R.

Other sets, the exact issues of which have not been ascertained, are at Manchester (Vols. I–III) and Bangor.

JAMES BISSET, 1800–1808

James Bisset was born in Perth in 1762 and came to Birmingham as an artist's apprentice in 1777. There he made a name as an artist, a designer of tokens and medals and a writer of verse. He belonged to the Minerva Club, also called ' The Twelve Apostles ', of which Charles Pye, a compiler of Birmingham directories, was another member. In 1813 he moved to Leamington, of which place he published a ' Picturesque Guide '. He died in 1832.[1] He is famous from our point of view as the first publisher of an illustrated directory (*Cf.* p. 13 above).

1800–1808

20. BISSET'S GRAND NATIONAL DIRECTORY OR LITERARY & COMMERCIAL ICONOGRAPHY . . . PUBLISHED BY J. BISSET, MUSEUM, BIRMINGHAM, MAY 1st 1800.
title + engraved plates numbered 1–14, XV, 16, XVII, 18, 4–8, A–X, 4, 6–22, [1 unnumbered], 26–28, [2 unnumbered].
$8\frac{3}{4} \times 5\frac{3}{8}''$. Issued in parts, wrappers, 2s. 6d. a part.
The plates, which were designed by Bisset, contain lists of commercial names engraved against pictorial backgrounds.

[1] *D.N.B.* ; B. Walker, ' Birmingham Directories ', *Birm. Arch. Soc. Trans.*, lviii (1937) ; W. Longman, *Tokens of the Eighteenth Century* (1916).

They cover some 30 towns. The project was advertised in *Aris's Birmingham Gazette*, 27 October 1800. The first part, which included the title, had appeared in the previous May. The others appeared irregularly until as late as 1808. Many of the plates were also published in Bisset's Birmingham directories for 1800 and 1808, *q.v.* The collected volume described above has the original wrappers of Pt. 2, with the name of the printers, Grafton & Reddell, 10, High Street. This, the only known copy, is the volume described by Walker (*op. cit.*) as belonging to Mr T. Whitmore Peck. *See also* p. 13 above.
Birmingham.

WILLIAM HOLDEN & THOMAS UNDERHILL, 1805–1816

No national directory was published for some years after the last edition of *The Universal British Directory*. The next attempt was made by William Holden, who began his career as a directory publisher in 1799, with a *Triennial Directory* covering London, of which a second and third edition, besides supplements, were published. His provincial series began in 1805, when he published the fourth edition of the *Triennial Directory* in two volumes, the second containing alphabetical directories for eighty-four towns in the United Kingdom. Holden, who is entered as a coal merchant and publisher in his 1802 directory, had an office in Clerkenwell and employed various printers, in some volumes as many as seven different firms, to print his directories. Whether by arrangement with Wilkes or not, much of the historical and descriptive parts of the first edition of his provincial directory are taken from *The Universal British Directory*. His ambition was to produce a classified directory but he found, he says, a large majority in favour of an alphabetical arrangement. The price of the 1805 directory was £1 19s. 6d. for the two volumes and he printed 11,000 copies. Evidently a number were left on his hands, for the same sheets were issued in 1808, with new titles but still called the fourth edition.

By this time he had moved to another office in Newgate St. His projects became more and more ambitious and his prices correspondingly higher. The price of the fifth edition was announced (on the title-page of the fourth) as three guineas for prompt payment (*i.e.* for subscribers) and four guineas after publication. This edition was published in 1809. It covered London and a larger number of provincial towns than before and the price was, in fact, five guineas. In the preface he announced that, from 1811, the directory was to be published annually and would cost five guineas to subscribers and six and a half guineas after publication. He announced at the same time a 'Large Work' to contain all the market towns in the United Kingdom, in seven volumes, at not less than a guinea and a half per volume, 'however few the sheets'. He also said that he intended to start a daily newspaper.

No more is to be heard of the 'Large Work' but the edition for 1811 is in three volumes. Holden complains in the preface of the difficulty of getting enough printers. The work was to be issued henceforth to subscribers only and there were three rates of subscription, £2 12s. 6d., £3 3s. and £5 5s. What advantages went with the higher rates is not specified but he published an imposing list of subscribers.[1]

After this Holden's business began to go to pieces. He was, no doubt, already suffering from the tedious illness from which he died. He had reverted to his always favourite idea of a classified directory and seems to have collected a considerable amount of material for it. In 1814 he published a volume covering the textile trades. In the preface he indicated that this 'fifth class' of his classified directory had given him great trouble, that it was much behind the promised time and that he had miscalculated the cost and was in financial difficulties. He died shortly afterwards.

His directory was taken over by Thomas Underhill, who published the first, second and third classes, presumably from material collected by Holden, in 1816. He abandoned the attempt to produce a fully classified directory and simply published alphabetical lists, for certain towns, of persons engaged in certain trades. He was struggling to fulfil Holden's obligations and had, he said, published and delivered many thousand volumes (of which singularly few have survived) of the provincial directory for Holden's subscribers but neither the fourth nor any subsequent classes of the classified directory are extant and perhaps they were never published.

Another edition of the London directory appeared in 1817 and Underhill said in the preface that he was determined to re-instate the directory and to publish another country volume in 1818. No such volume seems, however, to have been issued and the project came to an end with the eleventh edition of the London directory in 1822.

1805

21. HOLDEN'S TRIENNIAL DIRECTORY FOR 1805, 1806, 1807 . . . LONDON : SOLD BY THE PROPRIETOR, No. 8 . . . NORTHAMPTON BUILDINGS, ROSOMAN STREET, CLERKENWELL . . . PRINTED BY W. GLENDINNING [and six other firms].
[Vol. II] [Title as above but] FOURTH EDITION . . . SECOND VOLUME . . . 1805.
   The second volume contains a general list for each of eighty-four towns in the British Isles. 304 pp.
   $8\frac{1}{4} \times 4\frac{7}{8}$". Price £1 19s. 6d. per vol.
Birmingham (Vol. II). Bod. B.M. Guildhall. Manchester.

1808

22. HOLDEN'S TRIENNIAL DIRECTORY, FOURTH EDITION, INCLUDING THE YEAR 1808 . . . [imprint as 1805 but the proprietor's address is 122 Newgate Street].
   Re-issue of the 1805 edition with cancel titles.
B.M. C.U.L. Guildhall.

[1] *See* p. 8 above.

1809

23. HOLDEN'S TRIENNIAL DIRECTORY (FIFTH EDITION) FOR 1809, 1810, 1811 . . . LONDON : PRINTED BY J. DAVENPORT [and others]. SOLD BY THE PROPRIETOR, 122 NEWGATE STREET . . .
[Vol. I]. London. (*See* Goss, *op. cit.*)
[Vol. II]. 4 + 444 + 18 + 11–14 + 46. [Gen.]
8¼ × 4⅞″. Price £5 5s.
Pp. 1–444 cover Aberdeen–York with addenda for Dublin, followed by a blank leaf. The remaining pages include Cork and a few other towns, Waterford (11–14) and a list of M.P.'s (1–46). The B.M. copy has not the directories after p. 444 but it has a different Cork directory, paged with the Waterford directory, 5–14, at the end of Vol. I.
Birmingham. B.M. Guildhall. Manchester (to p. 444 only).

1811

24. HOLDEN'S ANNUAL LONDON & COUNTRY DIRECTORY OF THE UNITED KINGDOMS & WALES, IN THREE VOLUMES, FOR . . . 1811 . . . LONDON : PRINTED BY W. GLENDINNING [and others]. PUBLISHED BY W. HOLDEN, THE ONLY PROPRIETOR, 122 NEWGATE STREET . . . 1811.
[Vol. I]. London. (*See* Goss, *op. cit.*)
[Vol. II]. 2 + Aberdeen–York, unnumbered. [Gen.]
[Vol. III]. Abergavenny-Yarm, unnumbered + 16 + 17–154. [Gen.]
8¼ × 4⅞″. Price from £5 5s. to £2 12s. 6d.
See pp. 8, 16, 21 above.
Bishopsgate. Guildhall (Vols. I & II only).

1814

25. HOLDEN'S ANNUAL DIRECTORY. CLASS THE FIFTH. COMBINING THE CALICO, COTTON, SILK, WOOLLEN & . . . OTHER CONNECTED MANUFACTURERS & TRADESMEN . . . IN LONDON & 455 . . . TOWNS [in the British Isles, including the Channel Islands] . . . FIRST EDITION FOR . . . 1814 & 1815 . . . LONDON : PRINTED FOR THE PROPRIETOR, W. HOLDEN, 5 VERNON PLACE, BLOOMSBURY SQUARE . . .
x + 268. [Tr.]
8⅜ × 5⅜″. Price £1 11s. 6d.
B.M. Manchester.

1816

26. HOLDEN'S ANNUAL DIRECTORY. CLASS FIRST, COMBINING THE MERCHANTS, SHIPOWNERS, BANKERS, &c . . . IN LONDON & 480 . . . TOWNS [etc. as 1814 but] FOR 1816 & 17 . . . LONDON : PRINTED FOR THE PROPRIETOR, 9 BAGNIO PLACE, NEWGATE STREET. [Printer, W. Flint, Old Bailey.]

viii + 230 (including *169–*170 & *173–*174). [Cm.]
8⅜ × 5⅛". Calf, red label. Price £1 11s. 6d.
Preface signed Thomas Underhill.
Bod. B.M. Manchester.

27. HOLDEN'S ANNUAL DIRECTORY, CLASS SECOND, COMBINING
THE AGENTS, BROKERS, BREWERS [and 17 other trades, mostly
connected with commerce,] IN LONDON [etc. as Class First
above, but the proprietor's address is 11 Coleman Street.
Printer, W. Flint].
viii + 268 (including *105–*112). [Cm.]
8⅜ × 5⅛". Price £1 11s. 6d.
B.M. (bound with Class First).

28. BIENNIAL DIRECTORY. CLASS THIRD, COMPRIZING THE . . .
ADDRESSES OF AGRICULTURAL IMPLEMENT MAKERS, BIRMING-
HAM WAREHOUSES [and 45 other metal trades] IN LONDON
[etc. as Class First above. Imprint and printer as Class Second].
viii + 9–244 (including *137–*144 & *217–*224) ; adverts.
[Cm.]
8⅜ × 5⅛". Price £1 7s. 6d.
B.M.

JAMES PIGOT & ISAAC SLATER, 1814–1855 (and after)

The provision of a national directory was taken up after the
failure of Thomas Underhill by James Pigot. His great series of
county directories had no rival during the early part of the nineteenth century. Parson's and White's directories were important
and successful but they were issued one or two counties at a time,
at irregular intervals, and some counties were never included at all.
Pigot abandoned London and the Home Counties after 1840 in face
of competition from Kelly's Post Office directories and his successor,
Isaac Slater, gradually withdrew to the northern and north-western
counties, besides Wales, Scotland and Ireland, leaving the southern
and eastern counties to Kelly. After 1857, Kelly began to publish
directories for the northern counties too but the Slater series
continued, carried on by a limited company for some years after
Slater's death, until, from 1892, the business became absorbed into
Kelly's Directories, Ltd.
James Pigot first appears upon the scene in Scholes's Manchester
directory for 1794 as an engraver and copper-plate printer at 13
Back Falkner St. Many years later Isaac Slater dated the beginning
of Pigot's directories from 1795 [1] but there is no trace of his connection with a directory until a map, engraved by him, was published in Dean's Manchester directory for 1804. In 1811 he
published the first of his long series of Manchester directories
from Fountain St., which remained the address of his Manchester
publishing office for the next forty-five years. An account of the

[1] *Slater's Directory of Lancashire*, 1882, title-page and preface.

Manchester directories is given under Manchester in the Local section below. Though his name does not appear on the title of *The Commercial Directory For 1814–15*, which covers some thirty manufacturing towns in the north, it does on that of the subsequent editions, and there can be little doubt that he was the originator of it. The preface shows a remarkable appreciation of the purposes which his later directories aimed at fulfilling and of the difficulties which lay in his way.

In 1820 he published a directory of Ireland, Scotland and the four northern counties of England. In 1822 he extended his activities to the south and published his first London directory, together with directories of two hundred and eighty places in the midland counties and in Wales. He completed his survey of the United Kingdom in 1823 with a volume covering the home and southern counties. In this year he opened an office in Basing Lane in London, and in 1834 he had an agent in Paris for the sale of his directories on the continent. In 1837 he moved his London office to 9 Fleet St. He continued to publish a volume every year, and sometimes more than one a year, covering London and different blocks of counties, as well as Ireland, Scotland and Wales. Some of the volumes are only re-issues of earlier editions but, roughly speaking, a fresh survey was completed every six or seven years.

For some years Pigot's son, James Pigot, jun., was associated with him in the publication of the Manchester directories, but he either died or went elsewhere and in 1839 Pigot took into partnership an engraver called Isaac Slater. Slater, who first appears in the Manchester directory for 1829, apparently began in a small way, combining engraving with selling boots and shoes and manufacturing straw hats. However, he seems to have prospered, and after sharing in the printing business and the Manchester directories for three years, took over the national directories as well on Pigot's death in 1843. The imprint of Pigot & Co.'s Royal National and Commercial directories became ' I Slater, late Pigot & Slater ' in 1844 and they became ' Slater's ' or ' Slater's (late Pigot & Co.) ' from 1846. Pigot's name was retained on the title of the county directories until 1882 and in 1921 the directory of Scotland, published by Kelly's Directories, Ltd., was still called Kelly's (Slater's) Royal National Directory. Pigot and Slater also issued some Birmingham directories in conjunction with Messrs Beilby.

The trade arrangement which Holden had found by inquiry to be the least popular and of which he had failed to make a success was adopted by Pigot for his county directories. He rarely used an alphabetical commercial list. The information was collected by personal canvass by himself and his agents, some of whom, like W. Parson and Joseph Bentley later became directory publishers themselves and considered it a recommendation to state that they had once been employed by James Pigot. As has been said, a fresh survey was made within every six or seven years but the same survey was often re-issued under different dates during the period, in volumes containing different combinations of the counties. Some of the component parts were also issued separately. The London directories were more frequently revised, though sometimes the revision only consists of an extra list of additions and alterations.

The directories were at first advertised in boards or bound, at slightly lower prices to subscribers than to non-subscribers. For a short period, between 1824 and 1827, they could be had at subscription prices varying from 21s. to 25s., in sheep with plain maps, or in calf with coloured maps. From 1828 they appeared in a characteristic plain or flowered green cloth with yellow labels, or in plain or diced calf, with Pigot's name gilt on the spine or on red labels. Prices in the '30's went up to 25s. or 30s. to subscribers and 5s. extra to non-subscribers. After 1846 they ranged up to as much as £2 for the calf edition to non-subscribers. In some cases it appears that the subscribers' edition was published some months before the non-subscribers'.

1814

29. THE COMMERCIAL DIRECTORY FOR 1814–15 CONTAINING . . . [31 places in Lancs, Chesh. & Yorks and Leek in Staffs] . . . MANCHESTER: PRINTED & PUBLISHED BY WARDLE & BENTHAM, GILLETT'S ENTRY . . . MARKET STREET.

xii + 252 + 16. [Tr.]

$9\frac{3}{8} \times 5\frac{7}{8}''$. Boards.

Preface dated 11 April 1814. *See also* pp. 18–19 above.

Gen. Soc. Leeds. Manchester. Sheffield. A.R.W.

1816

30. THE COMMERCIAL DIRECTORY FOR 1816–17 CONTAINING . . . [places as in 1814 with Birmingham & Wolverhampton added] . . . MANCHESTER: PRINTED BY WARDLE & PRATT, GILLETT'S ENTRY . . . & PUBLISHED BY THEM & JAMES PIGOT, FOUNTAIN STREET. 1816.

8 + 366 + xvi. [Tr.]

$8\frac{7}{8} \times 5''$. Price, subsc, 10s. 6d. boards, 11s. 6d. bound.

Preface dated 12 June 1816. The lists have been revised since 1814.

Birmingham. Guildhall. Liverpool. Manchester. Sheffield.

1818

31. THE COMMERCIAL DIRECTORY FOR 1818–19–20. CONTAINING [about 52 towns in the Midlands] . . . MANCHESTER: PUBLISHED BY JAMES PIGOT, FOUNTAIN STREET & R. & W. DEAN, MARKET STREET . . . 1818.

510 ; adverts, 2 pp., 2 eng ; map. [Tr.]

$8\frac{1}{4} \times 5''$. Price, 10s. 6d. boards, 12s. bound ; non-subsc, 11s. 6d. & 13s.

Preface dated 3 August 1818.

Birmingham. I.H.R. Leeds. Manchester. A.R.W.

1819

32. THE COMMERCIAL DIRECTORY FOR 1819–20. CONTAINING [as 1816, with additional towns. Imprint as 1818]. 1819.

2 + 5–550 + 14. [Tr.]

8¼ × 5″. Price 10s. 6d. boards, 12s. 6d. bound.

Re-issue of 1818, with preface re-dated 17 April 1819, and directories of a number of towns in Cheshire added. The adds. & alts. in the 1818 edition are neither included nor incorporated.

Huddersfield. A.R.W.

Pigot's national directories from now onwards can be divided into groups, each group being based on one of five separate surveys of the United Kingdom. Generally speaking, any appearance of a county directory after the first, within any group, is a re-issue and not a new directory. The following list is divided into groups according to the different surveys and it is indicated which directories are not new but only re-issues of an earlier edition. Pigot's own numbering of his editions is misleading as he seems to have often counted re-issues as new editions. As many copies as possible of each issue have been examined but it is almost impossible to check minor variations in every copy, and for any particular piece of information it will always be as well to consult more than one issue, especially if accuracy of date is important.[1] The pagination of each county directory in a volume is given and this should enable readers to identify the edition if they should come across a volume or a separate county issue which the author has missed. The Irish and Scottish directories have been included only when they also contain English or Welsh sections, so that the tale of them as given here is not complete.

The titles in this list are summarised. They all begin ' Pigot & Co.'s ', or later ' Slater's ', and continue with variations of ' Commercial Directory ' or ' National Commercial Directory ' or similar words, and these are only specified when they have some special significance, as when they change from ' Pigot ' to ' Slater '. Nearly all the directories are trades directories and the size from 1822 is uniformly 9¼ × 5½″. The imprints are also nearly uniform. Later editions have a varying number of pages at the end containing lists of bankers and advertisements and these have not, as a rule, been specified. The prelims. also vary slightly in some copies. The calf-bound copies do not, as a rule, contain the maps until 1836, as before that year these were issued separately except in the cloth copies.

FIRST GENERAL SURVEY, 1820–1826

1820

33. THE COMMERCIAL DIRECTORY OF SCOTLAND, IRELAND & THE FOUR MOST NORTHERN COUNTIES OF ENGLAND FOR 1820–21 & 22 . . . PUBLISHED BY JAMES PIGOT & CO. 16 FOUNTAIN

[1] See also p. 21, n. 3, on addenda lists in Pigot's directories.

STREET . . . PRINTED BY T. WILKINSON, 19 RIDGFIELD.
1820.
    viii + 338 + 2 + 9–248 + xxviii ; 2 maps, table. [Tr ; Ct.
also for Dublin and Edinburgh.]
    8¼ × 5″. Price, 18s. bound.
Includes Nthumb, Cumb, Westm, Dur. *See also* p. 19
above.
B.M. Manchester. A.R.W.

1821

34. SECOND EDITION OF THE COMMERCIAL DIRECTORY OF IRELAND,
SCOTLAND [etc. as above] FOR 1821–22 & 23 . . . [imprint as
above]. 1820.
    viii + 9–248 + 462 + xxviii ; 2 maps, table. [Tr. etc. as
above.]
    8¼ × 5″. Price, non-subsc, 21s. bound.
Re-issue of 1820–2 with additional directories for the English
counties. The adds. & alts. for Scotland in the 1820–2
edition are neither included nor incorporated.
Newcastle-on-Tyne.

1822

35. PIGOT & CO.'S LONDON & PROVINCIAL NEW COMMERCIAL
DIRECTORY FOR 1822–3 . . . PUBLISHED BY J. PIGOT & CO.
FOUNTAIN STREET, MANCHESTER . . . [Containing London and
280 towns in Chesh, Derby, Glos, Heref, Lancs, Leics, Lincs,
Monm, Norfolk, Notts, Rutl, Shrops, Som, Staffs, Warw,
Wilts, Worcs, Yorks & Wales].
    10 + (London), 238, xviii, 104 + (other towns), ii, 749, 3 ;
map.
    9¼ × 5½″. Price, non-subsc, 30s.
Preface dated 24 June 1822. All Pigot directories are in
this larger format from now on.
B.M. Gloucester. Guildhall. Manchester.

1823

36. [As above.] FOR 1823–4 . . . PUBLISHED BY J. PIGOT & CO.
24 BASING LANE, LONDON & 16 FOUNTAIN STREET, MAN-
CHESTER. [Containing London, Mdsx and places within 12
miles of London and 300 places in Beds, Berks, Bucks, Cambs,
Cornwall, Devon, Dorset, Essex, Hants, Herts, Hunts, Kent,
Nhants, Oxon, Suffolk, Surrey & Sussex].
    xvi + (London), 372, 142 + (Mdsx, etc. & other towns),
526 ; 2 maps.
    Price, non-subsc, 30s. plain, 35s. calf, maps coloured.
The preface, which is undated, calls this the second volume
of the *London & Provincial Directory*. Pigot's advertisement
on p. [526] is dated 16 September 1823.
Bod. B.M. Folkestone. Guildhall.

1824

37. PIGOT & CO.'S NEW COMMERCIAL DIRECTORY FOR 1824 . . .
[Containing Mdsx, places within 12 miles of London and 300
places in Beds, Berks, etc. as above, also Birmingham, Bristol,
Liverpool, Manchester, Sheffield and Isle of Man].

> viii + (London street list), 17–48 + (Mdsx, etc. and 300
> other towns), 1–526 ; [remainder not included in only copy
> found].
> This is a re-issue of the corresponding parts of 1823, above.
> The missing sections are presumably the same as in the
> DUBLIN & HIBERNIAN DIRECTORY below.

Guildhall.

38. . . . DUBLIN & HIBERNIAN . . . DIRECTORY . . . [with London, Birmingham, Bristol, Liverpool, Manchester, Sheffield and
Isle of Man] . . . PUBLISHED AUG. 12th, 1824. [Imprint as
1823.]

> xxiv + (Ireland), 428 + (London, re-issue of 1822 with
> 91–104 of last section omitted) + (other towns), 91–206 + 12 ;
> map.

B.M.

39. [Another issue.] Same title, Ireland as above + re-issue of
London, 1823, omitting 133–42 of last section + other towns
as above, repaged 133–248 ; map.

> Price (both issues), 21s. sheep, 25s. calf with coloured map ;
> non-subsc, 30s. & 35s.

Gen. Soc.

1825

40. . . . NEW COMMERCIAL DIRECTORY OF SCOTLAND FOR 1825–6
. . . WITH [London, etc. as 1824] . . . PUBLISHED BY J.
PIGOT & CO. AT THEIR DIRECTORY OFFICES, [addresses as 1823].

> 10 + (Scotland), 7–706 + (re-issue of London & other towns
> as in No. 39) + xxiv ; 3 maps.
> Prices as 1824.

B.M.

1826

41. . . . DUBLIN & HIBERNIAN . . . DIRECTORY FOR 1826–7 . . .
[with Birmingham, etc. as 1824 and Leeds. Imprint as 1823].

> Re-issue of 1824, without London, other towns with Leeds
> added, paged 1–116, and xiv pp. instead of 12 at end ; 2 maps.
> Price, 30s. sheep, 35s. calf with coloured maps.

B.M.

42. . . . NEW COMMERCIAL DIRECTORY OF SCOTLAND FOR 1826–7
. . . [with Birmingham, etc. as above. Imprint as 1825].

> Re-issue of 1825, without London, other towns with Leeds
> added paged 1–72 + 205–248 ; map.
> Prices as above.

B.M.

SECOND GENERAL SURVEY, 1826–1830

1826

43. THIRD EDITION . . . LONDON & PROVINCIAL . . . DIREC-
TORY FOR 1826–7 . . . [containing London, Mdsx, Essex,
Herts, Kent, Surrey and Sussex] . . .

> 12 + (London), cxvi, 9–384, 3, *1–*7, 7–104 + (counties as
> title), 385–516, 517–556, 557–590, 591–664, 665–684, 685–
> 728 + 729–744.
>> Price, non-subsc, 30s. plain, 40s. calf with maps coloured
>> and bound separately.

B.M.   Gen. Soc.   Guildhall.

44, 45. This directory was twice re-issued with cancel titles
bearing the dates 1827–8 (Guildhall, Chet.) and 1828–9 (Guildhall).
The prices and contents are the same in all three issues except
that there is a new list of bankers after p. 372 of the London
directory in the third issue.

1827

46. . . . METROPOLITAN NEW ALPHABETICAL DIRECTORY FOR
1827 . . . [London, Mdsx & places 12 miles round London] . . .

> 4 + (London), iv, 442, 138 + (Mdsx & places round), iv,
> 224 ; map.
>> Price 14s. ; calf, 17s.

Re-issued with title dated 1828 and extra adds. & alts. for
London.

Gen. Soc. (1827).   B.M. (1828).

1828

47. . . . DIRECTORY FOR 1828–9. [Chesh, Cumb, Derby, Dur,
Lancs, Leics, Lincs, Nthumb, Notts, Rutl, Shrops, Staffs, Warw,
Westm, Worcs, Yorks, N. Wales] . . .

> 8 + (counties as title), 9–62, 63–104, 105–148, 149–206,
> 207–472, 473–504, 505–564, 565–624, 625–666, 666–668,
> 669–700, 701–760, 761–842, 843–854, 855–892, 893–1142,
> 1143–1180 + 12 ; 16 maps.
>> Price 30s. ; calf, £2.

The Manchester directory has 2 pp. adds, 363*–364* inserted.
Bangor.   B.M.   Guildhall.   Manchester.   N.L.W.

This volume was also published in parts.   I. Chesh, Derby, Lancs.
II. Cumb, Dur, Nthumb, Westm, Yorks.   III. Leics, Lincs, Notts,
Rutl, Warw.   IV. Shrops, Staffs, Warw, Worcs, N. Wales.   Copies
of three of these parts have been found, as follows.

48. . . . [Chesh. Derby. Lancs] . . . 1828.

> 6 + counties paged as above + 24 ; 3 maps.
>> Price, subsc, 9s. 6d. boards, 11s. 6d. calf.

This volume does not contain the 2 pp. adds. for Manchester
and was issued before the complete volume was ready.

Derby.   I.H.R.   Liverpool.   Manchester.

49. Re-issued with date 1 September 1829 on title and priced
10s. 6d. and 12s. 6d. This was presumably the non-
subscribers' issue.
Liv. Ath.

50. Also re-issued with title dated 1830–1 and an additional page
for Derbyshire, 148*.
Chetham.

51. . . . [Cumb, Dur, Nthumb, Westm, Yorks] FOR 1828–9 . . .
4 + counties paged as above + 12 ; 5 maps.
Price, subsc, 9s. 6d. boards, 11s. 6d. calf.
I.H.R.   Newcastle-on-Tyne.

1829

52. . . . [Staffs, Warw, Worcs, Shrops, N. Wales] . . . [n.d.].
4 + counties paged as above ; 5 maps.
Price, subsc, 10s. 6d. boards, 12s. 6d. calf.
Salt.

1830

[Re-issue of Chesh, Derby, Lancs, 1828]. *See* No. 50 above.

53. . . . DIRECTORY OF [Beds, Berks, Bucks, Cambs, Cornwall,
Devon, Dorset, Glos, Hants, Heref, Hunts, Monm, Norfolk,
Nhants, Oxon, Som, Suffolk, Wilts, S. Wales] . . . 1830.
8 + (counties as title], 9–26, 27–68, 69–98, 99–132, 133–172,
173–272, 273–303, 304–399, 400–482, 483–498, 499–512,
513–526, 527–607, 608–632, 633–664, 665–738, 739–788,
789–808 and 809/9½–816/16½, 817–866 ; 19 maps.
Price, subsc, 21s. ; 30s. calf.
Gen. Soc.

54. Re-issued with cancel title dated 1830–1, price 30s. and £2
(non-subscribers' issue).
B.M.

55. Also issued with ' Essex ' added on title and the directory of
Essex, pp. 517–556 from the 1826 edition at the end.
Bristol.

THIRD GENERAL SURVEY, 1831–1840

1831

56. . . . DIRECTORY FOR [Derby, Leics, Notts, Rutl] . . . 1831.
4 + (counties as title), 5–62, 63–102, 103–162, 163–166 ; 3
maps.
Price, subsc, 10s.
Leicester.

1832

57. FIFTH EDITION . . . LONDON & PROVINCIAL . . . DIRECTORY
FOR 1832-3-4 . . . [London, Essex, Herts, Kent, Mdsx, Surrey,
Sussex] . . .
4 + 9-16 + (London), 17-650, cxxiv + (counties as title),
2, 653-724, 725-768, 769-886, 887-944, 945-1001, 1002-
1056 + 16 ; 7 maps.
Preface dated July 1832.
B.M. Guildhall.

58. Re-issue with preface dated October 1832, price, non-subsc,
30s. and £2, apparently the non-subscribers' issue.
Gen. Soc.

1833

59. FIFTH EDITION [as above] FOR 1833-4 . . .
Re-issue of above with cxxii pp. adds. & alts. for London
only.
Guildhall.

60. [Another issue] FIFTH EDITION IMPROVED . . . FOR 1834 . . .
Contents as No. 59, price, non-subsc, 30s. & £2, preface dated
January 1834.
B.M.

1834

61. . . . DIRECTORY OF [Chesh, Cumb, Dur, Lancs, Nthumb,
Westm, Yorks] . . . 1834.
8 + (counties as title), 9-76, 77-130, 131-210, 211-558,
559-638, 639-656, 657-1024 + 16 ; 5 maps.
Price non-subsc, 25s. ; 30s. calf.
Gen. Soc. Guildhall. Manchester.

1835

62. . . . DIRECTORY OF [Derby, Heref, Leics, Lincs, Monm, Notts,
Rutl, Shrops, Staffs, Warw, Worcs, N. & S. Wales] . . . 1835.
8 + (counties as title), 9-84, 85-108, 109-162, 163-246,
247-266, 267-336, 337-342, 343-388, 389-492, 493-624,
625-678, 679-730, 731-796 + 20 ; 12 maps.
Price, non-subsc, 25s. ; 30s. calf.
Preface dated May 1835. The directories for Derby, Leics,
Notts & Rutl. are new since 1831. A copy at Birmingham
contains a receipt signed by Samuel Francis as agent for
Pigot & Co., promising to deliver ' the Work subscribed for '
as soon as possible after publication, ' each volume to be
paid for on delivery '. It is filled in for Vol. II, 25s. and
is not dated.
Birmingham. B.M. Guildhall. Manchester. Salt. N.L.W.

The directories above, together with the one published in 1839,
cover all the English counties except Bucks, Cornwall, Devon,
Dorset, Glos, Hants, Nhants, Oxon, Som and Wilts. A volume

covering these counties must have been issued about this date but
there seems to be no copy extant.

1836

63. SIXTH EDITION . . . LONDON . . . DIRECTORY FOR 1836 [London & six miles round] . . .
  6 + 5–448 + 88 ; map.
     Price, non-subsc, 30s. ; 35s. calf.
  Preface dated January 1836.
Bod. B.M.

1837

64. . . . DIRECTORY OF SCOTLAND & THE ISLE OF MAN [with trade
directories for Manchester, Liverpool, Leeds, Hull, Birmingham,
Sheffield, Carlisle & Newcastle-on-Tyne] . . . 1837.
  8 + (Scotland), 19–818 + (Man), 2, 821–844 + (towns),
  146 + 147–174 ; 2 maps.
     Price, non-subsc. 25s. ; 30s. calf.
  Preface dated August 1837.
Bod. B.M. Guildhall. Manchester.

1838

65. . . . LONDON . . . DIRECTORY . . . 1838.
  452 + 420 + (places six miles round), 421–482 + cix.
     Price, 25s. ; 30s. calf ; non-subsc. 30s. & 35s.
  Preface, dated March 1838, calls this the seventh edition.
Bod. B.M.

66. A directory of Ireland was advertised for 1838. No copy has
been seen but it presumably contains the same town directories as Scotland, 1837.

1839

67. . . . DIRECTORY . . . OF [Beds, Cambs, Essex, Herts, Hunts,
Kent, Mdsx, Norfolk, Suffolk, Surrey, Sussex & London] . . .
Sept. 1839.
  8 + (counties as title), 9–40, 41–78, 79–170, 171–222, 223–
  238, 239–386, 387–452, 453–526, 527–584, 585–648, 651–
  718 + (London), 12, 80, 17–452, 453–536 + 32 ; maps.
     Price 25s. ; 30s. calf ; non-subsc. 5s. extra.
  The London directory has 80 pp. adds. & alts. up to August
  1839 ; pp. 17–452 from the 1838 edition ; and a new
  conveyance list.
67a. The counties were also issued with the same title but undated
    and a London directory, 10, 3–266, 84, which appears to be
    slightly earlier than the 1840 directory below.
  A.R.W. (Sept. 1839). B.M. (n.d. but dated 1839 on the

modern binding). Gen. Soc. (n.d., 1840 on modern binding & 1841 in their catalogue). Guildhall (Sept. 1839).

68. R. Simms, *Bibliotheca Staffordiensis* (1894), lists a volume containing Derby, Dorset, Glos, Staffs, 1839. This seems likely to be a re-issue, perhaps with additions, of the 1835 edition but no copy has been located.

1840

69. . . . DIRECTORY OF LONDON FOR 1840 . . . [with Beds, Cambs, etc. as 1839] . . .
14 + (London), 11–350, 270, 84 + (counties as 1839), 9–718 + 32 ; maps.
Preface dated December 1839. The London directory is as No. 67a above, with a street directory and an extensive list of adds. & alts.
Bod. B.M. Guildhall (London section only).

FOURTH GENERAL SURVEY, 1841–1847

1841

70. . . . DIRECTORY . . . OF [Yorks, Leics, Rutl, Lincs, Nhants, Notts, with Manchester & Salford, etc] . . . AUGUST, 1841.
6 + 16 + (counties as title, each with fly-title and index, and text beginning on p. 1), 416, 58 (Leics & Rutl), 92, 32, 64 + (directory of Manchester & places round, May 1841, as No. 516, below) + 28 ; 8 maps.
Price 25s., 30s. calf ; non-subsc, 5s. extra.
Preface dated August 1841. The Manchester section differs slightly on pp. 117–18 from No. 516 and it omits pp. 157–8. One of the copies at Manchester omits the places round section and ends on p. 157.
B.M. Guildhall. Manchester (2 copies).

71. . . . DIRECTORY . . . OF [Warw, Leics, Rutl, Lincs, Nhants, Notts, Staffs, Worcs, Yorks] . . . DECEMBER, 1841.
6 + 16 + re-issue of counties in August 1841 above, with the following added : Warw 168, Staffs 112, Worcs 59 ; 8 maps.
Price 25s., 30s. calf ; non-subsc, 5s. extra.
Preface dated December, 1841. There is an issue at Birmingham containing Warw, Leics, Rutl, Nhants, Staffs, Worcs only. Nhants is not mentioned on the title. The preface has the same date and the price is 15s., non-subsc, 2s. 6d. extra.
Gen. Soc.

1842

72. DIRECTORY . . . OF [Derby, Leics, Lincs, Notts, Rutl, Shrops, Staffs, Yorks] . . . JANUARY, 1842.

Re-issue of some of counties above, with Derby, 82 pp. and Shrops, 54 pp. added; 7 maps.
Bangor. Newport.

73. . . . DIRECTORY . . . OF [Dorset, Glos, Heref, Monm, Oxon, Som, Wilts] . . . JULY, 1842.
    4 + (countries as title), 36, 142, 22, 24, 40, 98, 46 ; 7 maps.
      Price 15s. ; non-subsc. 2s. 6d. extra.
A.R.W.

74. A combination volume containing Dorset, etc. as in July 1842, above, with Derby, Shrops, Staffs, Warw, Worcs, as in December 1841 and January 1842, above, was issued with title dated July 1842.
B.M. Gen. Soc. A.R.W.

75. Another combination of Derby, Heref, Notts, Shrops, Staffs, Warw, Worcs, Yorks, all as above, was issued with title dated 1842.
Guildhall.

76. . . . DIRECTORY FOR [Berks, Bucks, Dorset, Glos, Oxon, Som, Wilts] . . . SEPTEMBER, 1842.
    Re-issue of some of the countries in July 1842 above, with Berks, 50 pp. and Bucks, 36 pp. added ; 7 maps.
      Price 15s. ; non-subsc. 2s. 6d. extra.
    Preface dated September 1842.
Reading.

1844

77. A DIRECTORY OF . . . AN EXTENSIVE MANUFACTURING DISTRICT ROUND MANCHESTER, WITH . . . TOWNS IN CHESHIRE & LANCASHIRE & THE WHOLE OF N. WALES . . . BY I. SLATER, LATE PIGOT & SLATER . . . MANCHESTER : PRINTED & PUBLISHED BY I. SLATER . . . JANUARY, 1844.
    4 + (sections as title), 2, 194 + 6, 106 + 4, 68 ; map. [Ct. Cm.]
      Price 9s. ; non-subsc. 10s. 6d.
    The district round Manchester was first issued in October 1843 (see No. 519). The whole directory was also issued with the Liverpool directory for 1843 (No. 484), with the same date as above on the title, price 21s., non-subsc. 25s.
Manchester. Chetham. A.R.W. (with Liverpool).

78. DIRECTORY . . . OF [Berks, Bucks, Cornwall, Devon, Dorset, Glos, Hants, Heref, Monm, Oxon, Som, Wilts, N. & S. Wales] . . . JUNE, 1844.
    6 + re-issue of counties from 1842 and N. Wales from Jan. 1844, with the following added : Cornwall, 50 ; Devon, 158 ; Hants, 100 ; S. Wales, 84 ; maps.
      Price 25s., 30s. calf ; non-subsc, 5s. extra.

Preface dated June 1844. The cloth bound issue has no date on title. The imprint is I. Slater, late Pigot & Slater. Bod. Gloucester. Newport. A.R.W.

79. DIRECTORY OF SHROPSHIRE [and N. & S. Wales, Liverpool and towns in Chesh, and Lancs] . . . JULY, 1844.

4 + a new directory of Shrops, 58 pp. + re-issues of the corresponding sections in January and June 1844, above; 2 maps.

Price 15s., non-subsc. 16s. 6d.

Birmingham.

80. . . . DIRECTORY . . . OF [Derby, Leics, Lincs, Notts, Rutl, Shrops, Staffs, Warw, Worcs, Yorks] . . . [n.d.]

All re-issues of 1841 and 1842 directories; 9 maps.

Price 25s., 30s. calf; non-subsc. 5s. extra.

Published shortly after Berks, etc. 1844. The only copy seen is cloth bound; the calf issue may have a date on the title.

Bod.

1846

81. I. SLATER'S . . . DIRECTORY OF IRELAND . . . [with Birmingham, W. Bromwich, Bristol, Leeds, Liverpool, Manchester, Sheffield & towns in Scotland] . . . 1846.

6 + (Ireland), 2, 9–248, 536 + (towns as title), 39, 40–42, 22, 18, 46, 74, 23, 76 + 16; map. [Tr. for towns.]

Price 25s., 30s. calf; non-subsc. 30s. & £2.

Preface dated March 1846.

B.M. Chetham.

81a. [Another issue. Title as above but with ISLE OF MAN added.]

Re-issue of above with Isle of Man directory, 32 pp.; 2 maps.

M.M.

81b. [Another issue] . . . DIRECTORY OF THE ISLE OF MAN [with towns as above] . . . 1846.

Re-issue of above without Ireland.

M.M.

1847

82. . . . DIRECTORY OF IRELAND & ISLE OF MAN . . . [with towns as 1846 & Derby, Leicester, Nottingham added] . . . 1847.

6 + Ireland, Man and towns as 1846, with Derby, 10 pp.; Leicester, 18 pp.; Nottingham, 26 pp.; map.

Price 25s., 30s. calf; non-subsc. 30s. & £2.

Preface dated February 1847.

B.M.

FIFTH GENERAL SURVEY, 1848–1853

1848

83. SLATER'S (LATE PIGOT & Co.) . . . DIRECTORY OF [Chesh, Cumb, Dur, Lancs, Nthumb, Westm, Yorks] . . . 1848.
   8 + (counties as title), 104, 105–112 & 9–72, 98, 540, 100, 30, 566 ; 8 maps.
   Price, 30s., 35s. calf ; non-subsc. 35s. & £2.
   Preface dated June 1848. The Manchester section is differently arranged from Slater's Manchester directory for 1848 (No. 523) but seems to contain the same names. The pagination of this section is very irregular and it contains 58 unnumbered pages. The B.M. copy of this directory is paged continuously (except for irregularities in the Manchester section) 1–1502 and has 6 extra pages for Cheshire.
   This is called the " Seventh Edition of the Northern Counties ". Even counting re-issues, not more than five editions of Northumberland, Cumberland, Durham and Westmoreland have been traced before this one, and it looks as though there must have been an edition of these counties between 1834 and 1848 of which no copy has been found.
   B.M. Guildhall.

1849

84. . . . DIRECTORY . . . OF YORKSHIRE & LINCOLNSHIRE . . . 1848.
   4 + (Yorks), 2, 566 + (Lincs), 2, 128 ; map.
   Price 15s., non-subsc. 17s. 6d.
   Yorks is as 1848 ; Lincs is new.
   Guildhall. Lincoln. A.R.W.

1850

85. . . . DIRECTORY . . . OF [Beds, Berks, Bucks, Cambs, Hunts, Leics, Lincs, Norfolk, Nhants, Notts, Oxon, Rutl, Suffolk] . . . 1850.
   8 + (counties as title), 36, 68, 40, 56, 20, 80, 128, 126, 44, 90, 46, 16, 76 + 16 ; 12 maps.
   Price 25s., 30s. calf ; non-subsc, 30s. & £2.
   Lincs is as in 1849.
   A.R.W.

86. . . . DIRECTORY . . . OF [Derby, Heref, Leics, Lincs, Monm, Nhants, Notts, Rutl, Shrops, Staffs, Warw, Worcs] . . . 1850.
   8 + (counties as title), 108, 26, 88, 128, 32, 44, 90, 16, 62, 160, 180, 76 + 16 ; 11 maps.
   Price as above.
   Preface dated January 1850. The corresponding counties are the same as in No. 85 except that there are additions to Leics. There are some Cm. lists for larger towns.
   Birmingham. B.M. Manchester. A.R.W.

87. . . . DIRECTORY . . . OF [Derby, Glos, Heref, Monm, Shrops, Staffs, Warw, Worcs, N. & S. Wales] . . . 1850.
   8 + same directories as January 1850 for counties included in both, with Glos, 174; N. Wales, 84; S. Wales, 106; maps.
      Price as above.
   B.M. Cardiff. Guildhall. Salt.

88. [Another issue.] Title dated 1850, without N. Wales but with Berks as No. 85 and Wilts, 62 pp.
   A.R.W.

89. [Another issue.] Title dated 1850, with Glos, Heref, Monm, Worcs, N. & S. Wales only.
   Cardiff.

1851

90. [Re-issue of No. 85, without Berks but with the longer Leics directory as in No. 86.] 1851.
   B.M. I.H.R.

91. [Another issue. Berks, Bucks, Glos, Hants, Heref, Monm, Oxon, Warw, Wilts, Worcs, S. Wales, all re-issues of 1850 directories except Hants, including Isle of Wight, 132 pp. which is new.] 1851.
   Guildhall. A.R.W.

92. . . . CLASSIFIED . . . DIRECTORY . . . OF LANCASHIRE & THE MANUFACTURING DISTRICT . . . 1851.
   4 + (Lancs, 7–278, 80, 357–521 (incl. 388½) + (parts of Chesh.), 522–572 ; 2 maps.
      Price 15s. ; non subsc. 17s. 6d.
   The Manchester section is slightly different from the Manchester & Salford directory for 1851 (No. 525).
   Guildhall.

93. [Another issue. Title as above but] EXCEPTING MANCHESTER . . . 1851.
   Re-issue of pp. 7–260 and 389–572 ; map.
   Manchester.

1852

94. . . . DIRECTORY OF MANCHESTER & SALFORD WITH THE WHOLE OF LANCASHIRE . . . 1852.
   The Manchester & Salford directory of 1852 (No. 527) + re-issue of 7–260 and 389–572 as above.
      Price, non-subsc. 17s. 6d.
      Preface dated July 1852.
   Chetham.

95. . . . Commercial Directory of the Isle of Man . . .
[with] Manchester, Birmingham, Carlisle, Hull, Leeds,
Liverpool, Newcastle on Tyne & Sheffield . . . 1852.
   2 + (Man), 34 + (towns as title), 72, 80, 6, 22, 26, 78, 18,
   30 ; map.
M.M.

96. [Another issue. Title as above but omitting Isle of Man.]
   Town directories as above. Price 15s., 17s. 6d., calf ; non-
   subsc. 20s. & 25s.
   Also issued as part of Slater's directory of Scotland, 1852
   and with Ireland and Scotch towns, n.d. but preface dated
   1857.
Chetham.

97. . . . Directory . . . of [Berks, Cornwall, Devon, Dorset,
Glos, Hants, Som, Wilts, S. Wales] . . . 1852–3.
   Re-issue of Berks, Glos, Wilts, S. Wales, 1850 and Hants,
   1851 with directories of Cornwall, 68 pp. ; Devon, 212 pp. ;
   Dorset, 46 pp. ; Somerset, 112 pp. ; 9 maps.
   Price 25s., 30s. calf ; non-subsc. 30s. & £2.
   Preface dated December 1852.
Manchester.

This concludes the last of the Pigot-Slater general surveys.
After this Slater concentrated on the North and the West Midlands,
with Ireland, Scotland and Wales. A new edition of the Northern
Counties comes just within our period.

1854

98. . . . Directory of the Northern Counties. Vol. I.
[Dur, Nthumb, Yorks] . . . 1854–5.
   8 + (counties as title), 120, 112, 618 ; 3 maps.
   Price 15s., 17s. 6d. calf ; non-subsc, 20s. & 25s.
   Preface dated 1 June 1854.
A.R.W.

1855

99. [Re-issue of above with title dated 1855 and] . . . Vol. II.
[Chesh, Cumb, Lancs, Westm] . . . 1855.
   8 + (counties as title), 134, 80, 1110, 28 ; 4 maps.
   Price for the two vols, 30s., 35s. calf ; non-subsc, 35s.
   & £2.
   Preface dated May 1855. Both volumes were re-issued in
   1856.
Guildhall. Newcastle-on-Tyne. Warrington.

WILLIAM ROBSON, 1838–1840

William Robson published directories of London nearly annually
from 1819 until 1842, when his business was taken over by Bowtell

& Co. They only published one more edition, however, because, they said, competition with Kelly had become impossible. Kelly included in his *Post Office London Directory* for 1843 a slip headed " Final Discontinuance of Robson's London Directory ", quoting Bowtell's reason for giving up.

In 1838 Robson made a sudden plunge into county directories and during the next two or three years he issued a number of volumes, generally forming second volumes to his London directory, covering the English counties except Northumberland, Cumberland and Westmoreland in the north and Leicestershire, Lincolnshire, Nottinghamshire, Northamptonshire and Rutlandshire in the midlands. Lancashire is represented only by Liverpool, Stafford-shire and Warwickshire only by Birmingham and places nearby and Yorkshire only by the West Riding and Sheffield. The county directories were issued in various combinations and none of the volumes is dated, though it can be seen from internal evidence that they mostly cover the years 1839–40. Robson was not above borrowing his descriptive text from other sources and his lists bear the marks of hasty and slipshod compilation.

The volumes entered below cover all the counties with which he dealt but there may be other combinations of the same directories in existence. For his Birmingham and Liverpool directories, *see* Nos. 739 and 483.

1838

100. ROBSON'S . . . DIRECTORY OF LONDON & THE SIX HOME COUNTIES [Essex, Herts, Kent, Mdsx, Surrey, Sussex with parts of Berks & Bucks] . . . WILLIAM ROBSON & CO. 16 GEORGE STREET, MANSION HOUSE. RICHARD CLAY, PRINTER, BREAD STREET HILL, LONDON. [Vol. I] London.
[Vol. II] 4 + (counties as title), 116, 76, 228, 96, 108, 122, 53 + 5 + (London Court Guide), 218 ; map for each county. [Cm. Tr.]
9⅜ × 5¾″. Price of Vol. II, 17s. 6d. Red calf, green label.
Dated 1838 on spine. Stapleton's directory of Canterbury, etc. (No. 402), of which the preface is dated August 1838, refers to a Robson volume containing a directory of Canterbury, which must be this. It says that both Pigot's and Robson's directories were " acknowledged on all hands " to be most incorrect.
Gen. Soc.

1839

101. ROBSON'S COMMERCIAL DIRECTORY OF LONDON & THE NINE COUNTIES OF [Beds, parts of Berks & Bucks, Cambs, Glos with Bristol, Hunts, Norfolk, Suffolk, Wilts] WITH . . . GUERNSEY & JERSEY . . . VOL. II CONTAINING THE COUNTRY DIRECTORY. WILLIAM ROBSON & CO . . . 4 CLOAK LANE, CHEAPSIDE . . . [Printer Richard Clay].

60GUIDE TO DIRECTORIES

4 + (counties as title), 34, 53 + 5, 64, 138 + 118, 30, 166, 102, 107, 2–54 ; map for each county. [Cm. Tr.]
9¾ × 5¾″. Red cloth, green labels. Price 25s. ; non-subsc, 30s.
The Berks & Bucks section is a re-issue from 1838.
Guildhall.

102. ROBSON'S COMMERCIAL DIRECTORY OF THE EIGHT COUNTIES OF [Beds, Bucks, Cambs, Hants, Hunts, Norfolk, Suffolk, Wilts with Guernsey & Jersey. Imprint as above].
Re-issue of parts of above with Bucks, 62 pp. and Hants (including Isle of Wight), 167 + 3, added.
9⅜ × 5¾″. Red cloth, green labels. Price 15s. ; non-subsc, 17s. 6d.
Dated 1839 on label.
I.H.R.

103. ROBSON'S COMMERCIAL DIRECTORY OF THE SIX COUNTIES FORMING THE NORFOLK CIRCUIT [Beds, Bucks, Cambs, Hunts, Norfolk, Suffolk] WITH OXFORDSHIRE . . . [imprint as above].
Re-issue of parts of above with Oxfordshire, 82 pp. added.
Binding and price as above.
Norwich. A.R.W.

104. ROBSON'S COMMERCIAL DIRECTORY OF THE SEVEN COUNTIES OF [Mdsx, Essex, Herts, Kent, Surrey, Sussex, Hants, with Isle of Wight] . . . FOR 1839. TWENTIETH EDITION. [Imprint as above.]
Re-issue of parts of above volumes.
Size, binding, price as above.
' Twentieth Edition ' refers to the whole of Robson's series, including London, and not to this particular volume.
Guildhall.

1840

105. ROBSON'S COMMERCIAL DIRECTORY OF LONDON & THE WESTERN COUNTIES [Berks, Cornwall, Devon, Dorset, Glos with Bristol, Heref, Som, Monm] WITH S. WALES [Brecon, Card, Carm, Glam, Pemb, Radnor] . . . VOL. II CONTAINING THE DIRECTORY OF THE COUNTIES. [Imprint as above.]
4 + (counties as above), 104, 84, 254, 82, 138 + 118 + 4, 40, 236, 54 + (S. Wales as above), 30, 16, 32, 64, 30, 10 ; map for each county. [Cm. Tr.]
Size, binding as above. Price 30s. ; non-subsc, £2.
The Gloucestershire section is a re-issue of 1839 with 4 pp. adds. for Bristol.
B.M. Gen. Soc. Manchester.

106. ROBSON'S COMMERCIAL DIRECTORY OF LONDON & THE COUNTIES OF [Chesh, Derby, Durham, Shrops, Worcs, Yorks (West Riding & Sheffield)] WITH N. WALES [Anglesey, Caern,

Denb, Flint, Merion, Mont] . . . Vol. II CONTAINING A
DIRECTORY OF THE COUNTIES. [Imprint as above.]
   22 + (counties as above), 154, 90, 150, 106, 118, 290 + 717–
834, 20, 26, 24, 20, 14, 30 ; maps. [Cm. Tr.]
      Size, binding as above.
   The Sheffield & vicinity section, 717–834, is the same as in
   Robson's directory of Birmingham & Sheffield, 1839
   (No. 739), which also has a street directory.
   Halifax. N.L.W. Warrington.

107. Bangor has a copy of Robson's *London & the Western Counties*,
      containing Glos, Heref, Monm, Shrops, Worcs and N. & S.
      Wales, all re-issues from the above directories.

KELLY'S POST OFFICE DIRECTORIES, 1845–1855

Frederic Kelly, who was an official in the London General Post
Office, began his career as a directory publisher by purchasing the
copyright of the *Post Office London Directory* in 1836.[1] In 1839 he
set up a printing and publishing office with his brother, W. Kelly,
in Old Boswell Court, from which place the London directory was
issued annually. In 1845 he began the publication of provincial
directories with a directory of the six home counties, replacing
Pigot, who published no directory of London or of these counties
after 1840. He directly competed with the Pigot-Slater series in
a directory of Birmingham, Warwickshire and part of Staffordshire
in the same year and went on to cover an increasing number of
counties in a widening circle round London. He did not reach the
far west or the north, except for Sheffield in 1854, until late in the
1850's and the last English county to be included was Monmouthshire in 1871. A directory of Brighton, in quite a different format
from the county directories, of which only one edition appeared,
was published in 1846. No other separate town directories were
attempted until much later, except those for Sheffield, of which only
one comes within our period, and some directories of Birmingham,
published with the county directories.
   It was popularly supposed that Kelly's position in the London Post
Office, which caused some scandal in connection with the production
of his London directory, gave him some special advantages, though
he was prohibited from making use of the services of post office
officials in 1847 and the work on the provincial directories seems
always to have been done by paid agents.[2] All his directories were,
however, called Post Office directories and were bound in bright
red cloth with the Royal Arms on the cover.
   New editions of the counties were issued at. irregular intervals
and there were never such complicated re-issues of the same edition
under different dates as occur in the Pigot-Slater series. Within
our period they generally contain alphabetical court and commercial
lists for each place with a combined classified trade directory for
all the counties in the volume and a combined court list. In the

[1] *See* p. 12 above.   [2] *Cf.* p. 17 above.

first series, 1845–9, some of the volumes are paged continuously with each other to form one whole. The full development of Kelly's activities falls outside our scope and the directories listed below are only a small part of what he subsequently achieved.

The entries in the following list are in summarised form. As has been said, all Kelly's titles begin ' Post Office Directory of . . .' and a list of the counties included seems sufficient to identify the directory. Similarly the imprint is always ' W. Kelly & Co. (or " Kelly & Co " from 1852) . . . Old Boswell Court, Temple Bar ', the size is uniformly 10 × 6½″ and the binding red cloth. These details are not given each time. The directories of Lincolnshire, which, for some reason, were issued singly and not with other counties, are included here instead of in the Local section as they really form part of Kelly's national series. The directories of Brighton and Sheffield will be found under their respective towns.

1845

108. [The Six Home Counties. Essex, Herts, Kent, Mdsx, Surrey, Sussex.] 4 + 9–1085 ; adverts, 1086–1144 ; 6 maps. [Ct. Cm. for each place ; Ct. Tr. for the six counties together.]
Price 25s. Preface dated July 1845.
Bod. B.M.

109. [Birmingham, Warw, part of Staffs.] 8 + (Birmingham), 9–340 + (S. Staffs & Warw), 500–766 ; adverts ; 2 maps. [Ct. Cm. for each place ; Tr. for Birmingham & S. Staffs together ; Ct. Tr. for Warw.]
Price 20s. Preface dated September 1845. The gap in pagination is intentional.
Birmingham. B.M.

1846

110. [The Norfolk Counties. Cambs, Norfolk, Suffolk.] 8 + 1087–1706 ; adverts ; 3 maps. [Ct. Cm. for each place ; Ct. Tr. for the three counties together.]
Price 20s. Maps dated 1846. Paged continuously with *The Six Home Counties*, 1845 (No. 108).
B.M.

111. [Another issue. The Nine Counties.] Contains *The Six Home Counties*, 1845 (No. 108), followed by *The Norfolk Counties* (No. 110), all paged as above. Preface dated October 1846.
B.M.

1847

112. [Berks, Nhants, Oxon, Beds, Bucks, Hunts.] viii + 1707–1964 + 6 + 1965–2369 ; adverts, 2370–2404 ; 6 maps.

[Ct. Cm. for each place ; Ct. Tr. for first three counties together and for last three together.]
    Price, subsc, 25s. Maps dated 1847. Published 1847 according to Kelly's advertisements. Paged continuously with *The Norfolk Counties* (No. 110).
Bod. B.M.

1848

113. [Hants, Dorset, Wilts.] viii + 2371–2940 ; adverts, 30 ; 3 maps. [Ct. Cm. for each place ; Ct. Tr. for Hants and for Dorset & Wilts together.]
    Maps dated 1848. Paged continuously with No. 112. The Hants directory includes Isle of Wight.
B.M.

114. [Derby, Leics, Notts, Rutl.] viii + 2371–2960 ; adverts, 2961–2988 ; 3 maps. [Ct. Cm. for each place ; Ct. Tr. for the four counties together.]
    Price 20s. Maps dated 1848. Paged continuously with the 1847 directory (No. 112).
B.M. Leicester.

1849

115. [Lincolnshire.] vi + 2961–3283 ; adverts, 3284–3309, 3 ; map. [Ct. Cm. for each place ; Ct. Tr. for the county.]
    Price 10s. Map dated 1849. Paged continuously with No. 114.
B.M.

1850

116. [Birmingham, Staffs, Worcs.] x + 9–698 ; adverts, xxxv, 5 ; 2 maps. [Ct. Cm. for each place ; St. also for Birmingham ; Ct. Tr. for all three sections together.]
    Price, subsc, 25s. Preface dated January 1850.
Birmingham. Bod. B.M.

1851

117. [The Six Home Counties. Essex, Herts, Kent, Mdsx, Surrey, Sussex.] 1198 pp. ; adverts, 1199 ; 6 maps. [Ct. Cm. for each place ; Ct. Tr. for the six counties together.]
    Preface dated November 1851.
B.M.

1852

118. [Jersey, Guernsey, etc. Hants.] 4 + (Hants, Isle of Wight,) 1199–1456 + (Jersey, etc.), 1457–1546 ; adverts, 1457–

1468, 2 ; map. [Ct. Cm. for each place ; Ct. Tr. for Hants
& for Jersey, etc. separately.]
 Price 10s. Map dated 1852. Paged continuously with
 No. 117.
B.M.

119. [Another issue. Hants, Essex, Herts, Kent, Mdsx, Surrey,
 Sussex.] Re-issue of 1851 and 1852 without Jersey, etc.
 Preface dated 1852.
Portsmouth.

1853

120. [Cambs, Norfolk, Suffolk.] xii + 680 ; adverts, 34 ; 3 maps.
 [Ct. Cm. for each place ; Ct. Tr. for all counties together.]
 Price 20s. Preface dated April 1853.
B.M. Norwich.

1854

121. [Birmingham, Warw, Worcs, Staffs.] 1854. xii + (counties),
 681 + (Birmingham), 684–1006 ; adverts, 1007–1094 ; 3
 maps. [Ct. Cm. for each place ; St. Tr. also for Birmingham ; Ct. Tr. for the three counties together.]
 Price 28s. Preface dated January 1854.
Birmingham. Bod. B.M.

122. [Berks, Nhants, Oxon, Beds, Bucks, Hunts.] 1854. viii +
 758 ; adverts, 30, 2 ; 6 maps. [Ct. Cm. for each place ;
 Ct. Tr. for first three counties together and for last three
 together.]
 Price 25s. Preface dated June 1854.
B.M.

1855

123. [Essex, Herts, Kent, Mdsx Surrey Sussex.] 1855. xx +
 1422 ; adverts 62 ; 6 maps. [Ct. Cm. for each place ; Ct.
 Tr. for the six counties together.]
 Preface dated February 1855.
Bod. B.M.

124. [Hants, Wilts, Dorset.] 1855. 4 + (counties as title), v–xiv,
 322 + 2, v–xii, 196 + 2, v–xii, 152 ; adverts, 40 ; 3 maps.
 [Ct. Cm. for each place ; Ct. Tr. for each county.]
 Preface dated April 1855. The Hants directory includes
 Isle of Wight.
B.M.

125. [Lincolnshire.] 1855. x + 374 ; adverts, 32 ; map. [Ct.
 Cm. for each place ; Ct. Tr. for the county.]
 Preface dated May 1855.
B.M.

126. [Derby, Leics, Notts, Rutl.] 1855. 4 + (Derby), v–x, 220 + (Notts), v–viii, 210 + (Leics & Rutl), 2, v–viii, 220 ; adverts, 36 ; 3 maps. [Ct. Cm. for each place ; Ct. Tr. for each section separately.]

Price 25s. Preface dated August 1855.

B.M.

WILLIAM WHITE AND HIS ASSOCIATES, 1817–1855

A notable series of directories mainly for places in the northern half of England, beginning with Edward Baines', directory of Leeds, 1817, was later taken over by William White and continued until the end of the century, when it was absorbed by Kelly & Co. Even then the Sheffield directory continued to appear with the old title, ' White's General & Commercial Directory ' and in the characteristic bright green cloth binding, until 1919 and the name of White did not finally disappear from the title till 1930.

Edward Baines, the head of a well-known Leeds family and owner of the *Leeds Mercury*, printed a directory of Leeds for M. Robinson & Co. in 1809 and published one in 1817, compiled with the help of William Parson. Baines wrote histories of York-shire and of Lancashire, published by him in 1822 and 1824, in both of which Parson was responsible for the directories. He printed and published other Leeds directories in 1834 and 1839 and printed one for J. Williams in 1845. William White's directories were printed by him until 1831.

William Parson is described in the 1817 Leeds directory as ' Mr W. Parson of Manchester, who has assisted in the compilation of several extensive publications of a similar description ', He first appears in a Manchester directory in 1811, when he is described as bookseller and stationer at 35 Market Street Lane. It seems likely, for reasons which will follow, that the extensive publications he had helped to produce were Pigot's early Commercial Directories. In 1818 a Lancashire directory in two parts was published by a printer called T. Rogerson, who had recently moved from Blackburn to Manchester. The second part was re-issued, with additions, printed by J. Leigh and sold by ' the proprietors '. This volume has a half title in which it is called ' Directory of the English Counties, Vol II, Pt. ii '. In the same year, 1818, there appeared a directory of Staffordshire by the same printer, uniform in appear-ance and general arrangement with the Lancashire directory, and compiled by W. Parson and T. Bradshaw. It seems probable that the ' proprietors ' of the Lancashire directory were also Parson and Bradshaw, who had taken it over from Rogerson and made it part of a projected directory of the English counties, of which the Staffordshire directory was another part. They may have originally compiled the Lancashire directory for Rogerson. Now the descrip-tive text of the Lancashire directory is partly the same as in Pigot's *Commercial Directory for 1816–17*, and though this may be merely a case of piracy, it is not unlikely that Parson wrote them both. In any case, the *Directory of the English Counties* seems to have been a spirited attempt to compete with Pigot, to which he did not fail to respond, for the preface to Pt. I of the Staffordshire directory refers to a ' formidable opposition ' with which the compilers had had to contend.

No other directories uniform with the Lancashire and Stafford-shire directories are extant and it appears that the ' English Counties ' project was given up. Both Bradshaw and Parson, however, continued to produce directories. Thomas Bradshaw, who was the father of George Bradshaw, the originator of *Bradshaw's Railway Guides*, was born in Belfast, to which place he returned in 1819, drawn there, he says, by the pleasure which he had frequently anticipated when working with Parson, of compiling a directory of the place of his birth. This directory of Belfast was published in 1819.[1] In 1820 he compiled a directory of Gloucester-shire with R. Gell, who later compiled two directories of Sheffield.

William Parson now acquired a new collaborator, William White of Newcastle-on-Tyne, who helped him with the directories in Baines' history of Yorkshire, 1822. Parson, while continuing to work for Baines, edited a directory of Hull, published by William White and printed by Baines in 1826. In this directory White announced that ' the task of preparing directories such as have for some years been issued from the Press of the Mercury Office at Leeds, has devolved on the Present Proprietors ' and said they proposed to extend their exertions to other suitable districts of the kingdom. This marks the real beginning of White's series, though in after-years the foundation of the business was dated back to 1822 [2] or even as early as 1818.[3]

The next Parson and White directory, for Durham and Northum-berland in 1827, was sold from their office at Bell's Court, Pilgrim St., Newcastle. It exhibits for the first time White's characteristic if inconvenient arrangement of places under the old county divisions into hundreds. In 1829 the publishers had also a publishing office in Leeds. During 1830 or 1831 Parson seems to have retired or died and White moved finally to Sheffield. From here he continued to produce, nearly every year, a number of directories, all for northern or eastern districts, apart from an unexplained excursion to Devonshire in 1850 and, outside our period, to Hampshire and to Birmingham.

White's directories were very popular and copies of them are to be found in the public libraries of most of the big northern towns. As has been said, he attached great importance to historical and scientific information and increasing space was given to articles on a variety of such subjects. The early editions were small volumes, very convenient to handle and moderately priced at round about six or seven shillings. They were bound in half or whole dark green cloth or in a yellowish calf, with marbled edges. Later in the cen-tury a larger format and a bright green cloth binding, with a device on the front cover, were adopted. The maps were issued separately and, as a rule, are not to be found bound up in the volumes.

[1] Copies in Bod, B.M. and C.U.L.
[2] White's *Directory of Hampshire*, 1878.
[3] Ditto for Leicestershire, 1863, where it is said that the business has been going for forty-five years.

Other publishers, as was common, helped themselves to the information in William White's directories, but he was particularly troubled by an individual called Francis White, who later claimed to be his uncle. Francis White first appears in Rogers' *Directory of Sheffield* for 1841, where he is described as a directory agent. Perhaps he was an employee of William White. In the same directory is John White, ' traveller ', with whom Francis White published his first directory, which was for Nottinghamshire, in 1844. William White calls this ' a pirated edition of William White's Nottinghamshire Work [*i.e.* his directory of that county for 1832] . . . published by an unprincipled and illiterate man in a very blundering manner '.[1] Francis White went on to publish a series of directories which not only made use of William White's material but imitated closely the binding and general appearance of his directories and were evidently intended to be confused with them.

William White refrained from taking any steps to protect himself, he says from ' a natural dislike to the entanglements of the law ' but perhaps because there really was a family connection. When he did finally apply for an injunction it was against E. S. Drake & Co. for pirating his directory of Leicestershire. An account of the case is given in the preface to W. White's *Directory of Norfolk* (1864).[2] In this he refers to ' the cupidity of certain illiterate individuals, who, in 1854, under the name of " Francis White & Co." published a pirated and spurious edition ' of his directory of Norfolk for 1845, in which ' most of the information was copied verbatim, whilst the form and general arrangement were identical '. Francis White's directories are certainly less honest and competent than William White's and should be clearly distinguished from them.

William White died about 1874, and in Francis White's *Directory of Warwickshire* for that year there is inserted the following note : ' Francis White begs to remind his subscribers and the public that, since the death of his late nephew, William White, Francis White & Co.'s are the only histories and directories published by any member of the family of " Whites ", the old and noted directory publishers of Sheffield '. It is difficult to see what he hoped to gain by this statement. He seems to have published no more directories himself except an enlarged edition of the Warwickshire directory in 1875, but William White's directories continued to appear, presumably carried on by his son, William White, Jun., who had joined his father's business in about 1860.

None of the directories by publishers mentioned in this note cover more than two counties and though William White, at any rate, may claim to rank among the publishers of national directories, his and other works referred to here will be found described in the Local section of the Catalogue. The attention of the reader may be again called to the warning about White's addenda lists on p. 21.

---

[1] W. White's *Directory of Leicestershire*, 1846, preface.
[2] Also in his *Leicestershire*, 1863.

LOCAL DIRECTORIES

BEDFORDSHIRE

1785

127. THE MERCHANTS' MISCELLANY & TRAVELLERS' COMPLETE COMPENDIUM . . . OF THE COUNTY OF BEDFORD FOR 1785 . . . BY JOHN FRANKLIN HENINGTON . . . BEDFORD : PRINTED BY BARTHOLOMEW HYATT . . .

22 pp. [Tr.]

$7\frac{1}{2} \times 5''$. Printed wrappers.   Price 6*d*.

Henington was an auctioneer and printer at Northampton. He seems, from various remarks in this directory, to have been of a radical turn of mind, saying (p. 15) that Woburn, ' like most towns that become the seat of partiality and persecution, by being under the influence of a particular family, is of small note '.   Let the government, he says on another page, ' crush aristocracy, and restore the commonweal, the only inheritance worthy of a briton ; and let us again find that laws to bind all shall be assented to by all.' His advertisement at the end is dated April 1785.   On the back wrapper Pt. II for Northamptonshire is announced for 14 May and speedily after, Pts. III–VI for Bucks, Leics, Cambs and Hunts.   Of this ambitious project only the Bedfordshire directory seems to have survived.   It was intended to be continued annually.   A facsimile reprint, without the wrappers, was published in 1885 by F. Hockcliffe, founder of the firm of F. R. Hockcliffe, Ltd. of Bedford.

Bod. (Gough. Bed. 1).   Guildhall (reprint).   F. R. Hockcliffe, Ltd.

BERKSHIRE

1842

128. THE POST OFFICE DIRECTORY. READING : COMPILED, PRINTED & PUBLISHED BY . . . JOHN SNARE, 16 MINSTER STREET. 1842.

10 + v–xx + 21–143 + 4 + v–xii + 153–306 ; adverts, 8, 50 ; errata slip ; another slip between 90/91 ; table of trains ; plan. [Gen ; St. also for Reading, Henley and Wokingham ; Tr. also for Reading ; Gen, for the county.]

$7\frac{1}{4} \times 4\frac{1}{4}''$.   Orange cloth.

Revised through the Post Office by permission of the postmaster. Train table revised to 1 July 1842. The errata slip occurs in a few copies only, in the others the errata have been corrected. There are numerous engravings in the text and the descriptions are by J. G. Robertson. They include an eulogy of Miss Mitford, who was alive at this date, and an engraving of her cottage.

Bod. C.U.L. Reading (2 copies, both with errata slip).

1846

129. HUNT'S ROYAL WINDSOR DIRECTORY . . . INCLUDING WINDSOR, SLOUGH, MAIDENHEAD [and places near in Berks, Bucks, Mdsx and Surrey] . . . 1846. WINDSOR : PUBLISHED BY EDWARD HUNT, 5 HIGH STREET. [Printer, J. Mallett, Wardour St., Soho.]

12 + 156 ; adverts, 34, xxxvi. [Ct. Cm ; Tr. also for Windsor.]

$6\frac{7}{8} \times 4\frac{1}{4}''$. Blue cloth. Price 3s. 6d.

Preface dated December 1845.

Bod.

1851

For Windsor and other places in the Thames valley, *see* SURREY, 1851.

1853

130. MACAULAY'S BERKSHIRE DIRECTORY . . . FOR 1853 . . . READING : PRINTED & PUBLISHED BY J. MACAULAY, BROAD STREET.

24 + 204 ; adverts, 2, 140. [Ct. Tr ; St. also for Reading.]

$7\frac{1}{4} \times 4\frac{3}{4}''$. Price 1s. 6d. wrappers, 2s. cloth.

James Macaulay also ran a circulating library.

Reading.

1854

131. M. BILLING'S DIRECTORY & GAZETTEER OF . . . BERKS & OXON . . . BIRMINGHAM : M. BILLING'S STEAM-PRESS OFFICES, NEW HALL STREET. 1854.

4 + iv + 406 ; adverts, 70. [Ct. Cm ; Tr. also for larger places.]

$8\frac{1}{8} \times 5\frac{1}{4}''$. Price 17s. 6d., with sheet map for subsc. only.

Preface dated April 1854.

Bod. Reading.

ABINGDON

(*See* OXFORDSHIRE, 1846.)

READING

1828

132. HORNIMAN'S READING DIRECTORY . . . READING : PRINTED
BY & FOR R. HORNIMAN, 66 BROAD STREET.
4 + 48. [Tr.]
$6\frac{3}{4} \times 4\frac{1}{8}''$.
Undated, but on p. 48 is an advertisement of *The Henley
Guide*, Hickman & Stapledon, 'just published,' which came
out in 1827. A printed list of additions is promised.
Reading.

1837

133. THE READING DIRECTORY . . . COMPILED BY C. INGALL . . .
READING : PRINTED BY CHARLES INGALL, 7 HIGH STREET
. . . 1837.
Title on wrapper + 3–47 ; adverts, 11. [Gen.]
$7\frac{1}{8} \times 4\frac{3}{8}''$. Mauve printed wrappers. Price 6*d*.
Reading.

WINDSOR
(*See* BUCKINGHAMSHIRE, 1853.)

BUCKINGHAMSHIRE

1846. *See* BERKSHIRE, 1846.
1850. *See* HERTFORDSHIRE, 1850.

1853

134. MUSSON & CRAVEN'S COMMERCIAL DIRECTORY OF THE COUNTY
OF BUCKINGHAM & THE TOWN OF WINDSOR . . . NOTTING-
HAM : PRINTED . . . BY STEVENSON & CO. MIDDLE
PAVEMENT. 1853.
8 + 5–280 ; adverts, 92. [Ct. Cm ; Tr. also for larger
places, many villages with description only and no directory.]
$8\frac{1}{2} \times 5\frac{1}{4}''$. Red cloth. Price, with map, 10*s*. 6*d*.
The binding is in obvious imitation of Kelly's Post Office
directories.
Guildhall.

ETON & SLOUGH
(*See* SURREY, 1851.)

CAMBRIDGESHIRE
1851

135. HISTORY, GAZETTEER & DIRECTORY OF CAMBRIDGESHIRE . . .
PETERBOROUGH : PRINTED & PUBLISHED BY ROBERT
GARDNER . . . MDCCCLI.

xiv + 2 + 744. [Ct. Cm ; Tr. also for larger places.]
8½ × 5⅛". Price 17s. 6d. or with map on rollers, £1.
Preface dated 31 December 1850.
Guildhall.

CAMBRIDGE
(*See* HUNTINGDONSHIRE, 1855.)

CHANNEL ISLANDS,
(*See* ISLANDS.)

CHESHIRE

(For places near Manchester *see also* Manchester directories.)

1781

136. THE CHESTER GUIDE . . . TO WHICH IS ADDED A DIRECTORY
. . . [of] THE CITY & MARKET TOWNS IN THE COUNTY.
CHESTER : PRINTED & SOLD BY P. BROSTER IN THE
EXCHANGE.

4 + 140. [Cm ; Ct. also for Chester.]
6 × 3¾". Price 1s.
The directory section is headed 1781. R. S. Brown (' The
Stationers, Booksellers & Printers of Chester ', *Hist. Soc.
of Lancs & Ches. Trans*, lxxxiii (1932), 101–42) mentions a
1780 edition but no copy has been found. The Brosters
were a well-known and much respected family of Chester
printers. Peter Broster become mayor of Chester. Both
he and his son, John Broster, took a great interest in the
history and antiquities of the city.
Bod. Chester. A.R.W.

1782

137. THE CHESTER GUIDE . . . SECOND EDITION . . . [imprint as
1781] . . . 1782.
8 (5/6 blank) + 144 (79/80 & 143/4 blank). [Cm ; Ct.
also for Chester.]
6 × 3¾". Grey wrappers. Price 1s.
Directory section headed 1782.
Guildhall. I.H.R.

1783

138. Re-issue of above, with same title dated 1782 but a new
edition of the directories, 81–142, headed 1783, and list of
Broster's publications, 143–4.
Bod. B.M. (10360.aaa.37).

For later issues of Broster's directory, *see under* CHESTER.

1789

139. THE DIRECTORY & GUIDE FOR CHESTER . . . [and] MARKET
TOWNS THROUGHOUT THE COUNTY . . . [and] WREXHAM &
ITS VICINITY . . . BY W. COWDROY, OF CHESTER, PRINTER,
1789 . . .

   108 pp. [Gen, or for some places, St.]
   $6\frac{1}{8} \times 3\frac{3}{4}''$. Price 1s.
   William Cowdroy edited *The Chester Chronicle* from about
   1785 and *The Manchester Gazette* in 1795. He is said to
   have set up his paragraphs in type straight from his head.
   He wrote poetry and was considered a wit. He died in
   1814. (*Gent. Mag.* lxxxv (1815), 572 ; R. S. Brown, *op. cit.*)
Bod. Chester. I.H.R.

1845

140. WILLIAMS'S COMMERCIAL DIRECTORY OF STOCKPORT [etc.] . . .
MANCHESTER : PUBLISHED BY J. WILLIAMS . . . VICTORIA
STREET . . . DEC. 1845.

   title + adverts, 12 + (Stockport), 62 + (Macclesfield),
   48 + (Congleton), 18 + (Leek), 14, 14 + (Glossop & Mot-
   tram), 10 + (Wigan), 14 + (Saddleworth), 12 + (Preston),
   80 + (Leeds), 3–12 + (Ashton-under-Lyne), 38 + (Dukin-
   field), 10. [Gen. except for Leeds, which is a few odd
   pages of a trades directory.]
   $7\frac{1}{8} \times 4\frac{1}{8}''$. Price, subsc, 12s. Leather.
Stockport, Congleton and the first 14 pp. of Leek are also
in Williams's directory of Stafford, etc. (*see* STAFFORDSHIRE,
1845). The Saddleworth directory is also in his directory
of Bolton, etc. (*see* LANCASHIRE, 1845).
Chetham.

1846

141. WILLIAMS'S COMMERCIAL DIRECTORY OF . . . CHESTER [etc,]
. . . LIVERPOOL : PUBLISHED BY J. WILLIAMS, SEN . . .
1846.

   (adverts), 42 + 6 + (Chester), 54, 18, 16 + (Birkenhead &
   places near), 40 + (Stockport, Macclesfield, re-issues of 1845
   above), 60, 48 + (Runcorn), 12 + (Warrington), 20 +
   (Stafford, Hanley, Shelton, Stoke, etc. Newcastle-under-
   Lyne, etc., as in Williams's directory of Stafford, etc. *see*
   STAFFORDSHIRE, 1846), 16, 8, 12, 16, 24 + (Shrewsbury),
   24 + (Wolverhampton), 24 + (Gorton, etc), 4 + (Altrinc-
   ham & places near), 16 + (Leeds), 3–12 + (Wrexham), 16.
   One copy has (Wigan), 14 after Hanley and no Wrexham.
   [Gen. Tr ; St. also for Chester ; Leeds as 1845.]
      $7\frac{1}{8} \times 4\frac{1}{8}''$. Price 10s. cloth, 12s. leather ; non-subsc,
   2s. extra.
Chester (including Wigan). Manchester.

1850

142. History, Gazetteer & Directory of the County . . . of Chester. By Samuel Bagshaw . . . Sheffield : Printed by George Ridge, 5 King Street : & Sold by Samuel Bagshaw, Wentworth Terrace . . . 1850.

iv + 712. [Misc. Tr. for larger places, Gen. for smaller.]
$8\frac{1}{2} \times 5\frac{1}{4}''$. Purple cloth. Price, subsc, 14s. 6d.
Preface dated 21 January 1850. Issued with a sheet map.
Guildhall. Salt. Warrington.

1852–54. *See* Lancashire, 1852, 1853, 1854.

ALTRINCHAM
1855

143. Charles Balshaw's Strangers' Guide & Complete Directory to Altrincham, Bowdon, Dunham, Timperley, Baguley, Ashley, Hale & Bollington. Altrincham : Printed by Charles Balshaw, High Street.

102 pp. ; plates. [Gen.]
$8\frac{1}{8} \times 5\frac{1}{8}''$. Red cloth, label.
N.d. but the list of mayors ends 1854. Other editions were published in 1857 and 1859.
Chetham. Warrington.

BIRKENHEAD
1843

144. 1843. Mortimer & Harwood's Directory of Birkenhead. Birkenhead : Printed & Sold by W. Osborne, Westminster Buildings, Chester Street.

(adverts), 32 + 2 + 10 + 22 + 15. [St. Gen.]
$6\frac{3}{4} \times 4''$. Brown printed wrappers.
Preface dated 1 September 1843. There are entries for W. W. Mortimer, accountant and Robert Harwood, keeper of the Market Inn, who may be the authors.
B.M. (10358.aa.41). Manchester.

1851

145. Pinkney's Directory of Birkenhead & its Environs. 1851. Birkenhead : R. Pinkney, Waterloo Buildings.

(adverts), 4 + 6 + ii + 5-100. [Gen.]
$6\frac{1}{8} \times 4\frac{1}{2}''$.
In 3 parts, Birkenhead, Rock Ferry & Bebington, Seacombe.
Liverpool. Manchester.

CHESTER

For 1780–3, *see* Cheshire. It seems likely that there were directories for some at any rate of the years between 1783 and 1787, published with re-issues of the second edition of the *Guide* as in 1783, but no record or copies have been found.

1787

146. THE CHESTER GUIDE . . . TO WHICH IS ADDED A DIRECTORY
. . . THIRD EDITION . . . CHESTER : PRINTED & SOLD BY
P. BROSTER.

Re-issue of the second edition of the guide (*see* CHESHIRE,
1782), with cancel title with corrections bringing the
information up to date on verso and a directory of Chester,
headed 1787, pp. 81–110. [Gen.]

B.M. (291.b.51). Guildhall.

1792

147. THE CHESTER DIRECTORY & GUIDE . . . CHESTER : PRINTED
FOR & SOLD BY JAMES POOLE, EASTGATE STREET.

40 pp. [Ct. Pr. Gm.]
$8\frac{1}{2} \times 5''$. Price 1s.

An offprint, with new title and dedication, of the Chester
directory in *The Universal British Directory* (No. 13). It
gives as mayor, Peter Broster, who was mayor in 1791–2.
Poole is entered as John Poole both here and in the 1787
directory. He published a *Concise History of Chester* in
1791, which contains the same account of the city as in
the above.

Bod. Chester.

1795

148. THE CHESTER GUIDE . . . TO WHICH IS ADDED A DIRECTORY
. . . THIRD EDITION. CHESTER, SOLD BY P. BROSTER &
SON & GEO. BULKELEY.

6 + 96 ; 5 plates. [Gen.]
$6\frac{7}{8} \times 4''$.

Directory section headed 1795. The guide has been re-
written since the 1787 edition which, in spite of its title
page, was apparently not now counted as a separate edition
by the publishers.

B.M. (10358.b.8. & 579.c.58). Chester. A.R.W.

1796

149. J. H. Cooke, *Bibliotheca Cestrensis* (1904), lists an edition of
the above dated 1796, which he says is rare. No copy has
been found. Presumably it is a re-issue of 1795 with a
new directory.

1797

150. Re-issue of 1795 with a new directory, pp. 73–99, headed 1797
and pp. 61–72 reprinted with the names of officials, etc,
brought up to date.

B.M. (579.c.58/2). Chester. Guildhall.

The fourth and later editions of Broster's *Chester Guide* have no directories. Cooke (*op. cit.*) cites *The Chester Guide & Directory* (1828), but this seems to be a confusion with *The Chester Guide or A Walk round the Walls . . .* Seacombe (1828), which is the seventh edition, enlarged, of Broster's guide, with no directory. It is entered in the B.M. catalogue as *The Chester Guide & Directory*, Broster & Son.

1840

151. THE CHESTER GENERAL DIRECTORY. PUBLISHED FOR THE PROPRIETORS BY PARRY & SON . . . EASTGATE STREET. CHESTER.

4 + 82 + 12 + 40 ; adverts, 50 pp. & interspersed. [Cm. Ct. Tr.]

$8\frac{1}{8} \times 3\frac{3}{4}''$. Green cloth, label. Price 3s.

Dated 1840 on label.

B.M. Chester.

MACCLESFIELD
1817

152. THE HISTORY OF MACCLESFIELD. BY JOHN CORRY . . . LONDON, SOLD BY J. FERGUSON, UNION STREET, SOMERS TOWN. 1817. [Printer, J. Leigh, Market Place, Manchester.]

12 + 292 ; 8 tables. [Tr. 280–87.]

$8\frac{1}{2} \times 5\frac{1}{8}''$.

John Corry was a native of Ireland and came to London, where he continued to reside, in 1792. He was the author of a number of biographies, local histories and other works. The directory in this volume was perhaps by W. Parson, for whom Leigh printed a directory in 1818 (*see* STAFFORDSHIRE, 1818).

Bod. B.M. Macclesfield.

1825

153. THE HISTORY & DIRECTORY OF MACCLESFIELD . . . MANCHESTER : PRINTED BY W. D. VAREY, RED LION STREET . . . 1825.

216 pp. [Gen. Tr.]

$6\frac{7}{8} \times 4\frac{1}{8}''$. Price 4s. 6d.

The directory was compiled by J. Plant and T. Gregory.

B.M. (lacking directory). Chetham. Macclesfield.

CORNWALL

1843–1855

Clergy and law directories for towns in Cornwall are included in *The Exeter Pocket Journal* for these dates (Nos. 193–206).

1847

154. Williams's Commercial Directory of the Principal Market Towns in Cornwall . . . J. Williams. Directory Publishing Offices, 11 Temple Court, Liverpool. 1847.
title + (adverts), 34 + vi + 7–240. [Ct. Cm ; Tr. also for larger towns.]
$8\frac{3}{8} \times 5\frac{1}{4}"$. Red or green cloth.
B.M. L.L. Morrab.

FALMOUTH

1815

155. The Ancient & Modern History of Falmouth . . . with a Directory . . . July, 1815 . . . By James Trathan. Falmouth : Printed & Sold by the Author . . . 1815.
vi + 7–86 ; table. [Gen.]
$6\frac{3}{8} \times 3\frac{7}{8}"$. Boards, label. Price 2s. 6d.
Bod. Falmouth.

1827

156. A Panorama of Falmouth . . . Falmouth : Printed at the Cornish Magazine Office by & for J. Philp . . .
title + 90 + 8 ; adverts, 12 pp., 5 eng ; 4 plates ; map. [Pr. Cm.]
$6\frac{3}{8} \times 3\frac{7}{8}"$.
N.d. but there is a reference to a ' recent ' death on 12 July 1827, on p. 89. Some copies are without the leaf containing a notice of the patronage of the duke of Clarence, official permission not having been received until some copies had been delivered. Pp. 39/40 are a cancel. It is possible that there were several issues of the book, with the information on these pages and on the 3 pp. of commercial names brought up to date. For purpose of identification it may be stated that in all three copies examined, the list of names contains 94 entries, from J. Arthur to Williams. If there were several issues it seems impossible to tell to which year the directory information applies. The plates were lithographed by C. Hullmandel.
Bod. B.M. (579.b.14). C.U.L. Falmouth. Morrab.

CUMBERLAND

1811

157. Jollie's Cumberland Guide & Directory . . . Carlisle : Printed by F. Jollie & Sons, 1811.
In two parts, each with separate title, also issued separately. [Pt. I]. [As above] . . . Part the First, containing Carlisle, Longtown, [etc.] . . .
viii + 84 + xl ; map, 2 plans, 3 plates. [Cm, butchers, Ct.]
Dedication dated December 1810. Besides the formal

directories, pp. 81–84 contain references to a number of local manufacturers. In all but one of the copies of the two parts bound together which have been examined pp. xxxv–xxxviii, and sometimes pp. xxxix–xl as well, are omitted. Presumably they were intentionally cancelled, though the reason is obscure. There are some corrections and additions on pp. xxxvii–xxxviii.

[Pt. II]. [As above] . . . PART THE SECOND [containing places in the western part of the county].

2 + 132 ; 2 plans. [Cm. etc. as Pt. I.]

$8\frac{3}{8} \times 5"$. Price 6s.

Jollie & Sons published a weekly advertising paper called *The Carlisle Journal.*

Barrow-in-Furness (with pp. xxxv–xxxviii). B.M. (2 copies, 290.e.35 and G.3192/1 and Pt. I alone, 578.c.36). Carlisle (in parts and together). Chetham (without xxxv–xl). Guildhall (as Chetham). A.R.W. (as Chetham).

1829

158. HISTORY, DIRECTORY & GAZETTEER OF . . . CUMBERLAND & WESTMORLAND, WITH . . . FURNESS & CARTMEL . . . BY WM. PARSON & WM. WHITE. PRINTED FOR W. WHITE & CO. BY EDWARD BAINES & SON, AT THE LEEDS MERCURY OFFICE : & SOLD BY THE PUBLISHERS, AT . . . 44 HUNSLET LANE . . . LEEDS ; & PILGRIM STREET, NEWCASTLE . . . 1829.

732 + xxxiv + 2 ; map ; notice inserted between 276/7. [Gen. for smaller places, Misc. Tr. for larger.]

$6\frac{7}{8} \times 4"$. Price, subsc, with an atlas and 3 tables, 14s. boards, 15s. 6d. calf ; with coloured maps, 3s. extra ; to purchasers of Parson & White's Durham directory, 12s.

Preface dated August 1829.

Barrow-in-Furness. B.M. Carlisle. Guildhall.

1847

159. HISTORY, GAZETTEER & DIRECTORY OF CUMBERLAND . . . BY MANNIX & WHELLAN. PRINTED . . . BY W. B. JOHNSON, MARKET STREET, BEVERLEY . . . 1847.

xvi + 9–632. [Gen. for smaller, Misc. Tr. for larger places.]

$8\frac{1}{4} \times 5\frac{1}{8}"$. Price 14s. 6d. ; non-subsc, 20s. ; map, 5s. 6d. Preface dated Whitehaven, 21 December 1847. ' Mannix ' seems to be a misprint for ' Mannex '. Mannex and Whellan parted company after this though they both went on to publish other directories. Probably both of them began as employees of one of the big directory publishers. All the Mannex directories, except one of Mid-Lancs in 1854, are by the same printer. In 1849 (Westmorland), he is called P. J. Mannex and in a directory of Lonsdale, published by Mannex & Co. in 1866, there is an entry for Patrick Mannex, publisher at Preston.

Barrow-in-Furness. B.M. (10352.cc.34). Carlisle. Guildhall.

LAKE DISTRICT

(*See also* WINDERMERE (Westmorland).)

1855

160. A COMPLETE GUIDE TO THE ENGLISH LAKES BY HARRIET
MARTINEAU . . . & A . . . DIRECTORY. WINDERMERE:
JOHN GARNETT. LONDON: WHITTAKER & CO.
4 + iv + ii + iv + 2 + 234; adverts, xvi; map, 16
plates, 6 outline plans. [Gen.]
6⅝ × 4". Green cloth, gilt. Price 5s.
Preface dated 12 March 1855. The directories were
compiled by the publisher who kept the post office at
Windermere and was also railway superintendent as well
as a printer and bookseller. The population of the Lake
district was a continually changing one (*see* p. 22 above).
W.S.L.

161. [Another issue.] Same title and binding but with a few
additions to the directory (*e.g.* first issue, p. 207, col. 1, 19
names; second issue, 20 names. First issue, p. 217, col. 2,
Youdel, John is corrected to Youdell in second issue) and
adverts. re-set and covering xix pp.
Bod. B.M. (10351.b.57). C.U.L. W.S.L.

The second edition of this guide (n.d. but *c.* 1857) also has a
directory. The third and later editions have shorter and much
inferior ones. The 4to editions do not contain directories.

BRAMPTON

(*See* NORTHUMBERLAND, 1851.)

CARLISLE

1792

162. THE CARLISLE DIRECTORY & GUIDE . . . PRINTED FOR &
SOLD BY LAUNCELOT SMITH . . .
32 pp. [Ct. Pr. Cm.]
8½ × 5".
An offprint, with new title and dedication, of the Carlisle
directory in *The Universal British Directory* (No. 13), with
some additions to the descriptive part. Dated from the
name of the mayor.
Carlisle.

1810

163. A PICTURE OF CARLISLE & DIRECTORY . . . CARLISLE:
PRINTED FOR A. HENDERSON IN THE MARKET PLACE. 1810.
xii + 164; map, plate. [Gen.]
6⅝ × 4". Boards.
Preface dated 13 October 1810.
Bod. B.M. (10368.cc.15). Carlisle. Guildhall.

1837

164. THE CARLISLE DIRECTORY FOR . . . 1837 . . . CARLISLE :
PRINTED BY JAMES STEEL, JOURNAL OFFICE. 1837.
iv + 88. [Gen. Tr. St.]
7 × 4⅛″.
The street directory has names of voters only.
Guildhall.

1840

165. THE CARLISLE DIRECTORY FOR . . . 1840. CARLISLE :
PRINTED FOR JAMES TAIT, KING'S ARMS LANE, BY H. LOWES,
ENGLISH STREET. 1840.
80 pp. [Gen. Tr. St.]
6⅛ × 3⅝″. Printed boards.
A.R.W.

1851 & 1852. *See* NORTHUMBERLAND, 1851, 1852.

PENRITH

(*See* NORTHUMBERLAND, 1852.)

WIGTON

(*See* NORTHUMBERLAND, 1851.)

DERBYSHIRE

(For places near Sheffield *see also* Sheffield directories.)

1829

166. THE DIRECTORY OF THE COUNTY OF DERBY . . . TAKEN
DURING THE YEARS 1827, '8 & '9 BY STEPHEN GLOVER.
DERBY : PRINTED . . . BY HENRY MOZLEY & SON . . .
1829.
xl + 120. [Gen.]
8⅞ × 5½″. Also L.P., 10 × 6⅜″. Green cloth, label.
Price 8s. ; non-subsc. 9s. ; L.P. 12s.
Uniform with and forming part of S. Glover, *The History,
Gazetteer, & Directory of the County of Derby*, ed. T. Noble,
Derby, 1829. Only two volumes of the *History* were
published. Besides two issues uniform with the two issues
of the *Directory*, there was a 4to edition, without the
directory.
Stephen Glover was an auctioneer and printer at Wirks-
worth, thirteen miles from Derby, in 1823. Soon after he
moved to Nottingham, of which place he compiled several
directories. He collected materials for the history of Derby
as well as for the directory, himself, travelling all over the
county for the purpose. He also issued a Peak guide in

1830 and assisted in *The Antiquities of Derbyshire*, published in 1848, besides compiling the Derby directories listed below. In 1843, he moved to Derby. The notice of his removal in the Derby directory for that year speaks of his twenty-five years' experience as a land-agent in Derbyshire, Nottinghamshire and other counties. He died in 1869 and was buried at Moreton in Cheshire. (*D.N.B.* ; Prefaces to directories of Derby and Nottingham.)

Bod. B.M. Derby. Guildhall. Salt.

1846

167. HISTORY, GAZETTEER & DIRECTORY OF DERBYSHIRE, WITH . . . BURTON-ON-TRENT . . . BY SAMUEL BAGSHAW. SHEFFIELD : PRINTED . . . BY WILLIAM SAXTON, HIGH STREET & SOLD BY SAMUEL BAGSHAW, PHILADELPHIA, SHEFFIELD . . . 1846.

4 + 702 ; map. [Gen ; Tr. also for all but smallest places.]
$8\frac{1}{2} \times 5\frac{3}{8}''$. Cloth. Price, subsc. 14s. 6d.
Preface dated 14 March 1846.
B.M. (10360.ff.31). Derby. Guildhall. Salt.

1852

168. FREEBODY'S DIRECTORY OF . . . DERBY, CHESTERFIELD [other towns in Derbyshire] . . . BURTON-ON-TRENT. DERBY : RICHARDSON & SON, 172 FLEET STREET, LONDON & 9 CAPEL STREET, DUBLIN. 1852.

title + vii–xxviii + 254 ; adverts, 70. [Gen. Tr. St. for Derby ; Tr. for other places.]
$7\frac{1}{4} \times 4\frac{3}{8}''$. Cloth.
Preface dated 10 May 1852.
Derby. Guildhall.

BUXTON
(*See* LANCASHIRE, 1854.)

DERBY

1823

169. BREWER'S DERBY CIRCULAR GUIDE & COMMERCIAL DIRECTORY FOR 1823 & 1824 . . . DERBY : PRINTED . . . BY G. WILKINS & SOLD BY J. DREWRY, IRON GATE & G. WILKINS, QUEEN STREET.

108 pp. [Pr. Ct. Tr. for Derby ; some short lists for other places.]
$7 \times 4\frac{1}{4}''$.
Said to be by Thomas Bathew of Sudbury, who died in 1824. According to the preface, ' a steady man was sent to obtain subscriptions and above 400 people put down their names and proper descriptions. Those who did not

must not complain of neglect '. The editor disclaims
any invidious distinctions between subscribers and non-
subscribers. Drewry was proprietor of the *Derby Mercury*.
Derby.

1843

170. THE HISTORY & DIRECTORY OF . . . DERBY . . . BY
STEPHEN GLOVER . . . DERBY : PRINTED & PUBLISHED FOR
S. GLOVER & SON BY HENRY MOZLEY & SONS. 1843.
    4 + 88 + 168 ; adverts, 16. [Gen. Tr.]
    $8\frac{5}{8} \times 5\frac{3}{8}''$. Cloth, label. Price 6*s*. 6*d*.
The history (1–88) and the directory with adverts (168 + 16)
were also issued separately at 2*s*. 6*d*., with new titles. The
B.M. copy of the history alone has a plan of Derby, dated
1835. No editions have been found between this and the
fourth edition, 1849. Perhaps the first edition was 1835
and this is either the second or the third.
Bod. B.M. Derby. Guildhall (directory alone).

1849

171. [Title as above but] FOURTH EDITION . . . PRINTED &
PUBLISHED FOR S. GLOVER BY W. ROWBOTTOM. 1849.
    vi + 104 + 2 + 128 ; adverts, 18. [Gen. Tr.]
    $8\frac{5}{8} \times 5\frac{3}{8}''$. Cloth.
Derby. Guildhall.

1850

172. [Title as above but] CORRECTED TO MAY, 1850 [and no date
at the end].
    Re-issue of 1849 with 10 pp. adds. Another edition was
    published in 1858.
Derby. A.R.W.

GLOSSOP

(*See* CHESHIRE, 1845 ; LANCASHIRE, 1851, 1852, 1853.)

DEVONSHIRE

1843–1855

There are clergy and law directories for towns in Devonshire in
The Exeter Pocket Journal for these dates (Nos. 193–205 below).

1845–54

Pr. directories for Devonshire towns are included in *The West of
England Pocket Book* (Nos. 209–212 below).

1848

173. HUNT & CO.'S DIRECTORY & TOPOGRAPHY FOR EXETER & BRISTOL & BRIDGEWATER, COLLUMPTON [and other towns in Devon and Somerset] . . . LONDON : PRINTED FOR E. HUNT & CO. BY B. W. GARDINER . . . PRINCES STREET . . . LONDON. 1848.

    viii + 122 + 176 + [2] + 192. [Ct. Cm. Tr. for Exeter ; Ct. Tr. for Bristol, etc.]

      7 × 4″. Price, subsc. 7s. 6d.

Guildhall.

1850

174. HISTORY, GAZETTEER & DIRECTORY OF DEVONSHIRE . . . BY WILLIAM WHITE . . . PRINTED BY ROBERT LEADER . . . & SOLD BY WILLIAM WHITE, BROOM BANK, SHEFFIELD . . . 1850.

    804 pp. ; in some copies one leaf adds. inserted ; map. [Gen. Tr.]

    $7\frac{3}{8} \times 4\frac{3}{8}''$. Half cloth, label, or calf. Price, subsc. 12s. 6d. boards, 14s. calf.

    Preface dated 10 June 1850.

B.M.   Exeter.   Guildhall (with adds. leaf). Plymouth. Salt.

EXETER

    J. Davidson, *Bibliotheca Devoniensis* (1852), has an entry, ' Trewman's Exeter Journal, 1790–1852 '. The earliest extant edition is that for 1807, of which the Guildhall has a copy. Exeter Public Library has 1816, 1825, 1827, 1828 and continuously, 1830–55. Until 1827 the title was *The Exeter Pocket Journal* ; in that year it became *The Exeter Journal*. The size, $6\frac{1}{2} \times 3\frac{7}{8}''$, and the price, 2s. 6d. roan or 4s. with a tuck-in flap, remained the same throughout in spite of sporadic competition and a slowly increasing number of pages. The directories were Pr. Cm. for Exeter until 1843, when clergy and law directories for towns in Cornwall and Devon were included. In 1848 the Exeter alphabetical list was extended to include private residents. The imprint was ' Trewman ' in 1807 ; ' Trewman & Son ', 1816 ; ' Trewman & Co ', 1825–33 ; and ' R. J. Trewman ', 1834 onwards. The title of the 1807 edition is given below and then a summarised list of the pagination of succeeding editions so far as copies have been found. Other Exeter directories follow.

1807

175. THE EXETER POCKET JOURNAL ; OR WEST COUNTRY GENTLEMAN & TRADESMAN'S MEMORANDUM BOOK FOR . . . 1807 . . . EXETER : PRINTED & SOLD BY TREWMAN . . .

    viii + (Almanac, etc.), 106 + 60.

1816

176. (blank), 26 + viii + (Almanac, etc.), 108 + 60 + 2 + (blank),
28 ; map. Map and varying number of blank and ruled
leaves continued in all editions ; Almanac until 1836.
In the Exeter copies, the blank and almanac pages are
sometimes partially or wholly lacking. Other pages are as
. follows :

1825, 1827, **177, 178.** xvi + 68.

1828. **179.** viii + 76.

1830–1833. **180–183.** xvi + 68. Exeter copy of 1831 ends p. 62,
incomplete.

1834. **184.** xxiv + 68.

1835. **185.** Only incomplete copy (Exeter) seen.

1836. **186.** xxxii + 72.

1837. **187.** xxxii + 74.

1838–1842. **188–192.** xxxii + 72.

1843–1847. **193–197.** xxxii + 76.

1848.ˑ **198.** xxxii + 83.

1849–1851. **199–201.** xxxii + 84.

1852. **202.** xxxii + 76.

1853–1855. **203–205.** xxiv + 84.

1828

207. EXETER ITINERARY & GENERAL DIRECTORY . . . JUNE, 1828.
EXETER : PRINTED & PUBLISHED BY T. & H. BESLEY, BELL
HILL, SOUTH STREET.
iv + iv + 9–226 ; adverts, 12 leaves ; plan. [Pr. Tr. Gen.]
$7\frac{1}{2} \times 4\frac{1}{2}''$.
Preface, dated 18 June 1828, says that many errors may
have occurred owing to ' the reserved manner in which some
persons have treated the necessary inquiries '.
Exeter.

1831

208. [Title as above but] JULY, 1831 . . . T. & H. BESLEY
DIRECTORY OFFICE . . .
viii + 9–236 ; adverts, 3 leaves ; plan, plate. [Pr. Tr. Gen.]
$7\frac{3}{8} \times 4\frac{3}{4}''$.
Preface dated 12 July 1831. Davidson, *op. cit.*, lists
editions for 1835, 1836 and 1837 but copies of these have
not been discovered.
A.R.W.

1845

209. THE WEST OF ENGLAND POCKET BOOK . . . 1845. EXETER :
PRINTED & PUBLISHED BY HENRY BESLEY, DIRECTORY
OFFICE . . .

248 pp. (217–236 unnumbered). [Gen. Also Pr. for towns in Devonshire.]

$6\frac{1}{4} \times 3\frac{7}{8}"$. Roan with tuck-in flap. Price 2s. 6d., 3s. or 3s. 6d.

This is an imitation in appearance and general contents of Trewman's *Exeter Journal*. Where it has been possible to compare the two directories for the same year Besley's has contained more names.

Exeter.

Three more editions of the West of England Pocket Book are extant, all with similar title, imprint and contents as 1845 and the same size, binding and price. Pagination as follows:

1847. **210.** 40 + (blank ruled), 112 + 149–252 (221–41 unnumbered) ; map. Exeter.

1853. **211.** 36 + (blank ruled), 112 + 149–252 ; map. Exeter.

1854. **212.** 38 + (blank ruled), 112 + 2 + 151–252 + iv ; map. B.M.

1849

213. Manchester P. L. catalogues a Hunt directory of Exeter and neighbourhood for 1849 but the copy seems to have been lost. It is probably the same as the Exeter section of DEVONSHIRE, 1848, *q.v.*

NEWTON ABBOT
1830

214. A HISTORY OF NEWTON-ABBOT & NEWTON-BUSHEL . . . BY THE REV. D. M. STIRLING . . . NEWTON-ABBOT. PRINTED BY F. FORORD. 1830.

xii + 180. [Pr. Gen.]

$7\frac{1}{8} \times 4\frac{1}{8}"$. Pink cloth, label. Price 5s.

Dedication dated May 1830.

B.M. (10352.a.37). Guildhall.

PLYMOUTH
1812

215. THE PICTURE OF PLYMOUTH . . . PLYMOUTH : PRINTED FOR REES & CURTIS . . . 1812. [Printer, J. M'Creery, Black Horse Court, Fleet Street, London.]

xii + 234 ; plan. [Gen.]

$5\frac{7}{8} \times 3\frac{5}{8}"$. Boards, orange label.

Address, dated 1 February 1812, says the book was written without the publishers' knowledge and very recently offered to them. It is attributed to Henry Woolcombe, who is entered in the directory as an attorney.

Bod. B.M. (10368.aaa.23). Guildhall. Plymouth. A.R.W. (in orig. boards).

1814

216. THE PLYMOUTH, PLYMOUTH-DOCK & STONEHOUSE GENERAL
DIRECTORY . . . FOR 1814. PLYMOUTH: PUBLISHED BY S.
ROWE, MARKET PLACE. [Printer, S. Rowe.]
    108 pp. [Gen. Also Ct. for vicinity.]
    $5\frac{5}{8} \times 3\frac{3}{8}''$.
Preface dated 1 March 1814. ' An intelligent person ' was
employed by the publisher to collect names from door to
door. Samuel Rowe (1793–1853) kept a bookshop and
circulating library with his brother, Joshua. He was the
author of a number of books, including one on Gothic
architecture, and his *Perambulation of Dartmoor* (1848) is
a standard work. In 1822 he took Holy Orders. (*D.N.B.* ;
R. N. Worth, ' Notes on Printing in Devon ', *Devon Assoc.
for Science, etc. Reports*, xi, 1879.)
Plymouth.

1822

217. THE PLYMOUTH, PLYMOUTH-DOCK, STONEHOUSE . . . DIREC-
TORY . . . BY N. TAPERELL. PLYMOUTH: PRINTED . . .
BY E. NETTLETON, 57 MARKET STREET . . . 1822.
    xxiv + 80 ; adverts interspersed. [Gen.]
    $6 \times 3\frac{3}{4}''$.
Preface dated 1 May 1822.
Exeter. Plymouth.

1823

218. THE TOURIST'S COMPANION BEING A GUIDE TO PLYMOUTH
. . . WITH A DIRECTORY . . . LONDON: PRINTED FOR LONG-
MAN, HURST, REES, ORME & BROWN, PATERNOSTER ROW.
1823. [Printer, J. Johns, Fore-street Dock, Plymouth.]
    xii + 316 ; 2 maps, plates. [Gen.]
    $5\frac{7}{8} \times 3\frac{5}{8}''$. Pink printed wrappers.
B.M. (10358.bb.55).

1830

219. THE PLYMOUTH, STONEHOUSE & DEVONPORT DIRECTORY . . .
BY ROBERT BRINDLEY . . . DEVONPORT: PRINTED & PUB-
LISHED BY W. BYERS . . . FORE STREET . . . 1830.
    vi + 6 + 9–212 ; addenda slip. [Gen.]
    $7\frac{1}{4} \times 4\frac{1}{8}''$.
Preface dated January 1830. Brindley was an architect,
surveyor and estate agent.
B.M. Exeter. Plymouth.

1835

220. R. N. Worth, *Three Towns Bibliotheca* (1873), p. 24, refers
to a Plymouth directory published by James Stevens, 1835.
No copy has been traced.

1836

221. THOMAS'S DIRECTOR : BEING AN ALPHABETICAL LIST OF THE INHABITANTS OF PLYMOUTH . . . PART I. JENKIN THOMAS, 9, CORNWALL STREET. 1836.

    viii + 112 ; eng. adverts ; errata slip, plan (1835). [Gen.] 6 × 4″. Price 2s. 6d.

    Preface dated 24 May 1836. The idea of a classified directory was given up because ' offence may be given to certain classes . . . and digust or ire may be raised by the name of a plebeian being arranged in the same page with that of an aristocrat.' (p. [47]) Pts. II and III for Stonehouse and Devonport were planned but probably not published. No copies or references to them have been found. Guildhall.

1844

222. FLINTOFF'S DIRECTORY & GUIDE TO PLYMOUTH, DEVONPORT [etc.] . . . PLYMOUTH : G. FLINTOFF, STANDARD OFFICE, 3 OLD TOWN.

    8 + 13–168 ; adverts, 26. [Tr ; Ct. also for Plymouth.] 7 × 4¼″. Blue cloth, printed label. Price 2s. 6d.

    Dated from the name of the mayor.

Plymouth. A.R.W.

1847

223. WILLIAMS'S COMMERCIAL DIRECTORY OF DEVONPORT, PLYMOUTH & STONEHOUSE . . . J. WILLIAMS, DIRECTORY PUBLISHING OFFICES, 11 TEMPLE COURT, LIVERPOOL. 1847. [Printer, L. E. G. Battenbury, Devonport.]

    (adverts), 76 + 264. [St. Cm. Tr.] 6¾ × 3¾″.

Plymouth.

1852

224. A DIRECTORY OF PLYMOUTH, STONEHOUSE [etc.]. COMPILED FROM ACTUAL SURVEY. PLYMOUTH : PUBLISHED BY F. BRENDON . . . CORNWALL STREET. 1852.

    xvi + 280. [St. Gen. Tr. Also Ct. for vicinity.] 7 × 4⅝″.

Exeter. Plymouth.

225. R. N. Worth, *op. cit.*, lists an 1853 edition of the above. No copy found.

SIDMOUTH
1836

226. A DESCRIPTIVE SKETCH OF SIDMOUTH . . . BY THEODORE H. MOGRIDGE, ESQ. M.D. . . . SIDMOUTH : PRINTED, PUBLISHED & SOLD BY J. HARVEY.

viii + 172 ; map. [Tr.]
   6⅞ × 4¼″. Dark blue figured silk, gilt edges.
The only clue to the date is the map which is dated 1836.
Mogridge was a consulting surgeon. A typical watering-
place directory in a pretty and unusual binding.
A.R.W.

TORQUAY

1832

227. The Panorama of Torquay . . . by Octavian Blewitt.
Second Edition . . . London : Simpkin & Marshall, &
Cockrem, Torquay. 1832.
   eng. title + xii + 288 ; map, plates. [Tr.]
   7⅛ × 4¼″. Cloth, black label. Price 7s. 6d.
Map dated 1 October 1832. Cockrem was responsible for
the directory section.   The first edition has no directory.
B.M. (579.b.44. Dated 1833 in Catalogue.) A.R.W.

1841

228. [*Guide to Torquay, Containing a General History & Miscellaneous Directory.* 1841.] The only known copy, which
was at the Plymouth Institute, was destroyed during the
late war.

DORSETSHIRE

1851

229. Hunt & Co.'s Directory of Dorsetshire with Part of
Hants & Wilts . . . 1851. Printed for E. Hunt & Co.
by B. W. Gardiner . . . London.
   viii + 248 + 2 + 88 ; adverts, 20. [Misc. Tr. for larger,
Gen. for smaller places.]
   7 × 4″. Green cloth. Price 5s. 6d.
The Dorsetshire section was re-issued in Hunt's Hampshire
directory, 1852 (*see* Hampshire, 1852).
Gen. Soc. A.R.W.

230. [Another issue] [title as above but] Also of . . . Bristol &
[places in Somerset].
   As above to p. 88 + 2 + 122 + 48 + 233–372 + 372*–
373* ; adverts.
   Green cloth. Price 9s.
The Somerset section is a re-issue of Hunt's Somerset
directory 1850 (*see* Somerset, 1850) and the Bristol section
is a re-issue of the court directory in Bristol, 1848 and
the Tr. directory as in Wales, 1850.
A.R.W.

WEYMOUTH

1816 & 1827

231–232. [*Weymouth Guide. To Which is Subjoined a Directory.*
G. Kay. 1816.] No copy found. It is listed in C. H.
Mayo, *Bibliotheca Dorsetiensis* (1885), which also mentions
New Weymouth Guide, G. Kay, 1827. No copy found either.

1828

233. BENSON'S WEYMOUTH GUIDE & COMMERCIAL DIRECTORY.
WEYMOUTH : PRINTED FOR & BY B. BENSON.
iv + 4 + 82 ; adverts, 2 ; plate. [Tr.]
$7\frac{1}{8} \times 4''$. Mauve printed wrappers.
Dated 1828 on front wrapper.
A.R.W.

COUNTY DURHAM

1827–1828

234. HISTORY, DIRECTORY & GAZETTEER OF . . . DURHAM &
NORTHUMBERLAND . . . & BERWICK-ON-TWEED . . . BY
WM. PARSON & WM. WHITE . . . PRINTED FOR W. WHITE
& CO. BY EDWARD BAINES & SON, AT THE LEEDS MERCURY
OFFICE & SOLD BY THE PUBLISHERS AT THEIR OFFICE, BELL'S
COURT, PILGRIM STREET, NEWCASTLE . . . 1827.
[Vol. I] 10 + clxviii + 504. [Misc, but Cm. for Newcastle ;
Tr.]
Adds (clxii–clxviii) dated August 1827. Preface dated
September 1827.
[Vol. II] Title dated 1828.
4 + 684. [Cm.] Preface dated 14 July 1828.
$7\frac{1}{2} \times 4\frac{5}{8}''$. Price per vol., 10s. 6d. boards, 12s. calf ;
non-subsc, 13s. 6d. or 15s. Maps 1s. 6d. each.
Vol. I contains market towns, Vol. II, villages.
B.M. Carlisle. Guildhall. Newcastle.

1847 *et seq.* *See* NORTHUMBERLAND, 1847, *et seq.*

1851

235. HAGAR & CO.'S DIRECTORY OF THE COUNTY OF DURHAM . . .
NOTTINGHAM : PRINTED . . . BY STEVENSON & CO. MIDDLE
PAVEMENT. 1851.
iv + 5–46 ; adverts, 74. [Ct. Tr.]
$8\frac{1}{2} \times 5\frac{3}{8}''$. Red cloth. Price, subsc, 10s. 6d. or 12s. with
map.
A sketchy affair. The binding is an imitation of Kelly's
Post Office directories.
Durham. Guildhall.

DURHAM

1845

236. WHITE'S DIRECTORY & ALMANACH FOR 1845 . . . DURHAM :
THOMAS WHITE, PRINTER, SADLER STREET.
    50 pp. [St.]
    $7 \times 3\frac{3}{4}''$.
A map seems to have been removed from the only known
copy. The issue for 1856 is said to be the fourteenth,
so there must have been two issues, of which no copies
seem to be extant.
Durham U.L.

At the end of 1845 Thomas White sold his printing business to
George Walker, Jun., owner of an old-established Durham business,
who continued White's directory. All Walker's issues are the same
size, with similar title and imprint and priced at 1s. in wrappers.
They were also issued in cloth. They are listed below in a summarised form. Durham U.L. has a complete set. There are also
copies of 1848 at Durham P.L., of 1849 and 1853 at the Guildhall
and of 1851, '57, '58, '60 in the A.R.W. collection.

1846

237. THE DURHAM DIRECTORY & ALMANACH FOR 1846. GEORGE
WALKER, JUN.
    52 pp. ; adverts, 10. [Gen.]
    $7\frac{1}{4} \times 4\frac{1}{4}''$. Price 1s.
Durham U.L.

1847. **238.** adverts, 4 + ftsp, eng. title, title + 72 ; adverts, 20.
    [Gen.] Preface dated December 1846.
1848. **239.** ftsp, title + v–x + 4 + 11–56 ; adverts, 16. [Misc.
    Tr.] Preface dated December 1847.
1849. **240.** ftsp + 4 + 74 ; adverts, 20. [Misc. St. Tr.] The
    same types of directory appear in all later issues.
1850. **241.** ftsp, title + 76 ; adverts, 20, 12.
1851. **242.** ftsp, title + ii + 3–78 ; adverts, 18, 12. The directory
    section is headed 1850 but is not the same as in the
    1850 issue.
1852. **243.** ftsp + iv + 5–76 ; adverts, 20, 12, 2.
1853. **244.** ftsp + 78 ; adverts, 18, 12.
1854. **245.** ftsp, title + 84 ; adverts, 48, 2.
1855. **246.** ftsp, title + 84.

ESSEX

1848

247. HISTORY, GAZETTEER & DIRECTORY OF . . . ESSEX . . . BY
WILLIAM WHITE . . . PRINTED FOR THE AUTHOR BY ROBERT
LEADER . . . & SOLD BY WILLIAM WHITE, 200 BROOK HILL,
SHEFFIELD . . . 1848.

725 pp. ; adverts, 7 ; map. [Misc. Tr.]
$7\frac{1}{2} \times 4\frac{1}{2}''$. Price, subsc, 12s. boards, 13s. 6d. calf.
Preface dated 1 August 1848.
Bod. B.M. C.U.L. Guildhall. Salt.

GLOUCESTERSHIRE

1820

248. The Gloucestershire Directory . . . by R. Gell &
T. Bradshaw. Gloucester: Printed by J. Roberts,
Herald Office, Westgate Street. 1820.
xx + 13–228 ; plan. [Gen ; Tr. also for larger places.]
$6\frac{3}{4} \times 4\frac{1}{8}''$.
For Gell and Bradshaw, *see* p. 66 above.
Bod. Cheltenham. Chetham. Gloucester. I.H.R.

1844

From 1844 a court directory for Gloucestershire was included in
the *Cheltenham Annuaire*. In 1855 and later this section was also
issued separately (*see* Cheltenham, Nos. 328–339).

1847

249. Hunt & Co.'s Gloucester & Cheltenham Directory . . .
[with] Surrounding Villages . . . also Berkeley, Cirencester [and other towns in Gloucestershire and Ross in Heref.]
. . . 1847. Printed for E. Hunt & Co. by B. W.
Gardiner . . . Princes Street . . . London.
8 + 64 + 148 + 12 ; adverts, 58, xviii. [Ct. Tr. for
Gloucester & Cheltenham ; Ct. for other towns.]
$7 \times 4\frac{1}{8}''$. Blue cloth. Price 6s. 6d.
Preface dated February 1847. The Gloucester section was
re-issued with Hereford, etc. in August (*see* Herefordshire, 1847).
Cheltenham (bound up with Cheltenham section first).
Gloucester.

1849

250. Hunt & Co.'s Directory & Topography for Gloucester,
Bristol [with] Berkeley, Cirencester [and other places in
Gloucestershire] . . . with Aberavon, Aberdare [and other
places in S. Wales & Monmouthshire] . . . [imprint as above].
March, 1849.
4 + 188 + 144 + 180 ; adverts. [Ct. Tr ; Gen. also for
Gloucester.]
$7 \times 4\frac{1}{8}''$. Green cloth.
The court and general directories for Gloucester were re-
issued in June 1849 with more Welsh towns (*see* Wales,

1849). The Welsh section was first issued in 1848 (*see* WALES, 1848).

Cheltenham. Gloucester. A.R.W.

1854. *See* SOMERSET, 1854.

BRISTOL
1775

251. SKETCHLEY'S BRISTOL DIRECTORY . . . BRISTOL : PRINTED BY JAMES SKETCHLEY . . . 27 IN SMALL STREET . . .

4 + 126 ; advert, 2 ; plate, list of conveyances, almanach. [Gen. merchants.]

$7\frac{1}{4} \times 4\frac{5}{8}''$.

Dated from the name of the mayor. The chief interest of the merchants is often specified, such as wine, timber, American or Irish. No copy with the list of conveyances or the almanach has been found. For Sketchley, *see* BIRMINGHAM, 1763.

Bod. Bristol.

1785

252. THE BRISTOL DIRECTORY . . . INCLUDING BEDMINSTER, CLIFTON & THE HOT-WELLS . . . BRISTOL : PRINTED FOR AR. BROWNE & SON, J. B. BECKET, J. NORTON, T. MILLS, W. BULGIN, E. SHIERCLIFF, J. LLOYD & J. THORBRAN. 1785.

4 + 78. [Cm.]

$6\frac{7}{8} \times 4''$.

Bristol.

1787

253. THE BRISTOL & BATH DIRECTORY . . . BEING THE THIRD NUMBER OF THE GENERAL DIRECTORY OF ENGLAND, WALES, &c. BRISTOL : PRINTED FOR THE AUTHOR BY W. ROUTH, BRIDGE STREET . . . 1787.

4 + 185–280. [Gen.]

$7 \times 4''$.

The dedication is signed William Bailey. This is the only known surviving part of his *General Directory*. There is no entry for Bailey and he says the executive part has had to be entrusted to others. *See also* BIRMINGHAM, 1787, LIVERPOOL, 1787 and Bailey's directories in the National section of this catalogue.

Bristol.

1792

254. THE NEW BRISTOL DIRECTORY FOR . . . 1792 . . . BY JOHN REED. PRINTED FOR & SOLD BY WM. BROWNE, TOLZEY [& 14 other Bristol booksellers].

4 + 84 ; adverts, 4.   [Ct. Cm.]
    $8\frac{1}{2} \times 5\frac{3}{8}''$.
An offprint, with new title, dedication, slightly different
errata list and a four-page list of Champante & Whitrow's
publications, of the Bristol section of *The Universal British
Directory* (*see* No. 13). John Reed is entered as an accountant. Among the participating booksellers is Joseph
Cottle.
    Bristol.

In 1793 began one of the longest and most complete series of
directories recorded in this catalogue. Published biennially from
1793 to 1805 (with also an edition for 1798), it then became annual.
William Matthews, who started it, was the son of a landowner and
took up printing and publishing in defiance of his father's threat
to disinherit him if he did so. He settled in Bristol and became
the founder of a large family of Bristol printers. In 1805 his son,
Edward Mathews (the family seems to have dropped the second
' t ' in 1803) succeeded him and at once announced his intention of
making the directory an annual one. He died in 1811 and in that
year the directory was only a re-issue of the 1810 edition, with
a supplement. It was continued from 1812 by his brother, Joseph
Mathews, who kept up an annual publication in spite of financial
difficulties, complicated by his ill-health. His sales were threatened
in the years 1816–18 by Evans's *Bristol Index* which contained a
classified trade directory. To meet this competition Mathews
added, in 1819, a classified directory to the simple alphabetical list
which was all that had been provided hitherto. This, which he
called *Mathews's Bristol Commercial List*, was published separately
from the directory in the first year and bound with it in 1820.
Afterwards it became an integral part of the volume. The price
was raised by 1s. to meet the extra cost. In spite of the defeat
of Evans's *Index*, which was not published again after 1818, the
production of the directory continued to be a struggle. The commercial list was omitted in 1822, owing to the expense, and in 1823
an announcement was made that it would only be published every
two years, though, in fact, it was continued annually. In the same
year it was announced that ' a compliment ' would be expected
from non-subscribers whose insertions occupied more than one line.
The charge was specified in 1824 as 6d. for two lines and 6d. for
every line over. The charge for one line was 1d. These charges
were reduced in 1829 to 3d. for two lines and 2d. for every line
over, but the price of the book was raised in 1830 to 4s. for non-
subscribers. In 1834 Joseph Mathews emigrated to America.
Thomas Mathews, who seems to have been a member of the family,
perhaps Joseph's son, appeared in Bristol in 1839 from New York
and set up as a printer. Matthew Mathews, another son of old
William Matthews, continued the directory. He had two sons,
Edward Hazard and William, both printers. Edward, who also
owned a patent baking powder, retired from printing in 1853 and
died shortly after, bequeathing the baking powder to his wife.
Matthew added an almanach to the directory in 1840 and a street

directory in 1844. From 1849 he included directories of neighbouring villages, perhaps to meet the competition of Hunt's Bristol
directories. The directory continued to be published by the
Mathews family until 1869, when it was taken over by Messrs
Wright & Co.

1793

255. MATTHEWS'S NEW BRISTOL DIRECTORY FOR . . . 1793–4 . . .
BRISTOL : PRINTED & SOLD BY WILLIAM MATTHEWS, NO. 10
BROADMEAD . . .
> 104 pp. [Cm.]
> $7\frac{1}{2} \times 4\frac{1}{2}''$. Price 3s. 6d.
> Also published with Matthews's *New History, Survey &
> Description of Bristol.* In several copies Matthews' trade
> card is attached to the last page. It was no doubt intended
> to be used as a label when the book was bound. A facsimile
> reprint of the history and directory was published by John
> Wright & Co. in 1898, to celebrate the centenary edition
> published by them in that year.
> Bod. Bristol. B.M. (579.c.42/2). Gloucester. A.R.W.

The rest of the Mathews' directories are listed below in summarised
form. There were small changes in the title but the book is called
' Matthews's ' (or ' Mathews's ' after 1803) directory throughout and
the format remains the same as that of the first edition. Changes
in contents or price are mentioned under the edition in which they
first occur and may be taken to have continued in subsequent
volumes. It should be noted that the adds. lists, which in later
editions are generally printed on a separate leaf or two leaves bound
before the title, are sometimes slightly different in different copies.
These variations are mentioned when they have been found but there
may be others in copies not examined. A summary of the location
of copies is given at the end of the series. The only other separate
Bristol directories are Evans's for 1816–18 and Hunt's and Scammell's directories between 1848 and 1853. These are described in
chronological order after the Mathews' series.

1795.	256.	William Matthews	128 pp.	[Cm.]
1797.	257.	,,	,,	146 pp.	
1798.	258.	,,	,,	144 pp.	Price 1s.
1799.	259.	,,	,,	144 pp.	
1801.	260.	,,	,,	148 pp.	Price 1s. 6d. Corrected to May.
1803.	261.	,,	,,	136 pp.	Corrected to May. A.R.W. copy, 7 names in adds. Bristol, 9 names.
1805.	262.	Edward Mathews	4 + 128.	Corrected to February.
1806.	263.	,,	,,	4 + 128.	Corrected to January.
1807.	264.	,,	,,	4 + 128.	Corrected to January.
1808.	265.	,,	,,	4 + 136.	1s. 6d. sewed, 2s. boards. Corr. to February.

1809. **266.** Edward Mathews　4 + 136.　Corr. to February. Bristol, 2 copies, diff. issues of errata on p. 135.

1810. **267.**　　,,　　　　,,　　4 + 144.　Corr. to February.

1811. **268.**　　,,　　　　,,　　4 + 146.　Re-issue of 1810 with corrections on 1–8, corrected list of coaches, etc. & adds. up to February 1811. *2s.* sewed, *2s. 6d.* boards.

1812. **269.** Joseph Mathews　2 + 140.　*See* p. 16 above.

1813. **270.**　　,,　　　　,,　　4 + 150.　Preface dated 25 January.

1814. **271.**　　,,　　　　,,　　4 + 156.　Unless otherwise stated prefaces are dated some time in January from now on. Application for entries was made regularly in October or November.

1815. **272.**　　,,　　　　,,　　4 + 180.

1816. **273.**　　,,　　　　,,　　4 + 212.　Professional names now included.

1817. **274.**　　,,　　　　,,　　4 + 196.

1818. **275.**　　,,　　　　,,　　204 pp.　Preface, 16 December 1817.

1819. **276.**　　,,　　　　,,　　208 pp.　A trade directory, the *Commercial List,* was published separately in March at 1s. No copy found.

1820. **277.**　　,,　　　　,,　　210 + (blank), 2 + 2 + 5–80. Price with commercial list, 1s. extra.

1821. **278.**　　,,　　　　,,　　280 pp.　Preface 8 January ; in some copies, 9 January. Trade directory now part of the volume.

1822. **279.**　　,,　　　　,,　　224 pp.　No trade directory.

1823. **280.**　　,,　　　　,,　　290 pp.　Trade directory resumed.

1824. **281.**　　,,　　　　,,　　292 ; adverts, 6 leaves.

1825. **282.**　　,,　　　　,,　　6 + 300 ; adverts, 8 leaves.

1826. **283.**　　,,　　　　,,　　6 + 304 ; adverts, 5 leaves.

1827. **284.**　　,,　　　　,,　　6 + 284 ; adverts, 6 leaves.

1828. **285.**　　,,　　　　,,　　6 + 304 ; adverts, 8 leaves. Preface, 27 December 1827.

1829. **286.**　　,,　　　　,,　　8 + 296 ; adverts, 16 pp.

1830. **287.**　　,,　　　　,,　　298 ; adverts, 14. Price 3s. 6d. boards. Persons outside the editor's canvass could be entered if they applied between 29 September and 20 October.

1831. **288.**　　,,　　　　,,　　320 ; adverts, 16.

1832. **289.**　　,,　　　　,,　　320 ; adverts, 12.

1833. **290.**　　,,　　　　,,　　314 ; adverts, 8. Preface, 23 December 1832.

1834. **291.** Matthew Mathews 314 ; adverts, 16
1835. **292.**   ,,   ,,   4 + 316 ; adverts, 32.
1836. **293.**   ,,   ,,   4 + 318 ; adverts, 28.
1837. **294.**   ,,   ,,   8 + 13–328 ; adverts, 8.
1838. **295.**   ,,   ,,   334 ; adverts, 48 ; errata slip.
1839. **296.**   ,,   ,,   ii + 336 ; adverts, 34 ; adds. slip pasted on p. ii. Price, non-subsc. 4s.
1840. **297.**   ,,   ,,   352 + 22 ; adverts, 24.
1841. **298.**   ,,   ,,   (adverts, with adds. on last page), 28 + 352 + 22.
1842. **299.**   ,,   ,,   12 + 17–360 ; adverts, 24 ; almanach.
1843. **300.**   ,,   ,,   10 + 15–360 ; adverts, 16 ; almanach.
1844. **301.**   ,,   ,,   10 + 15–368 ; adverts, 16 ; almanach. First street directory.
1845. **302.**   ,,   ,,   8 + 15–368 ; adverts ; almanach.
1846. **303.**   ,,   ,,   8 + 13–366 ; adverts, 18 ; almanach ; slip pasted at end of adds. (Bristol copy, 3 names ; A.R.W. 5 names).
1847. **304.**   ,,   ,,   8 + 13–368 ; adverts, 12 ; almanach ; slip pasted at end of adds. (Bristol copy).
1848. **305.**   ,,   ,,   8 + 13–376 ; adverts, 12 ; almanach. B.M. copy lacks adds. list.
1849. **306.**   ,,   ,,   380 ; adverts, 28 ; almanach. First directories of surrounding villages.
1850. **307.**   ,,   ,,   384 ; adverts, 24 ; almanach ; slip pasted at end of adds. (not in Bristol copy, which is also imperfect otherwise).
1851. **308.**   ,,   ,,   10 + 7–390 ; adverts ; almanach.
1852. **309.**   ,,   ,,   404 ; adverts, 14 ; almanach ; slip pasted at end of adds. (Bristol copy).
1853. **310.**   ,,   ,,   410 ; adverts ; almanach ; map. Price 4s. 6d.
1854. **311.**   ,,   ,,   416 ; adverts, 28 ; almanach ; slip pasted at end of adds. (Bristol. B.M.).
1855. **312.**   ,,   ,,   8 + 7–412 ; adverts ; almanach. One extra name in adds. in A.R.W. copy.

Bristol, 1793–1855. B.M. 1793, 1801, 12, 13, 15–18, 30, 48–55. Gen. Soc. 1814, 40, 52, 54. I.H.R. 1850, 52, 54. A.R.W. 1793, 95, 98, 1801–6, 09, 12, 21, 26, 31, 32, 34, 35, 37, 39, 44–7.

1816

313. THE BRISTOL INDEX OR EVANS'S DIRECTORY FOR . . . 1816 . . . BRISTOL : PRINTED & PUBLISHED BY JOHN EVANS & CO. AT NO. 7 ST JOHN STREET . . .

xii + 118 ; adverts, 10 leaves. [Tr. Ct.]

$8\frac{3}{4} \times 5\frac{1}{4}"$. Price 2s. 6d. boards.

Preface dated 18 April 1816. 500 copies were printed. This, though the editor later disclaimed any intention of trying to ' supersede any other publication ', was clearly intended to be an improvement on Mathews' directories. Though the price is the same, the paper is better and the directory is a classified one, an arrangement which the editor considered very much more useful than an alphabetical list which was all that Mathews had hitherto attempted. John Evans was a printer and edited the *Bristol Observer*. He says in the preface to the above volume that he had published a prospectus describing the plan of his directory as early as 1800. He also wrote *A Chronological Outline of the History of Bristol*, published in 1824. He was killed in the collapse of the Brunswick Theatre in London, in 1828 (Timperley, *Dictionary of Printers* (1839), p. 904). He is to be distinguished from John Evans, schoolmaster of Bristol, who died in 1832. Joseph Mathews said that the latter part of this edition was pirated from his directory. The competition must have added to the financial difficulties which beset him but Bristol remained, on the whole, faithful to him, for Evans' venture came to an end in 1818. Bristol.

1817

314. THE BRISTOL INDEX [etc. as above but] FOR 1817.

(blank), 2 + 6 + 1 + 90 ; adverts, 2 & 5 eng. [Gen. Tr.]

$8\frac{3}{4} \times 5\frac{1}{4}"$. Price 2s. 6d. boards.

Preface dated 7 January 1817.

Bristol.

1818

315. THE BRISTOL INDEX . . . FOR 1818 . . . BRISTOL : PRINTED BY & FOR BROWNE & MANCHEE, NO. 19 CLARE STREET . . .

6 + lvi + 96 ; plan. [Gen. Tr.]

$8\frac{3}{8} \times 4\frac{7}{8}"$. Stiff printed wrappers. Price 2s. sewed, 2s. 6d. boards.

Preface dated 20 January 1818. The plan is a reprint of a 1671 map of Bristol. Browne & Manchee took over the directory from Evans, encouraged, they said, ' by its adoption in London ', a reference apparently to the similar arrangement of Johnstone's *London Commercial Guide*, 1817. William Browne, who was perhaps the same as the William Browne, agent for the 1792 directory, went into partner-

ship with Manchee in 1817 and they set up a printing office at 30 Quay in the following year.
Bristol. B.M.

1848

316. HUNT & Co.'s . . . BRISTOL, CLIFTON & HOTWELLS DIRECTORY . . . 1848. PRINTED FOR E. HUNT & Co. BY B. W. GARDINER . . . LONDON.
xiv + 232 + 8 + 144. [Ct. Cm. Tr.]
7 × 4″. Price 5s.
Adds. list up to May 1848. This directory was also issued, with a different adds. list and directories of Welsh towns, in January, 1848 (see No. 863). Parts of it, sometimes repaged, were issued in conjunction with directories of other places between 1848 and 1851. See DEVON, DORSET, GLOUCESTERSHIRE, SOMERSET, WILTSHIRE, WALES for these years. There is little difference between these re-issues, except in WALES, 1850 (No. 867) and DORSET, 1851 (No. 230), where there is a street directory and some other additions.
I.H.R.

1852

317. SCAMMELL & Co.'s . . . BRISTOL & S. WALES DIRECTORY . . . FEBRUARY, 1852. PRINTED FOR W. SCAMMELL & Co. BY C. T. JEFFERIES, 97 REDCLIFF STREET, BRISTOL.
xxiv + (Bristol), 204 + (S. Wales), 224; adverts, 82. [Ct. Tr.]
7 × 4″. Green Cloth. Price, non-subsc. 5s.
Mathews' complaint in 1853 of a piracy of his directory presumably refers to this, but in general appearance and contents it is rather an imitation of Hunt's directories. The names do not altogether correspond with those in Mathews' directory of Bristol for the same year. It was re-issued with Scammell's Gloucester directory, 1853, *q.v.*
Cardiff. Newport. A.R.W.

1853

318. SCAMMELL & Co.'s BRISTOL GENERAL DIRECTORY . . . JANUARY, 1853. [Imprint as above].
xxiv + 562; adverts, 2, 84; map. [St. Gen. Tr.]
7 × 4″. Blue cloth. Price, non-subsc. 5s. 6d.
Bristol. A.R.W.

CHELTENHAM
1800

319. CHELTENHAM DIRECTORY, 1800 . . . CHELTENHAM: PRINTED BY J. SHENTON AT THE MERCURY PRESS & SOLD BY W. BUCKLE AT . . . NO. 167, OPPOSITE THE GEORGE INN.

32 pp. [St. Pr. Laundresses.]
6¾ × 4". Price 8*d*.

It is clear from the preface that Shenton was the editor. A reprint was included in the *Royal Cheltenham & County Directory*, 1872–3, H. Edwards. There is also a facsimile reprint, n.d. (copy in the Gloucester P.L.).

Cheltenham. Guildhall.

1802

320. CHELTENHAM DIRECTORY FOR . . . 1802 . . . [imprint as above].

44 pp. ; plate. [Pr. St. Laundresses.]
6⅞ × 4".

The plate is said to be a portrait of Shenton. It is on different paper from the rest of the volume and it is not clear whether it is an original part of it. There seems from the preface to have been an edition in 1801.

Gloucester.

1837

321. THE CHELTENHAM ANNUAIRE FOR . . . 1837 . . . CHELTEN-HAM : PUBLISHED BY H. DAVIES, MONTPELLIER LIBRARY & SIMPKIN & CO. LONDON [Printer, H. Davies.]

xvi + 17–174 ; adverts, 24 ; 2 plates. [Ct. Pr.]
6¼ × 4". Stiff printed wrappers, label.

Preface, dated January 1837, says that the directory was the main object, the other sections having been added when planning the work (*cf*. p. 14 above). A note on p. [138] indicates that the names were got by advertising for entries and that the response had not been wholly satisfactory.

Bod. B.M. Cheltenham.

The *Annuaire* continued to be published annually until 1916 and throughout our period the main part of the title and the imprint are the same ; so is the size. From 1839 the directories are Ct. Pr. St. Cm. and from 1844, Ct. for the county was added. The volume appeared early in January every year except in 1850 when it was delayed until the end of February, owing to the illness of the publisher. The binding was wrappers or boards until 1849 when the first cloth bound edition appeared. The rest of the series will now be listed in summarised form and the other Cheltenham directories will follow. There is a complete set of the *Annuaire*, 1837–1916, in the Cheltenham P.L. Other copies may be found as follows : Bod. 1837, '38, '41, '42, '43, '48–'51, '54 ; B.M. 1837, '38 ; Gen. Soc. 1854 ; A.R.W. 1852.

1838. **322.** viii + 148 ; adverts, 26. [Ct. Pr. Cm.]
1839. **323.** lvi + 146 ; adverts, 20 ; adds. 2 pp. after p. 58. [Ct. Pr. St. Cm.]
1840. **324.** vi + ix–lviii + 59–212 ; adverts, 18 & 2 eng.
1841. **325.** 2 + vi + v–lvi + 57–186 ; adverts, 50 & 1 eng.

1842. **326.** xxxvi + 37–168 ; adverts, 20.
1843. **327.** xxxvii + 38–184 ; adverts, 30.
1844. **328.** xxxvi + 37–170 + xxviii ; adverts, 28. The editor
apologises for the incompleteness of the new court list
for the county.
1845. **329.** 2 + vii–viii + 9–32 + xxxiii + 4 + 38–170 + xxx
adverts, 8, 20 and 1 eng.
1846. **330.** 2 + (adverts), 14 + vi + 9–176 + xxviii ; adverts, 16
& 1 eng.
1847. **331.** viii + 9–168 + xxxvi ; adverts, 28, 2.
1848. **332.** viii + 9–176 + xxxviii ; adverts, 24.
1849. **333.** viii + 9–180 + xxxviii ; adverts, 24.
1850. **334.** viii + 9–176 + xlii ; adverts, 28.
1851. **335.** viii + 9–180 + xl ; adverts, 32.
1852. **336.** viii + 9–180 + xlii ; adverts, 22.
1853. **337.** viii + 9–196 + xliv ; adverts, 34.
1854. **338.** viii + 9–208 + xl ; adverts, 36.
1855. **339.** viii + 9–212 + xxxviii ; adverts, 22. The county section, 4 + 9–100, was also issued separately with title,
THE ANNUAIRE ; & DIRECTORY OF THE PUBLIC
AUTHORITIES & RESIDENT GENTRY OF GLOUCESTER-
SHIRE FOR 1855 (Copy in the Gloucester P.L.).

1839

340. THE ORIGINAL CHELTENHAM DIRECTORY FOR 1839 . . .
CHELTENHAM : PUBLISHED BY T. E. WELLER, COLONNADE
. . . [printers, W. Paine & Co. 127 High Street.]
8 + 102 (no pp. 59/60) + 14 ; adverts, 2, 28 ; errata slip.
[Ct. Pr. Tr.]
$7\frac{1}{8} \times 4''$. Printed wrappers. Price 1s. 6d.
Gloucester.

1843

341. HARPER'S COMMERCIAL & FASHIONABLE GUIDE FOR CHELTEN-
HAM & THE ADJOINING HAMLETS. 1843. CHELTENHAM :
S. C. HARPER, FREE PRESS OFFICE, HIGH STREET.
2 + vi + 296. [St. Cm. Clergy. Ct ; hamlets, Gen.]
$5\frac{1}{2} \times 3\frac{1}{2}''$.
Gloucester.

1844

342. [Title as above but] 1844.
iv + 400 ; table. [St. etc. as 1843]. Size as 1843.
Cheltenham. Gloucester.

1845

343. ROWE'S ILLUSTRATED CHELTENHAM GUIDE. [Imprint on
p. 3 of index, Cheltenham ; Published by George Rowe.

Printed by Rowe & Norman, Examiner Office, 9 Clarence
Street.]

vi + 104 + 4 ; adverts, xlviii, 2. [St. Tr.]

$7\frac{5}{8} \times 4\frac{3}{4}''$. White cloth, gilt.

Besides the classified trades under which the index is
arranged, each street is described, giving the names and
occupations of the inhabitants of the chief buildings. There
are a number of small engravings showing the shops, with
names over them. A pretty example of the illustrated
directory. The title is engraved and without date or
imprint. One advertisement is dated Christmas 1844.
R. Austin, *Catalogue of the Gloucester Collection in the
Gloucester Public Library* (1928), says the date 1850 has been
attributed but that 1845 is more likely. George Rowe calls
himself an artist in Rowe & Norman's advertisement. He
was head of their lithographic department. Hyett &
Bazeley, *Bibliographer's Manual of Gloucestershire Literature*
(1895–7), mention a copy in private possession with thirty-
nine tinted plates. The present whereabouts of this copy
has regrettably not been traced.

Cheltenham. Gloucester.

1848

344. EDWARDS'S NEW CHELTENHAM DIRECTORY FOR 1848 . . .
CHELTENHAM : R. EDWARDS, 82 HIGH STREET.

vi + 5–72 + 99 ; adverts, 100–112. [St. Ct. Tr.]

$5\frac{1}{2} \times 3\frac{1}{2}''$. Brown cloth. Price 1s. 6d.

Preface dated 15 January 1848. Hyett & Bazeley, *op. cit.*,
refer to an 1847 edition, but this must be a mistake, as
the preface to the 1852 edition speaks of the *four* previous
issues.

Cheltenham.

The next four editions of Edwards' directory will be summarised.
The title, size and price are the same as in 1848 throughout. The
directories are the same, except that from 1849 a separate professional directory is included. The street directory was enlarged
in 1850 to include commercial as well as residential areas. The
volume was published early in January each year. No edition has
been traced after 1852 until 1862. In the '70's it became *The
Royal Cheltenham Directory*.

1849. **345.** 208 ; adverts, 209–240. Bod.

1850. **346.** 156 + xxxvii ; adverts, xxxviii–liv. Cheltenham.
I.H.R.

1851. **347.** (adverts), 2 + 108 + xc ; adverts, xci–c, 4. Cheltenham.

1852. **348.** (adverts), 2 + 2 + 154 + xxxviii ; adverts, 30. Bod.
Cheltenham.

1853

349. HARPER'S CHELTENHAM DIRECTORY, 1853 . . . CHELTENHAM :
S. C. HARPER. CAMBRAY OFFICES.

4 + 262; adverts, 4. [St. Cm. Ct. Tr.]
$7\frac{1}{4} \times 4\frac{3}{4}''$. Price 3s. 6d.
The only known copy is interleaved and corrected in ink.
It looks as though there might be some pages missing after
p. 262.
Gloucester.

CIRENCESTER
1847

350. [Dropped heading.] A DIRECTORY CONTAINING . . . GENTLE-
MEN, MERCHANTS [etc.] IN CIRENCESTER. [Printed by Baily
& Jones, Market Place, Cirencester.]
22 pp., without title or imprint appended to *Moore's
Almanack* for 1847, with running headlines, ' Baily & Jones'
Appendix to Moore's Almanack '. Contains an alpha-
betical list for Cirencester and short lists for Fairford,
Cricklade, Northleach and Swindon.
$7\frac{3}{4} \times 4''$.
Cirencester.

FAIRFORD
(*See* CIRENCESTER, 1847.)

GLOUCESTER
1802

351. THE GLOUCESTER NEW GUIDE . . . GLOUCESTER, PRINTED
FOR THE EDITOR BY R. RAIKES . . . 1802.
viii + 168; errata slip. [Pr. Gen.]
$7\frac{5}{8} \times 4\frac{7}{8}''$. Marbled boards. Price 2s. 6d:
The Guide is by T. Rudge (1754–1825), antiquary and
clergyman, but Raikes probably compiled the directory.
He was Robert Raikes, the well-known philanthropist and
founder of Sunday Schools.
B.M. (10352.b.15). Gloucester. Guildhall. Salt.

1841

352. A DIRECTORY FOR . . . GLOUCESTER FOR 1841 . . .
GLOUCESTER: PRINTED & SOLD BY LEWIS BRYANT, CITY
LIBRARY, COLLEGE GREEN.
vi + 7–94; adverts, 95–134; plan. [Gen. Tr.]
$7\frac{1}{4} \times 4\frac{1}{4}''$.
Preface dated January 1840. This must be a misprint as
both the directory lists are headed 1841.
Gloucester.

1853

353. SCAMMELL & CO.'S GLOUCESTER, BRISTOL & S. WALES
DIRECTORY FOR 1853 . . . PRINTED FOR W. SCAMMELL &
CO. BY C. T. JEFFRIES, 97 REDCLIFF STREET, BRISTOL.

xvi + v–xxi + 3 + (Gloucester), 48 + (adverts), 16 +
(Bristol), 204 + (S. Wales), 224 ; adverts, 84. [Ct. Tr.]
    7 × 4″. Green cloth. Price, non-subsc. 7s. 6d.
Preface dated September 1852. Pp. v–xxi + 3 and the
Bristol and S. Wales sections are re-issues of Scammell's
BRISTOL, etc., 1852, q.v.
  Bristol.

NORTHLEACH

(See CIRENCESTER, 1847.)

HAMPSHIRE
1784

354. THE HAMPSHIRE DIRECTORY . . . WINCHESTER. PRINTED
  BY J. SADLER. 1784.
    4 + 170 + 8. [Pr. Cm.]
    $7\frac{3}{8} × 4\frac{1}{4}″$.
  Preface dated 2 March 1784. Includes Isle of Wight. A
  list of additions is promised free to subscribers by 10 April.
  Winchester.

1790

355. THE HAMPSHIRE POCKET COMPANION . . . FOR . . . 1790.
  SOUTHAMPTON. PRINTED BY & FOR A. CUNNINGHAM, OP-
  POSITE THE MARKET HOUSE, HIGH STREET & BOUND BY
  A. GILMOUR, SALISBURY.
    viii + 9–192. [Tr.]
    $6 × 3\frac{1}{2}″$. Price 2s.
  Pp. 9–116 are not paginated. Includes Isle of Wight and
  Channel Islands. There was perhaps a 1783 edition (*The
  Hampshire Antiquary*, i (1891), 31). A copy of the 1788
  edition in the B.M. was destroyed in the late war.
  Southampton.

1851. *See* DORSETSHIRE, 1851.

1852

356. HUNT & CO.'S DIRECTORY OF HAMPSHIRE & DORSET . . .
  [with] ISLE OF WIGHT . . . 1852. PRINTED FOR E. HUNT
  & CO. . . . BY BENSON & BARLING, ROYAL LIBRARY,
  WEYMOUTH . . .
    18 + (Hants, 352 + (Isle of Wight), lviii + (Dorset), 4,
    248 + (Salisbury), 28 ; adverts, 28. [Ct, with Cm. for
    small places & Tr. for large.]
    $7 × 4\frac{1}{8}″$. Price, subsc. 10s. 6d.
  The Dorset section is the same as in Hunt's DORSETSHIRE,
    1851, q.v.
  Southampton.

SOUTHAMPTON

1803

357. THE DIRECTORY FOR . . . SOUTHAMPTON . . .
SOUTHAMPTON : PRINTED BY & FOR A. CUNNINGHAM. 1803
44. [Gen.]
$6\frac{3}{4} \times 4''$.   Price 1s.
Southampton Univ. Coll.

1811

358. THE DIRECTORY FOR . . . SOUTHAMPTON IN 1811 . . .
SECOND EDITION.   SOUTHAMPTON : PRINTED BY A. CUNNING-
HAM, 75 FRENCH STREET . . .
4 + 40 + 2 + 30.   [Gen.]
$6\frac{5}{8} \times 4''$.   Price 3s. 6d.
The second section (2, 30) has title *The Southampton Register
for 1811 . . . Fourth Edition* and imprint as above.
Southampton (without h.t. or title to directory and the
Register bound first).   Southampton Univ. Coll.

1834

359. FLETCHERS' SOUTHAMPTON DIRECTORY. 1834. SOUTHAMP-
TON : PRINTED & PUBLISHED BY FLETCHER & SON . . .
4 + 128 ; adverts, 32 & 16 eng.   [St. Gen. Pr.]
$7\frac{1}{8} \times 4\frac{1}{8}''$.   Printed boards.   Price 3s.
This is the first edition.
Southampton (P.L. & Univ. Coll.).

1836

360. FLETCHER'S DIRECTORY OF . . . SOUTHAMPTON, INCLUDING
THE NEIGHBOURING VILLAGES.   CORRECTED TO AUGUST 1836.
[Imprint as 1834.]
xxxiv + 3–92 ; adverts, 8 pp. & interspersed.   [Gen. Tr.]
$7 \times 4\frac{1}{8}''$.   Cloth, label.   Price 2s. 6d.
Southampton (P.L. & Univ. Coll.).

1843

361. POST OFFICE DIRECTORY OF . . . SOUTHAMPTON & THE
NEIGHBOURHOOD . . . COMPILED BY WILLIAM COOPER . . .
SOUTHAMPTON : FLETCHER, FORBES & FLETCHER . . . 1843.
viii + 196 ; adverts, 114 & 15 eng.   [Gen. St.]
$7\frac{1}{8} \times 4\frac{1}{8}''$.   Cloth.
Preface dated January 1843.   The contents were compiled
within the previous two months.   William Cooper was
chief clerk in the Southampton Post Office.   He says the
directory was specially designed to help in the correct
addressing of letters.   He also published a pamphlet
called *The Penny Postage. A Letter.*, in 1839.
Bod.   B.M.   Southampton (P.L. & Univ. Coll.).

This directory continued to be published biennially for at least ten years. From 1849 it was compiled by E. D. Williams, second clerk in the Southampton Post Office. From 1847 to 1851 it was published by Forbes & Knibb and from 1853 by Forbes & Marshall. The details of the editions to 1855 are given below in summarised form. The title is similar and the format the same as in 1843 throughout. The Southampton Public Library has a complete set. There are copies of 1843, '47, '49, '53 in the B.M. and of 1845, '49 in the A.R.W. collection.

1845. **362.** cxxii + 64 ; adverts, 65–202 & 23 eng ; plan. [Gen. St. Tr.] Preface dated December 1844.

1847. **363.** 8 + clii + 72 ; adverts, 156 & 10 eng. [Gen. St. Tr. Also Ct. for the county.] Preface dated December 1846.

1849. **364.** cxxviii + 88 ; adverts, 120 & eng ; plan. [Gen. Tr. St. Also Gen. for villages & Ct. for the county.] Preface dated November 1848.

1851. **365.** viii + 28 + cxxxiv + 76 ; adverts, 128 & 18 eng. [Gen. etc. as 1849.] Preface dated December 1850.

1853. **366.** viii + 180 + 104 ; adverts, 160. [Gen. etc. as above but Tr. now confined to employers only.] In spite of the notice that publication would be annual, the directory continued to appear biennially.

1855. **367.** xii + 318 (including 196*–199*) ; adverts, 112. [Gen. etc. as 1853.]

1849

368. RAYNER'S DIRECTORY OF . . . SOUTHAMPTON FOR 1849. SOUTHAMPTON : PRINTED & PUBLISHED BY C. & J. RAYNER, 180 HIGH STREET. 1849.

viii + 9–104 ; adverts, 66, 74, 6 eng. [Gen. St. Tr. Also Ct. Cm. for places near and Ct. for the county.]

$7\frac{3}{4} \times 4\frac{5}{8}''$. Printed boards.

The publishers refer to attempts by ' certain designing persons ' to create prejudice against them. They claim to have made use of the services of various letter-carriers. The directory contains rather more names than Forbes & Knibb's directory of the same date. No further editions seem to have appeared.

Southampton.

WINCHESTER
1854

369. GILMOUR'S WINCHESTER ALMANACH & POST OFFICE DIRECTORY FOR 1854 . . . WINCHESTER : PRINTED, PUBLISHED & SOLD BY G. & H. GILMOUR. SQUARE.

24 + 21–48. [Ct. Tr. Also Ct. for vicinity.]

$7\frac{3}{8} \times 4\frac{3}{8}''$.

Winchester.

HEREFORDSHIRE

1847

370. HUNT & Co.'s COMMERCIAL DIRECTORY FOR . . . GLOUCESTER HEREFORD & WORCESTER . . . ALSO OF [other places in Glos, Heref & Worcs] . . . 1847. PRINTED FOR E. HUNT & Co. BY B. W. GARDINER . . . LONDON.

 viii + 236 + 12 ; adverts, 68, 12. [Ct. Tr. for towns, Gen. for villages.]

 $6\frac{7}{8} \times 4''$. Cloth. Price 6s.

Preface dated August 1847.

Bod. A.R.W. N.L.W. Worcester.

1851

371. LASCELLES & Co.'s DIRECTORY & GAZETTEER OF HEREFORD-SHIRE . . . PRINTED . . . BY SWAN BROS, 45 ANN STREET, BIRMINGHAM. 1851.

 272 pp. ; adverts, 68. [Ct. with Cm. for smaller & Tr. for larger places.]

 $8\frac{1}{4} \times 5\frac{1}{2}''$.

Preface dated September 1851. The names differ considerably from those in Slater's directory of Herefordshire for 1850 but, though the history at the beginning is not the same as in Slater, the descriptions further on are adapted from him and sometimes copied *verbatim*. This evident intention to deceive makes the reliability of the whole directory doubtful.

Birmingham. Cardiff. A.R.W.

ROSS

(*See* GLOUCESTERSHIRE, 1847.)

HERTFORDSHIRE

1850

372. WILLIAMS' DIRECTORY OF THE PRINCIPAL MARKET TOWNS IN HERTFORDSHIRE . . . LONDON : PUBLISHED BY J. WILLIAMS . . . 1850.

 title + (Barnet), etc. 14 + (St Albans, etc.), 25–48 + (towns in Bucks), 40 + (Watford), 16 + (towns in Kent, *see* KENT, 1850, for details). [Gen.]

 7 × 4''. Price, subsc. 4s. 6d., non-subsc. 5s. 6d.

Only one copy of this oddly patched-up volume has been found. It seems unlikely that it was issued by the publishers in this condition.

A.R.W.

HUNTINGDONSHIRE
1854

373. HISTORY, GAZETTEER & DIRECTORY OF THE COUNTY OF
HUNTINGDON . . . HUNTINGDON : PRINTED & PUBLISHED
BY JAMES HATFIELD, FOR SUBSCRIBERS ONLY . . . 1854.
title + ii + iv + 786 ; adverts, 28. [Ct. with Tr. for
towns and Cm. for villages.]
$8\frac{3}{8} \times 5\frac{1}{2}''$. Red cloth. Price with map, 17s. 6d.
Preface dated September 1854.
Guildhall.

1855

374. CRAVEN & Co.'s COMMERCIAL DIRECTORY OF THE COUNTY
OF HUNTINGDON & THE TOWN OF CAMBRIDGE . . . NOTTING-
HAM : PRINTED FOR & PUBLISHED BY THE PROPRIETORS.
1855.
4 + 196 + 4 ; adverts, 52. [Gen ; Tr. also for Huntingdon
and Cambridge.]
$8\frac{5}{8} \times 5\frac{1}{2}''$. Red cloth.
Gen. Soc.   Guildhall.

ISLANDS
CHANNEL ISLANDS

1790. *See* HAMPSHIRE, 1790.

1826

375. A GUIDE TO . . . GUERNSEY . . . WITH A COMMERCIAL
DIRECTORY . . . GUERNSEY : PRINTED FOR & PUBLISHED
BY J. T. COCHRANE, MARKET STREET. 1826. [Printer,.
Brouard.]
viii + 146 ; errata leaf, 4 plates. [Cm. for St Peter Port.]
$7\frac{1}{8} \times 4\frac{1}{2}''$. Printed boards. Price 4s. 6d.
Bod.   B.M. (10368.bbb.39).   Chetham.

1833

376. THE STRANGERS' GUIDE TO . . . GUERNSEY & JERSEY . . .
WITH A COMPLETE COMMERCIAL DIRECTORY . . . GUERNSEY :
PUBLISHED BY J. E. COLLINS, STATES ARCADE LIBRARY . . .
S. BARBET, PRINTER, 1833.
In two parts, each with separate title and pagination,
probably also issued separately.
[Pt. I.] THE STRANGERS' GUIDE TO . . . GUERNSEY [imprint
as above]. 1833.
4 + 146 + 24 ; map. [Tr. for St Peter Port.]
[Pt. II.] THE STRANGERS' GUIDE TO . . . JERSEY [imprint
as above but printer T. J. Mauger]. 1833.
130 pp. ; map. [Tr. for St Helier.]
$7 \times 4\frac{1}{4}''$. Green flowered cloth, yellow labels.

Copies are variously found without the collective title,
with the parts in reverse order or with an undated title to
the Guernsey Guide.
Bod. (without last 24 pp. in Guernsey section). B.M.
(10351.cc.13). Guildhall. A.R.W.

1834

377. GUIDE TO . . . JERSEY, CONTAINING . . . A COMMERCIAL
DIRECTORY TO . . . ST HELIER . . . JERSEY: A. J. LE
CRAS, NEWS & PATRIOT OFFICE, 5 HOPE STREET, ST HELIER.
1834.
  viii + 162. [Tr.]
  $5\frac{1}{2} \times 3\frac{1}{2}''$. Pink cloth, label. Price 2s. 6d.
Bod. B.M. (10368.aa.26).

1837

378. THE ROYAL ALMANACK OR DAILY CALENDAR . . . FOR . . .
JERSEY, GUERNSEY [etc.] . . . FOR 1837 . . . JERSEY:
PRINTED BY P. PAYN. ROYAL SALOON.
  adverts, 4 + 94. [Tr. for St Helier.]
  $6\frac{1}{8} \times 3\frac{1}{2}''$. Printed wrappers. Price 1s. plain, 1s. 3d.
  coloured.
Jersey.

1840

379. THE PRIVILEGED ISLANDS, BEING A COMPANION TO . . .
GUERNSEY, JERSEY, ALDERNEY, SERK, [etc.] . . . BY A
TWENTY YEARS RESIDENT. JERSEY: PUBLISHED BY P.
PAYN, 45 KING STREET . . . 1840.
  x + 120 + 54 + 24 ; map, 2 plates. [Ct. Pr. for Guernsey,
  St. for St Peter Port.]
  $5\frac{1}{2} \times 3\frac{1}{2}''$. Blue cloth, printed labels.
Mr J. L. Douthwaite.

1845

380. THE BRITISH PRESS ROYAL ALMANAC . . . FOR THE ISLAND
OF JERSEY, 1845 . . . SOLD AT NO 7 LIBRARY PLACE . . .
JERSEY ; ALSO BY PAUL NAFTEL, 29 ARCADE, GUERNSEY.
  (adverts), 32 + 74 + 28 ; table. [Tr. for St Helier.]
  $6\frac{1}{8} \times 3\frac{1}{2}''$. Blue wrappers. Price 1s. or 1s 6d. with map.
Guildhall (without map).

1847

381. [Title as above but] 1847.
  127 pp. ; adverts, 39 ; table. [Tr.]
  $6\frac{1}{4} \times 3\frac{5}{8}''$.
  Preface dated 9 November 1846.
B.M. (10368.a.30/1).

1853

382. The Royal Jersey Almanac. Compiled by Capt.
Childers. 1853. Printed & Sold at the British Press
Office, No. 13 Broad Street, St. Helier . . .
  132 pp. ; adverts, 32. [Tr. for St Helier, Ct. for the
  Island.]
    $6\frac{7}{8} \times 3\frac{3}{4}''$.   Cloth.
  Preface dated 27 October 1852.
Jersey.

ISLE OF MAN

1808

383. Manks Almanac for . . . 1808 . . . with an Appendix,
Comprising a View of the Principal Estates in the
Island with the Proprietors . . . Douglas : Printed
by Geo. Jefferson.
  A set of these Almanacs 1808–55 lacking 1810, '12, '14,
  '15, '17, '21, '23, '24, '27, '31, '41, '44, '48–'50, is to be
  found in the Manx Museum. The Appendices include,
  besides private estates, the farms, with their tenants or
  owners, in each parish.

1836

384. The Illustrated Guide & Visitor's Companion through
the Isle of Man . . . [with] A Directory of Douglas . . .
by a Resident . . . Douglas : Printed & Published
by J. Quiggin, North Quay. 1836.
  4 + 124 ; map, plates. [Tr.]
    $6\frac{1}{4} \times 3\frac{7}{8}''$.   Purple cloth, label.
B.M. (10368.aaa.55).   M.M.

1837

385. [Title as above but] 1837. Re-issue of 1836 with cancel
title, bound blue cloth with label.
Bod.

1839

386. Quiggin's Illustrated Guide . . . Through the Isle of
Man . . . Second Edition. Fifth Thousand. [Imprint
as above.] 1839.
  4 + 130 ; adverts, 2 ; map, plates. [Tr.]
    $6\frac{1}{4} \times 3\frac{3}{4}''$.   Purple cloth, label.
  Preface dated July 1839.
B.M. (10360.b.3).

1840

387. [Title as above but] 1840. Re-issue of 1839 with cancel title, bound blue cloth.
A.R.W.

388. JEFFERSON'S ISLE OF MAN NEW GUIDE . . . WITH A DIRECTORY OF . . . DOUGLAS. FIFTH EDITION. TWELFTH THOUSAND . . . DOUGLAS : PRINTED & PUBLISHED BY G. JEFFERSON, DUKE STREET. 1840.
viii + 132 ; map. plates. [Tr.]
$6\frac{1}{2} \times 4''$. Purple cloth, label.
Four previous editions, 1823, '24, '31 and '34, have no directories. This, though called the fifth edition, has a map dated 1836 and it may, like many of Quiggin's directories, be a re-issue of an earlier edition.
B.M. (10369.aaa.21). M.M.

1842

389. [Title as *Quiggin's Guide*, 1839 but] 1842. Re-issue of 1839 with cancel title, bound blue printed boards or purple cloth.
Bod. A.R.W.

1843. *See* MANCHESTER, 1843.

1844

390. [Title as *Quiggin's Guide*, 1839 but no ' Second Edition ' and] PRINTED & PUBLISHED BY M. A. QUIGGIN, CUSTOM HOUSE QUAY. 1844.
4 + 130 ; adverts, 2 ; map, plates. [Tr.]
$6\frac{1}{4} \times 3\frac{3}{4}''$. Purple cloth.
Same pagination as 1839 but a new edition of the directory. The map is by J. Pigot.
B.M. (10360.b.41).

1845

391. [Title as 1844 but] 1845. Re-issue of 1844 with cancel title, bound purple cloth. It has a new map by I. Slater and a population table.
B.M. (10360.b.35).

1847–1849

392. [Title as *Quiggin's Guide*, 1844 but] THIRD EDITION . . .
viii + 164 ; adverts, 2 ; map. [Tr.]
The actual date of the directory (which covers 14 pp.) in this edition is uncertain. The B.M. has a copy of the *Guide*, without directory, 150 pp., third edition, dated 1847. Among the advertisements is one of the *Guide* ' with a directory of Douglas '. The copy described above is

undated but has ' 1849 ' written on it in pencil. This may
be the date of the ' guide ' section but it seems likely that
the directory section is a re-issue, as in so many of Quiggin's
editions, and dates from 1847. The Manx Museum has a
copy of the *Guide*, without directory, third edition, dated
1848, which differs from the guide section in the undated
issue described above.

M.M.

1852

393. [Title as above but] FOURTH EDITION . . . 1852.
     viii + 184 ; adverts, 2 ; map. [Tr.]
     $6\frac{1}{4} \times 3\frac{3}{4}''$.

M.M.

1853

394. [Title as above but] 1853.
     Re-issue of 1852 with cancel title.

M.M.

ISLE OF WIGHT

(*See also* Hampshire directories.)

1839

395. THE VECTIS DIRECTORY OR ISLE OF WIGHT GENERAL GUIDE
    . . . NEWPORT : PUBLISHED BY WILLIAM LAMBERT . . .
    1839.
     4 + 140 ; adverts, 36 & 8 eng, also a number interspersed.
     [Cm. for towns, yeomen for villages.]
     $7\frac{1}{4} \times 4\frac{3}{8}''$.   Purple cloth, label.
    Preface dated 4 June 1839.
Bod (lacking 1–6).   B.M. (10358.cc.1).

396. THE VECTIS DIRECTORY . . . THIRD EDITION. [Imprint as
above.] 1839.
     4 + 7–20 + 109–120 + (adverts), 2 + 80 + 127–140 ; errata
     slip ; adverts, 72, 8, 20 eng. & others interspersed. [Cm ;
     Ct. also for larger places.]
     $7\frac{1}{4} \times 4\frac{3}{8}''$.   Light brown cloth, label.
    Preface dated 16 September 1839. The numbered pages
are a re-issue of the first edition. The 80 unnumbered
pages contain a new edition of the directory. Pp. 121–6
of the first edition are replaced by the last pages of the
directory section which contain the same information
brought up to date. No copy of the second edition has
been found but it seems unlikely that it contains yet
another version of the directory.
Bod.   B.M. (796.d.9).

RYDE
1846

397. GABELL & CO.'S GUIDE & DIRECTORY TO . . . RYDE. 1846.
PRINTED & PUBLISHED BY GABELL & CO, 43 UNION STREET,
RYDE.

> 6 + 5–54 ; adverts, 14. [Ct. St.]
> $5\frac{1}{2} \times 3\frac{1}{4}''$. Printed wrappers.
> The directory was ' copied from official lists of the occupiers
> of houses, corrected by personal knowledge and inquiry '.
> B.M.

KENT
1803

398. AN HISTORICAL SKETCH OF . . . KENT . . . BY W. FINCH
. . . LONDON : PRINTED BY WAKE, COW LANE, SNOW HILL
FOR THE EDITOR, 50 LAMBETH MARSH . . . 1803.

> 178 pp. ; 5 plates, map, table. [Gen.]
> $6\frac{7}{8} \times 4''$. Price 1s. 6d. per part.
> In three parts, though title to Pt. I says in two. Pt. I
> ends on p. 66 and Pt. II on p. 126. Dedication dated
> 10 December 1803.
> Canterbury. Gen. Soc (Pt. II only).

1807

399. [A CONCISE . . . PROVINCIAL DIRECTORY . . . TO BE
PUBLISHED WITH THE HISTORY & ENGRAVED VIEW OF ALL
THOSE TOWNS . . . WHICH ARE DESCRIBED IN THE IMPERIAL
ATLAS.]

> The above is the dropped heading to ten pages containing
> commercial directories of a number of Kent towns, ending
> abruptly in the middle of Folkestone, which are to be found
> at the end of a volume in the Guildhall Library, with title
> *The Maritime Imperial Guide*. They were printed by
> Caddel of Rochester, whose imprint appears on p. 4 and
> they seem to be specimen pages from a prospectus of *The
> Imperial Atlas*. Their date is uncertain ; *The Maritime
> Guide* was a sequel to *The Imperial Guide* by J. Baker, of
> which the title is dated 1802, but it was published in parts
> over several years. An account of J. Baker, who was an
> engraver, may be found in J. Ballinger, *An Artist Typo-
> grapher* (1916), also published in *The Library* (April 1916).
> The Guildhall volume contains fragments of *The Maritime
> Guide* and so does a volume in the Margate Public Library,
> which has the title of *The Imperial Guide*. No further
> trace of *The Imperial Atlas* or of any more directories has
> been found.

1831–1833

400. THE WATERING PLACES OF GREAT BRITAIN & FASHION-
ABLE DIRECTORY . . . LONDON : PUBLISHED FOR THE PRO-
PRIETORS BY I. T. HINTON, 17 WARWICK SQUARE. 1831.
    11 parts, containing 216 + 48 + 2 ; eng. title, plates.
[Ct. Pr. Tr.]
    11 + 8″. Grey or buff wrappers. Price 5s. per part.
Issued in parts consisting of 6 leaves each, generally 10 pp.
of text and 2 pp. of directories but Pt. 9 seems to have
had 12 pp. text and Pts. 10 and 11, 8 pp. text and 4 pp.
directories. The text ends in the middle of Ramsgate.
Pt. 11, which was published in 1833, comes from a new
publisher, Joseph Robins, who republished the parts, with
additions to the text, in the same year. The directories
are revised in later editions but no further towns were
added to them. The first page of the directory section is
headed FASHIONABLE DIRECTORY./[rule]/. The trades and
professions included are confined to those likely to be
patronised by fashionable visitors.
B.M. (Pts. 1–11, with proof copies of the plates and front
wrapper of Pt. 11 bound in. Shelf mark, 789.f.2). Folkestone
(Pts. 7, 8, 9, including pp. 121–84, text and 25–32, directories,
with adverts, 4 leaves ; orig. grey wrappers bound in).

There are several later issues of this book. The copies available
seem to be collections of odd parts and their exact make-up presents
bibliographical problems which cannot be gone into here, but each
contains a different issue of the directories, though the exact dates
at which these were compiled are uncertain. The distinguishing
marks of each issue of the directories are detailed below. The
plates vary both in subject and publisher in all the copies examined.
See also No. 403.

1833

401. THE WATERING PLACES OF GREAT BRITAIN & FASHIONABLE
DIRECTORY . . . JOSEPH ROBINS. LONDON. 1833.
    264 + 28 + 48 ; eng. title, plates. [Ct. Pr. Tr.]. Format
as above.
Text revised and extended ; new edition of the directories.
The first page of the directory section is headed by a large
cut of the Royal Arms and different printers' rules above
and below the word BRIGHTON.
Margate (shelf mark, 7302).

401a. [Another issue.] Same title and pagination but text reset
and directories revised. The gathering signed L in the two
editions above is here unsigned and in the directory section
there is k^2, k*^{2} instead of k^7. The first page of the directory
section has the large cut of the Royal Arms but the same
printers' rule above and below the word BRIGHTON.

Mr Graham Pollard. Folkestone P.L. has a copy with the second section of the text extended to 72 pp. and no directories (shelf mark, 914.2).

1838

402. STAPLETON & CO.'S TOPOGRAPHY, HISTORY & DIRECTORY OF CANTERBURY, FAVERSHAM [and other places in East Kent] . . . LONDON : STAPLETON & CO, 284 STRAND.

viii + 120 + 58 ; adverts, 18 ; 2 plates. [Ct. Tr.]

$7\frac{1}{4} \times 4\frac{1}{4}''$. Buff printed wrappers.

Preface dated August 1838. The separate directories are variously dated from May to August 1838. The preface says that Pigot's and Robson's Kent directories are generally acknowledged to be most incorrect. It also refers to a campaign of 'the grossest mis-statements and cowardly innuendoes' in the local press, intended to prevent publication. A directory of Dover and places round by Stapleton & Co. is advertised here but no copy has been found.

Canterbury.

1840

403. THE FASHIONABLE GUIDE & DIRECTORY TO THE PUBLIC PLACES OF RESORT IN GREAT BRITAIN . . . LONDON : PUBLISHED FOR THE PROPRIETORS BY T. FRY, BRIDE COURT, FLEET STREET. 1840.

256 + 284 (pp. 271–80 mispaged 671–80) + 48 ; eng. title, plates. [Ct. Pr. Tr.]

$11 \times 8''$. Pale green printed wrappers. Price 3s. per part.

Another edition of *The Watering Places of Great Britain*, in parts, by a different publisher. It has additions to the text and revised directories, including the same places, except Herne Bay. The first page of the directory section is headed by a small cut of the Royal Arms with clouds behind.

Margate (Rowe Bequest, 173, with no title but the wrapper of Pt. 2 bound in, giving title as above. It lacks pp. 281–4).

Margate (Parker Collection, 7355, with title as above. This has only pp. 1–8 of the directories).

1847

404. HISTORY, GAZETTEER & DIRECTORY OF . . . KENT . . . BY SAMUEL BAGSHAW. SHEFFIELD : PRINTED FOR THE AUTHOR BY G. RIDGE. MERCURY OFFICE, KING STREET . . .

[Vol. I.] 4 + 712 + x. [Misc. Tr.]

[Vol. II.] 2 + 662 + x ; map. [Misc. Tr.]

$7 \times 4\frac{1}{4}''$. Black cloth. Price, subsc. 10s. 6d. per vol.

Preface to Vol. I dated 25 June 1847.

Folkestone. Guildhall. Margate.

1849

405. SOUTH-EASTERN COAST DIRECTORY . . . LONDON : PUB-
LISHED BY J. WILLIAMS . . . 1849.
    24 + (Dover), 52 + (Canterbury), 36 + (Ramsgate, Mar-
    gate, Broadstairs), 84 + (Folkestone), 18 + (Sandgate,
    Herne Bay, Street), 13–32 + (adverts), 4 + (Greenwich),
    56 + (Deptford), 42 + (blank), 2 + (Blackheath, Woolwich,
    etc.), 72 + 24 + 12 + 4 ; adverts, 62. [Gen.]
        7 × 4″. Red cloth. Price 8s. 6d., non-subsc. 10s.
    Folkestone.

405a. [Another issue.] ISLE OF THANET DIRECTORY . . . [imprint
as above]. JUNE, 1849.
    Containing Ramsgate, etc. Deptford, Greenwich, Black-
    heath, etc. as above but with 64 pp. for Greenwich. Price
    6s., non-subsc. 7s. Grey cloth.
    Margate.

1850

Williams' directory of Hertfordshire, 1850, contains the following
Kent towns : Dartford, etc. 12 pp. ; Sheerness, 12 pp. ; Greenwich, 66 pp. ; Gravesend, 24 pp. ; Chatham, 34 pp. ; Lewisham,
36 pp. ; Bromley, 16 pp. ; Woolwich, 72 + 16 + 12 pp. [Gen. ;
Woolwich has also St. Tr.] *See* HERTFORDSHIRE, 1850.

BROMLEY
1797

406. AN ACCURATE DESCRIPTION OF BROMLEY . . . BY THOMAS
WILSON. LONDON : PRINTED FOR J. HAMILTON, 46
PATERNOSTER ROW : & T. WILSON, BOOKSELLER, BROMLEY,
KENT. 1797.
    118 ; adverts, 119–20, 2 ; 3 plates. [Pr. Tr.]
        6 × 3¾″.
    Thomas Wilson also wrote a book on the use of circulating
    libraries and some other small works.
    Bod. B.M. (579.a.25, with MS. notes, & two other copies).

CHATHAM

1838. *See* ROCHESTER, 1838.

1842

407. FORDHAM'S KENTISH ADVERTISER . . . & CHATHAM DIREC-
TORY FOR . . . 1842 . . . PRINTED & SOLD BY A. T.
FORDHAM . . . 127 HIGH STREET, CHATHAM.
    14 pp. [Gen.]
        7⅛ × 4½″. Price 2d.
    B.M. (10368.e.4/35).

DEAL
(*See* DOVER, 1792.)

DOVER
1792

408. THE DOVER & DEAL DIRECTORY & GUIDE . . . DOVER :
PRINTED FOR & SOLD BY J. HORN . . . AT THE APOLLO
LIBRARY . . . & BY R. LONG, DEAL.   ·
    4 + 52. [Ct. Pr. Cm.]
    $8\frac{1}{8} \times 5\frac{1}{8}$". Price 1s. 6d.
A reprint, on the same paper and from the same setting of
type, of the Dover and Deal sections of *The Universal
British Directory* (*see* No. 13), repaged, with some additions
and with a few alterations in the Deal section.   The words
' at this time, 1792 ' occur in the list of the corporation.
Horn was an organist as well as printer, bookseller and
perfumer.   The later editions of this guide, 1807 and 1817,
have no directories.
Birmingham.   B.M. (10358.e.5).   Dover.

GRAVESEND
1842

409. JOHNSTON'S APPENDIX TO THE ALMANACKS & GRAVESEND
ADVERTISER . . . .FOR 1842.   GRAVESEND :   PRINTED &
PUBLISHED BY J. JOHNSTON, 46 HARMER STREET.
    48 pp. ; adverts, 56. [Gen.]
    $6\frac{1}{4} \times 3\frac{7}{8}$". Price 3d. or with Moore's Almanack, 9d.
Maidstone.

1845

410. JOHNSTON'S APPENDIX TO THE ALMANACS & GRAVESEND
ADVERTISER . . . FOR 1843. [Imprint as above.]
    56 pp. ; adverts, 57–64. [Gen.]
    Size, price as above.
Also issued with *Johnston's New Guide to Gravesend*, 1843.
Guildhall (with the *New Guide*).

1853

Hall's Gravesend, Milton & Northfleet Directory, 1862, is marked
' Tenth Year ' on the title but no copies have been found of the
earlier editions.

MAIDSTONE
1839

411. TOPOGRAPHY OF MAIDSTONE & ITS' ENVIRONS . . . MAID-
STONE :   PRINTED & PUBLISHED BY J. SMITH.   1839.

viii + 108 + 38 ; adverts, 26 ; plan, map, plate. [Ct. P1.
Cm.]
   6⅜ × 4″. Purple cloth.
Bod. B.M. (796.b.17). C.U.L. Folkestone. Maidstone.

1850

412. NEW & ENLARGED DIRECTORY FOR MAIDSTONE & ITS
ENVIRONS . . . BY JAMES PHIPPEN. MAIDSTONE : PRINTED
& PUBLISHED BY W. WEST . . . HIGH STREET . . . 1850.
   vi + 5–96 ; adverts, 44 ; map. [Ct. Cm. Tr. for Maidstone,
Gen. for villages.]
   6⅜ × 3⅞″. Purple cloth, green label. Price 2s. 6d.
Preface, dated January 1850, refers to an earlier edition.
Phippen was editor of the *Weald of Kent Mail*.
Guildhall. I.H.R.

1854

413. MONCKTON'S DIRECTORY FOR MAIDSTONE & NEIGHBOURING
VILLAGES. 1854. MAIDSTONE : PRINTED & PUBLISHED BY
W. MONCKTON, 11 KING STREET.
   viii + 5–116 ; adverts, 32 ; map. [Ct. Cm. for Maidstone,
Gen. for villages.]
   7⅛ × 4¾″. Stiff red wrappers.
Preface dated August 1854.
Bod.

ROCHESTER
1838

414. WRIGHT'S TOPOGRAPHY OF ROCHESTER, CHATHAM, STROOD
. . . ETC . . . PUBLISHED BY I. G. WRIGHT, CHATHAM HILL
. . . 1838. [Printer, W. H. Cox, Lincoln's Inn Fields.]
   vi + 140 ; adverts, 141–56 ; 2 plates. [Gen.]
   6¼ × 3¾″. Green cloth.
I.H.R. Rochester. A.R.W.

TUNBRIDGE WELLS
1808

415. THE DIRECTORY : OR, THE ANCIENT & PRESENT STATE OF
TUNBRIDGE WELLS . . . ABRIDGED FROM THE TUNBRIDGE
WELLS GUIDE . . . TUNBRIDGE WELLS : PRINTED & SOLD
BY JASPER SPRANGE. 1808.
   ii + 40. [St. lodgings.]
   5⅞ × 3⅝″.
Contains chief commercial names only.
Mr. J. L. Douthwaite.

1845

416. THE TONBRIDGE WELLS GUIDE & DIRECTORY . . . TON-
BRIDGE WELLS : PUBLISHED AT THE ROYAL PARADE LIBRARY
. . . [Printer, W. Stapley, Parade.]
  iv + iv + 76 ; adverts, 77–92. [Ct. Tr.]
  $6\frac{1}{8} \times 3\frac{1}{4}''$. Price 1s.
There is a reference on p. 69 to the ' present year, 1845 '.
B.M. (10351.aaa.55/1).

1849

417. COLBRAN'S HANDBOOK & DIRECTORY FOR TUNBRIDGE WELLS
& ITS NEIGHBOURHOOD . . . TUNBRIDGE WELLS : PRINTED
& PUBLISHED BY JOHN COLBRAN. HIGH STREET.
  6 + 138. [Lodgings, Ct. Pr.]
  $6\frac{1}{4} \times 3\frac{3}{8}''$.
Dated 1849 on cover. The directory section was also sold
separately for 6d. This is the second edition. The first
edition (*Colbran's New Guide for Tunbridge Wells*, ed.
J. Phippen, 1840) contains an eleven-page list of subscribers
which, it is said in the preface, is so long as to make the
directory, promised in the prospectus unnecessary.
A.R.W.

1850

418. [Title as 1849. Third edition.]
  6 + 144 ; adverts, 30. [Ct. Pr. lodgings.]
  $6\frac{3}{4} \times 4\frac{1}{4}''$. Purple cloth.
Preface dated July 1850. Directory section also sold
separately for 6d. The fourth edition, 1852, has only
lodging houses and a short list of professions.
Guildhall. A.R.W.

LANCASHIRE

(For the district round Manchester *see also* Manchester directories,
1821, 1824 and from 1832.)

1787. *See* LIVERPOOL, 1787.

1818

419. LANCASHIRE GENERAL DIRECTORY FOR 1818, PART FIRST
. . . MANCHESTER : PRINTED & PUBLISHED BY T. ROGER-
SON, No. 11, MARKET PLACE . . .
  In three sections, each with separate title, dated 1818,
imprint as above, and pagination, probably also issued
separately.
419a. [Sec. I] THE BLACKBURN DIRECTORY . . . [with Accring-
ton, Church, Clitheroe, Darwen & Whalley] . . .
  68 pp. [Gen.]

419b. [Sec II.] The Bolton Directory . . . [with Astley Bridge, Breightmet, Burnden, Chowbent, Dean Church & Leigh] . . . 76 pp. [Gen.]

419c. [Sec. III.] The Preston Directory . . . [with Chorley & Walton] . . .

76 + xxx ; map. [Gen.]

7 × 4". Price 5s. 6d. sewed, 6s. bound.

P. 8 of Sec. I is dated January 1818. In some copies Sec. III ends with 2 pp., fairs and an announcement of Pt. II for May or June, instead of the xxx pp. list of bankers.

Blackburn. Bolton (Sec. II only). Chetham. Manchester.

420. Lancashire General Directory for 1818. Part Second. Containing . . . Rochdale, Bury, Burnley, Haslingden & Colne ; [with Bacup, etc.] . . . [imprint as Pt. I].

xxxvi + 5–134 + 2 ; advert, 2. [Gen.]

7 × 4". Price 4s. 6d. sewed, 5s. bound.

Bury. I.H.R. (lacking pp. 11/12). Rochdale.

421. Lancashire General Directory for 1818–19–20. Part Second. Containing . . . Ashton, Burnley [etc.] . . . Manchester : Printed by J. Leigh, Market Place ; & Sold by the Proprietors . . .

4 + iii–xxxvi + 5–226 + 4. [Gen.]

421a. [Another issue.] 5–232 pp. instead of 5–226 ; slip pasted at end of index.

7 × 4". Price 5s. 6d. sewed, 6s. bound.

See p. 65 above for a comment on this directory. The proprietors were probably W. Parson and T. Bradshaw. The half title runs ' Directory of the English Counties. Vol. II. Part II. Lancashire.' Pp. iii–xxxvi and 5–134 are a re-issue from Part Second above. The additional pages, 135–226 and 227–32, contain directories of more places. All copies have pp. xxxi–xxxii removed, presumably because the information on them (public officers, etc.) was out of date. Some copies have, instead of the last four pages, the list of bankers from Part Second above pasted on to p. 226.

Chetham (with pp. 227–32). I.H.R. Manchester. A.R.W.

1824–1825

422. History, Directory & Gazetteer of the County of . . . Lancaster . . . by Edward Baines. The Directory Department by W. Parson . . . Liverpool : Published by Wm. Wales & Co, Advertiser Office, 68 Castle Street . . . 1824. [Vol. II, 1825.] [Printer, W. Wales.] [Vol. I.] viii + 660. [Misc. or Gen ; Tr. also for larger places and St. for Liverpool.]

[Vol. II.] xii + 744. [Misc., etc. as Vol. I, St. for Manchester], Preface dated 19 September 1825.

[Supplement.] LIVERPOOL . . . SEPT. 24, 1825 . . . WM. WALES & CO.

24 pp. [adds. for Liverpool.]

$7\frac{5}{8} \times 4\frac{5}{8}''$. Price 24s. for the two vols; supplement presented free to patrons.

[Maps.] The very handsome maps were issued separately, half with Vol. I and half with Vol. II. With Vol. I, map of Lancashire, plan of Liverpool, plans of Lancaster and Preston, two tables. With Vol. II, plan of Manchester, plans of six other towns, map of canal system. Also issued together, in buff printed wrappers. On front wrapper, ILLUSTRATIONS. HISTORY, DIRECTORY & GAZETTEER OF LANCASTER . . . LIVERPOOL: PUBLISHED & SOLD BY WILLIAM WALES & CO. 1824-5.

Bod. B.M. (010351.h.7 & maps, 1.c.10 & another copy, with supplement, 10349.c.6). Halifax. Liv. Ath. (supplement only). Manchester.

1845

423. WILLIAMS' DIRECTORY OF BOLTON [etc.] . . . MANCHESTER: PRINTED FOR J. W. SENR . . . 1845.

(adverts), 18 + 2 + (Rochdale), 52 + (Bolton), 78 + (Heywood & Heap), 14 + (Todmorden), 22 + (villages) 26 + (Bacup), 24 + (Manchester), 36 + (Leeds), 4 + (Bury), 40 + (Oldham), 56 + (Saddleworth), 12 + (Burnley), 32. [Gen. except Manchester, Tr. and Leeds, a few odd pages.]

$7\frac{1}{8} \times 4\frac{1}{8}''$. Price, 12s., non-subsc, 14s.

Manchester.

424. WILLIAMS'S DIRECTORY OF ROCHDALE [etc.] . . . ROCHDALE: PRINTED FOR J. WILLIAMS . . .

(adverts), 12 + 2 + (Rochdale), 72 + Heywood–Leeds as above; adverts interspersed. [Gen. Tr. for Rochdale.]

$7\frac{1}{8} \times 4\frac{1}{8}''$. Purple cloth, label or orange leather.

The Rochdale directory is as in Williams' *Bolton, etc.* above, with a trades directory added. The Leeds section is another fragment.

Manchester (for some reason dated 1841 in pencil).

1847

425. Wm. White's directory of Leicestershire, 1846, contains an announcement of a *History, Gazetteer and Directory of Lancashire* by W. White, to be published in two vols. in 1847-8, but no other trace of this has been found.

1852

426. A NEW GENERAL & COMMERCIAL DIRECTORY OF MANCHESTER & SALFORD, ASHTON-UNDER-LYNE, ETC., [including places in

Cheshire & Yorks] . . . By W. Whellan & Co. . . . Manchester : Printed . . . by Booth & Milthorpe, 28 New
Cannon Street. 1852.

> xl + 360 + 365–516 + 615–656 + 679–932 + 18 ; adverts, viii ; map. [Misc. or Gen. ; Tr.]
>
> $8\frac{1}{4} \times 5\frac{1}{8}''$. Price 11s. 6d., non-subsc, 13s.
>
> Preface dated 12 October 1852. The gaps in pagination are to allow for expansion in future issues.

Chetham. Rochdale. A.R.W.

1853

427. A New Alphabetical & Classified Directory of Manchester & Salford, Bolton [etc. with places in other counties] . . . by William Whellan & Co., [imprint as above]. 1853.

> Re-issue of above with new title and pp. 657–8 and 933–1072, covering more places, added.

428. [Another issue.] As above with pp. 1073–1258, more places, added.

> Price 14s. 6d., non-subsc, 16s. 6d.
>
> Preface dated February 1853.

B.M. (1258 pp., impf). Bury. Chetham (1072 pp). Manchester (1258 pp.). A.R.W. (1072 pp.).

1854

429. A New . . . Directory of Chester, Bolton, Bury [etc. with places in other counties] . . . By William Whellan & Co. . . . Manchester : Printed . . . By Galt, Kerruish & Gent, 28 New Cannon St. . . . 1854.

> viii + 679–1320.
>
> Price, subsc, 10s. 6d. cloth, 12s. 6d. calf.
>
> Re-issue of part of above without Manchester and with places in various counties added.

Bangor. Chester.

430. History, Topography & Directory of Mid-Lancashire . . . by Mannex & Co. Preston : Printed . . . by William Bailey & Henry Thomson. 1854.

> xii + 764 ; adverts, 4. [Misc. Tr. for larger places ; Gen. for smaller.]
>
> $7\frac{1}{8} \times 4\frac{3}{4}''$. Price, subsc, 14s. 6d., cloth, 15s. 6d. half bound.
>
> Preface dated January 1854.

Bury. Blackburn. Guildhall. Liv. Ath. Southport.

ASHTON-UNDER-LYNE
(*See* Cheshire, 1845.)

BLACKBURN

1818. *See* Lancashire, 1818 (No. 419a).
1846. *See* Staffordshire, 1846.

1852

431. BLACKBURN AS IT IS . . . INCLUDING . . . A DIRECTORY FOR
1852 . . . BY P. A. WHITTLE . . . PRESTON : PRINTED BY
H. OAKEY, FISHERGATE . . . 1852.
    x + 400 ; plan. [Ct. Tr.]
      $8\frac{1}{8} \times 5\frac{1}{2}''$. Cloth, label.
For P. Whittle *see* No. 531.
Blackburn. Bod. B.M. (10349.gg.12). Rochdale.

BLACKPOOL
(*See* SOUTHPORT, 1831.)

BOLTON

1818. *See* LANCASHIRE, 1818 (No. 419b).

1829

432. THE BOLTON DIRECTOR FOR 1829 . . . MANCHESTER :
PRINTED & PUBLISHED BY M. WARDLE, 29 BACK KING STREET
& T. WILKINSON, 19 RIDGFIELD.
    4 + 40. [Gen.]
      $8 \times 4\frac{3}{4}''$.
Preface dated 1 May 1829.
Bolton. Manchester.

1848

433. MACKIE'S BOLTON DIRECTORY, WITH ALMANACK FOR 1849.
BOLTON : PRINTED BY R. M. HOLDEN, 13 MEALHOUSE
LANE. 1848.
    2 + (adverts), xiv + 60. [Ct. Tr.]
      $7\frac{1}{8} \times 4\frac{3}{8}''$. Green cloth, label. Price 1s. 6d.
Preface, dated 29 December 1848, says the compiler took
nearly three months collecting the material. Alexander
Mackie was house-agent, debt-collector and teacher of
shorthand. He also invented a typesetting machine. He
founded *Mackie's* (later *The Bolton*) *Advertiser* in 1848 and
started *The Bolton Guardian* in 1852, which he continued
to publish from Warrington, where he moved in 1853.
(P. Whittle, *Bolton-le-Moors* (1852), p. 69 ; J. C. Scholes,
Bolton Bibliography (1886), p. 134.) Whittle says there
was an edition of the directory in 1851 and another proposed
for 1852 but no copies have been found.
Bolton. A.R.W.

BURY
1850

434. THE BURY DIRECTORY . . . BURY : PRINTED & PUBLISHED
BY JOHN HEAP, 7 UNION SQUARE. 1850.
    viii + 70 ; adverts, 71–88. [Ct. Tr.]
      $6\frac{3}{8} \times 4''$.
Manchester. A.R.W.

CARTMEL
(*See* CUMBERLAND 1829.)

CHORLEY
1835

435. AN HISTORY & DESCRIPTIVE ACCOUNT OF . . . CHORLEY . . . TO WHICH IS ADDED A DIRECTORY . . . CHORLEY: PRINTED & PUBLISHED BY C. ROBINSON, MARKET STREET. 1835.

    4 + 48. [Ct. Tr.]
    $6\frac{7}{8} \times 3\frac{7}{8}''$.
    Preface dated October 1835.
Chorley.

1851. *See* PRESTON, 1851.

FURNESS
(*See* CUMBERLAND, 1829.)

LIVERPOOL

An exhaustive account of Liverpool directories and of John Gore, their originator appears in the reprint of the earliest of them, edited by G. T. & I. Shaw, under title *Liverpool's First Directory* (1907).[1] There is little any one can add to Mr Shaw's researches, though one directory (1787) of which he could find no copy has since been acquired by the Liverpool Public Library and a few other points have been cleared up. Mr and Miss Shaw also edited reprints of the next four Liverpool directories. These reprints contain the alphabetical lists from the original editions, with street directories compiled from the lists by the editors.

Unless specified 'P.L.' or 'Ath.', copies designated 'Liverpool' below are to be found both in the Liverpool Public Library and in the Liverpool Athenaeum Library. The long run of Liverpool directories owned by the Liverpool Lyceum was recently disposed of to the Argosy & Sundial Libraries, Ltd., who have since sold them. The manager courteously informed the author that they had no record of the name of the purchaser.

1766

436. THE LIVERPOOL DIRECTORY FOR THE YEAR 1766 . . . LIVERPOOL: PRINTED BY W. NEVETT & CO. FOR J. GORE, BOOKSELLER, NEAR THE EXCHANGE. 1766.

    40 pp. ; 2 pp. (adds) inserted between 32/3. [Gen.]
    $6\frac{7}{8} \times 4\frac{1}{4}''$.

[1] See also A. C. Wardle. 'John Gore', *Hist. Soc. of Lancs. & Chesh. Trans.*, xcvii (1946), 223-4.

Contains less than one-fifth of the estimated number of inhabitants, according to Shaw. Besides Shaw's edition, there are at least two (not very accurate) earlier reprints and one by Messrs Rockcliffe Bros. for T. J. Walmsley, 1924.
Liv. Ath.

1767

437. GORE'S LIVERPOOL DIRECTORY FOR . . . 1767 . . . LIVERPOOL : PRINTED BY WILLIAM NEVETT & CO. IN PRINCES STREET.

50 pp. [Gen.]
$6\frac{1}{8} \times 3\frac{1}{2}''$. Price 6d.

An advertisement asking for additions appeared in the *Liverpool General Advertiser* on 13 February 1767. The book was advertised, 'This Day Published', in the same paper on 29 May. Reprint, edited G. T. Shaw, *Liverpool's Second Directory*, 1928.
Liverpool.

1769

438. [Title as above but] FOR . . . 1769.

54 pp. [Gen.]
Format, price as 1767.

Advertised, 'This Day Published', in the *Liverpool General Advertiser*, 30 June 1769. Reprint, edited G. T. & I. Shaw, *Liverpool's Third Directory*, 1930.
Liverpool.

1772

439. [No title found.]

3–62 + 2. [Gen.]
Format as 1767.

The only known copy of this lacks the title. It has ' 1773 ' written on it in ink and Shaw tentatively dates it between 1769 and 1774. However the list of Archbishops, which generally bears the same date as the title, is here dated 1772 and 'Gore's Liverpool Directory for 1772' was advertised, 'This Day Published', on 28 August 1772 in the *Liverpool General Advertiser* and in *Williamson's Advertiser*. The editor promises a list of additions free to subscribers to the directory. He also says that the very small sale of former editions has nearly prevented him from going on. Reprint, edited G. T. Shaw, *Liverpool's Fourth Directory*, 1931.
Liv. P.L.

1774

440. THE LIVERPOOL DIRECTORY FOR . . . 1774 . . . LIVERPOOL :
PRINTED FOR JOHN GORE, NO. 1 CASTLE STREET.
    80 pp. [Gen.]
      Format as 1767.
    The general survey for this edition was taken by about
June 1773 but publication was delayed owing to the re-
numbering of the houses. There are 4 pp., adds. to bring
it up to date. (*See* Shaw's preface to his reprint of the
1772 directory.) Reprint, edited G. T. Shaw, *Liverpool's
Fifth Directory*, 1932.
    Liverpool. Manchester.

1777

441. GORE'S LIVERPOOL DIRECTORY FOR . . . 1777 . . . [imprint
as 1774].
    124 pp. [Gen.]
      Format as 1767.
    Liv. P.L. (lacking 121–3). Liv. Ath. B.M. (lacking 99–102
and 112–24. Pp. 99–112 can be found in a volume containing
fragments of a number of Liverpool directories, shelf mark,
10349.cc.7).

1781

442. GORE'S LIVERPOOL DIRECTORY . . . PRINTED BY WILLIAM
NEVETT, FOR J. GORE . . . 1781.
    2 + 136. [Gen.]
      Format as 1767.
    B.M. Liverpool.

1787

443. [Bailey's directory. No title found.]
    iii–iv + 5–128. [Gen.]
      $6\frac{1}{2} \times 4\frac{1}{2}''$.
    Includes, besides Liverpool, Prescot, Warrington, Ormskirk
and St Helens. The dedication is signed William Bailey,
33 Duke St. and dated 26 January 1787. This is apparently
not part of Bailey's *General Directory of England, Wales, etc.*,
of which the only surviving number is No. 3 Bristol, 1787.
This is not on the same sized paper or in the same type.
Perhaps Bailey gave up the idea of a general directory and
published his Liverpool material separately. Shaw, who
had not seen a copy, refers to this directory (*Liverpool's
First Directory*, p. 22, n.1) as perhaps a separate issue of
part of Bailey's *Western & Midland Directory* (1783), but
it is not this nor is it the same as the Liverpool section of
Bailey's *British Directory*, Vol. III, 1784.
    Liv. P.L.

1790

444. THE LIVERPOOL DIRECTORY FOR . . . 1790 . . . BY CHARLES
WOSENCROFT . . . PRINTED & SOLD BY THE AUTHOR AT HIS
OFFICE IN COOK STREET . . .

152 pp. [Gen.]
$6\frac{3}{8} \times 4\frac{3}{8}''$.

Dedication dated 28 January 1790. This has fewer names
than Gore's directory for the same year. Besides being a
printer and patent medicine vendor, Wosencroft ran a
registry office for servants.

Liverpool.

445. GORE'S LIVERPOOL DIRECTORY . . . LIVERPOOL: PRINTED
FOR JOHN GORE. 1790.

2 + 258. [Gen.]
$7\frac{3}{8} \times 4\frac{3}{8}''$.

Dated August 1790 on p. 256 and advertised in the *Liverpool
Advertiser* on the 30th of that month. *Lewis's Liverpool
Directory, 1790*, published in 1890, is a reprint of this with
the list of adds. omitted and the *Sketch of Liverpool* from
Gore's 1796 directory added.

B.M. Liverpool.

1794

446. THE LIVERPOOL DIRECTORY & GUIDE . . . LIVERPOOL:
SOLD BY ALL THE BOOKSELLERS. 1794.

2 + 66. [Ct. Pr. Cm.]
$8\frac{1}{2} \times 5''$.

The paper and type and the lists of names, as well as the note
about the new baths at the end are the same as the Liverpool section of *The Universal British Directory (see No. 15,
above).* In the *U.B.D.* the preliminary account of Liverpool
is much longer and much of the material for it is taken
from Gore's 1790 directory. In this issue the preliminary
matter, apart from the first page which is taken from *The
Liverpool Memorandum Book* (1753), is based on Gore, 1790,
but brought up to date. *The Memorandum Book* was also
used by Gore's son for his 1805 directory. It is possible
that John Gore supplied the information to the editor of
the *U.B.D.*, but it seems more likely that some other person,
Charles Wosencroft has been suggested, was responsible.

Liv. Ath.

1796

447. GORE'S LIVERPOOL DIRECTORY . . . LIVERPOOL: PRINTED
IN THE YEAR 1796.

4 + 272. [Gen.]
$6\frac{1}{4} \times 4\frac{7}{8}''$.

B.M. Guildhall. Liv. P.L. (impf). Liv. Ath.

1800

448. [Title as above but dated 1800.]
    4 + 228. [Gen.]
    $6\frac{1}{4} \times 4\frac{7}{8}''$.
B.M. Liv. P.L.

449. SCHOFIELD'S NEW LIVERPOOL DIRECTORY . . . LIVERPOOL:
PRINTED BY J. SCHOFIELD, DALE STREET, FOR T. SCHOFIELD
. . . 1800.
    2 + 112 + 20 (or, another issue, 24). [Gen.]
    $7\frac{1}{8} \times 4\frac{1}{4}''$.
Fewer names than in Gore, 1800.
B.M. (to p. 112 only). Liv. Ath. (ends p. 24). Liv. P.L.
(ends p. 20).

1803

450. GORES' LIVERPOOL DIRECTORY . . . LIVERPOOL: PRINTED
BY J. GORE & SON, CASTLE STREET, 1803.
    4 + 248. [Gen.]
    $7 \times 4\frac{3}{8}''$. Price 2s. 6d. sewed, 3s. 6d. bound.
Advertised, ' To-morrow will be published ', in the *Liverpool
General Advertiser*, 26 May 1803.
B.M. (impf. but most of the missing pages are in the volume of
fragments from Liverpool directories, shelf mark, 10349.cc.7).
Guildhall. Liverpool.

1804

451. WOODWARD'S NEW LIVERPOOL DIRECTORY . . . LIVERPOOL:
PRINTED BY J. LANG, 13 FENWICK STREET & SOLD BY
C. WOODWARD, LORD STREET . . . 1804.
    4 + 254; table. [Gen.]
    $6\frac{7}{8} \times 4\frac{3}{8}''$.
Liverpool. N.L.W.

1805

452. [Appendix to above with dropped heading.] APPENDIX 1805.
    32 pp. [adds.]
Liv. Ath. (bound with 1804 directory).

Johnson Gore, who had been in partnership with his father since
1800, succeeded him on his death in 1803. From 1805 Gore's
directory appeared very nearly regularly every two years. In
1825 Johnson Gore was joined by his son John and the directory
became Gores' instead of Gore's. In 1834 Gore's business was
taken over by Messrs J. & J. Mawdsley, and the directory was
published by this firm for many years. It continued, however, to
be called Gore's and it remained ' Gore's ' even after it had been
taken over by Kelly's Directories Ltd. in 1898. The rest of Gore's
directories will now be listed in summarised form. The rare

attempts to compete with them will be given in detail afterwards.
Gore's editions are all dated on the title. The size remained at
$6\frac{3}{4} \times 4\frac{3}{8}''$ until 1829, when a narrow oblong, $8\frac{1}{8} \times 3\frac{1}{2}''$, was adopted.
It was abandoned in 1857 for an octavo, $9\frac{5}{8} \times 5\frac{3}{4}''$. A green or
maroon cloth binding, with printed label, was used from 1829, with
later an alternative form in black leather. A professional directory
was added to the general list in 1821, a trades directory in 1827
and streets in 1839. Copies may be found as follows.

  Bod. 1810, 11, 18–23, 29, 32–55. B.M. 1805–35 (except 1813,
  23, 27, 28), 1849. Guildhall 1805–53 (except 1813, 28, 30, 37,
  43). Liv. Ath. 1805–55 (except 1813). Liv. P.L. 1805–55
  (except 1830).

1805. **453.** 4 + 228 + 120. Contains extracts from *The Liverpool
  Memorandum Book* (1753). Preface dated September
  1805. Some of the lists of officials are for 1806.

1807. **454.** 4 + 5–270 + 112. Pp. 1 and 7 of the second pagination
  are cancels, probably indicating that this section was
  ready some time before publication and the lists of
  officials, etc. on these pages had to be brought up to
  date.

1810. **455.** 264 + 82. The Appendix (second pagination) is dated
  1809 but the list of magistrates on p. 73 is for 1810.
  The title is a cancel. Perhaps it had been intended
  to publish in 1809 but the list of names had not been
  ready.

1811. **456.** 264 + 92. The Bod. and B.M. copies are imperfect.

1813. **457.** 2 + ii + 276 + 144. Both sections are dated 1813.
  The Liverpool P.L. copy, the only one found, lacks
  title and some of the last pagination.

1814. **458.** As above, with title dated 1813, but the list of names
  is new and headed 1814. These two issues are not
  distinguished by Shaw. B.M. copy lacks the last
  section.

1816. **459.** 290 + 149.
1818. **460.** 316 + 164 ; plan.
1821. **461.** x + 5–328 + 194.
1823. **462.** 276 + 164 ; plan.
1825. **463.** 300 + 180.
1827. **464.** 392 + 84 ; plan. A note on p. [4] is dated May 1827.
1828. **465.** Supplement to Gores' Directory . . . 42 pp. [adds.]
  Dated June 1828 on p. [3]. Liv. Ath. copy, the only
  one found, is bound with the 1827 directory.
1829. **466.** 356 + 100 ; plan.
1830. **467.** Supplement to Gores' Directory . . . 1830. 32 pp.
  [adds.] Dated June 1830 on p. [3]. Both known
  copies are bound with the 1829 directory.
1832. **468.** (adverts), 24 + 4 + xxvi + 5–406 + 114 ; plate, plan.
1834. **469.** (adverts), 116 + 2 + xiv + 3–426 + 124 ; plan.
1835. **470.** (adverts), 102 + 470 + 128 ; plan.
1837. **471.** (adverts), 92 + 2 + 492 + 144 + *143–*144 ; plan.
1839. **472.** (adverts), 144 + 4 + vi + 5–520 + §72 + *156 ; plan.

1841. **473.** (adverts), 130 + 4 + x + 5–572 + §64 + *152. Bod.
      copy lacks last 2 pp.
1843. **474.** (adverts), 146 + 4 + viii + 5–608 + §72 + *160.
1845. **475.** (adverts), 144 + 31 + x + 32–650 + 88 + *176.
1847. **476.** viii + 3–738 + 88 + *140 + (adverts), iv, 162. The
      street list and the general list are dated 1846/7.
      The Appendix is dated 1846.
1849. **477.** viii + 3–698 + 80 + *144 + (adverts), 2, 74 ; slip. The
      slip (in Bod. & B.M. copies) is dated 1 November 1848
      and promises a corrected list of the new town
      council to be delivered free as soon as possible after
      9 November.
1851. **478.** viii + 3–710 + 88 + *148 + (adverts), 120, iv.
1853. **479.** viii + 3–738 + 96 + *152 + (adverts), 88.
1855. **480.** viii + 3–818 + 112 + *156 + (adverts), 120.

DIRECTORIES OTHER THAN GORE'S FROM 1827

1827

481. PICKEN'S ANNUAL DIRECTORY OF LIVERPOOL . . . FOR 1827
. . . ANDREW PICKEN & SON . . . 23 CASTLE STREET . . .
iv + 314 ; folding sheet. [Gen.]
$6\frac{5}{8} \times 4''$.
This is said to contain all persons in business on their own
account and all householders of respectability. It was
intended to be published annually but Picken's business in
Liverpool was a failure and shortly after this he went to
London. His idea seems to have been to provide something
shorter and more up to date than Gore. The folding sheet,
which contained local and historical information, does not
seem to have survived. Andrew Picken (1788–1833) was
born at Paisley. In London he found friends in literary
circles and had some success as a writer of novels. He
seems to have been a simple, unworldly and engaging
character. (*Gents. Mag.* N.S.I. (1834), 111 ; R. Brown,
Memoirs of Ebenezer & Andrew Picken, 1878).
Liverpool. Manchester.

1830

482. THE HISTORY OF EVERTON . . . BY ROBERT SYERS . . .
LIVERPOOL ; PUBLISHED BY G. & J. ROBINSON, CASTLE
STREET & D. MARPLES, LORD STREET. 1830.
xvi + 480. [St. Gen.]
$8 + 5\frac{1}{8}''$.
History of the Everton district of Liverpool. Gives no
occupations but indicates the type of dwelling, practically
all residential.
B.M. (10349.e.5). Liv. P.L.

1840

483. ROBSON'S LIVERPOOL DIRECTORY, STREET KEY & CLASSIFICA-
TION OF TRADES . . . WILLIAM ROBSON & CO. . . . . 4 CLOAK
LANE, CHEAPSIDE . . .

4 + xvi + 114 + 101–258 + 301–562 + 36 ; adverts, 48 ;
map. [Gen. Tr. ; also Gen. for surrounding villages.]
$9\frac{3}{4} \times 6''$. Price 10s. 6d., non-subsc, 12s. 6d.

The street list is dated 1840 but the directories were probably
compiled earlier. The text is condensed and adapted from
Gore. Not a reliable production.

B.M.

1843

484. PIGOT & SLATER'S GENERAL & CLASSIFIED DIRECTORY
& STREET REGISTER OF LIVERPOOL . . . MANCHESTER :
PRINTED & PUBLISHED BY PIGOT & SLATER . . . 1843.

28 + 9–220 + 82 + 84 + 28 ; adverts, 90 ; map. [Gen.
Tr. St.]
$9\frac{3}{8} \times 5\frac{1}{8}''$. Price 9s., non-subsc. 10s.

Preface dated May 1843. Also issued with Manchester &
Isle of Man (*see* MANCHESTER, 1843). Re-issued January
1844, with Chesh, Lancs, etc. (*see* No. 77).

B.M. Guildhall. Manchester. Warrington.

1846

485. Shaw lists a Liverpool, Dublin, Chester directory by J.
Williams, Sen. 1846. The Liverpool copy of this was
destroyed in the late war and no other copy has been traced.
There is a Liverpool trades directory in Williams' directory
of Leamington, etc., 1846.

1848

486. M'CORQUODALE'S ANNUAL LIVERPOOL DIRECTORY . . . LIVER-
POOL : GEORGE M'CORQUODALE & CO. 38 CASTLE STREET.
NOVEMBER. 1848.

xiv + 288 + 150 + 120 ; adverts, 60. [Gen. St.]
$9\frac{7}{8} \times 6\frac{1}{8}''$. Price 5s.

The prospectus, issued 27 May 1848, points out the superiority of this directory in type, paper, convenience of size
and up-to-dateness. A card for entering name and address
was sent with the prospectus. A trades directory, not
ready in time for the volume, was promised free, for
December.

Guildhall. Liv. P.L.

LYTHAM

(*See* SOUTHPORT, 1831, 1836.)

MANCHESTER

For an account of early Manchester directories *see* J. Harland, ' Collectanea relating to Manchester ', *Chetham Soc. Pubs.*, lxviii (1866), 119–66. Unless specified ' P.L.' or ' Chetham ', copies designated ' Manchester ' below are to be found in both the Manchester Public Library and in the Chetham Library.

1772

487. THE MANCHESTER DIRECTORY FOR . . . 1772 . . . LONDON : PRINTED FOR THE AUTHOR & SOLD BY R. BALDWIN, NO. 47 PATERNOSTER ROW ; & BY THE AUTHOR IN MANCHESTER.

title & preface on wrapper + 60 + adverts on back wrapper. [Gen. country tradesmen.]

$7\frac{3}{8} \times 4\frac{3}{8}''$. Blue printed wrappers.

Preface signed Elizabeth Raffald, dated 20 March 1772. Mrs Raffald (1733–81), better known as the author of *The Experienced English Housekeeper*, settled in Manchester after her marriage. She kept a confectioner's shop and a registry office for servants. As owner of the Bull's Head Inn and later of the King's Head, Salford, she came into contact with commercial travellers and foreign buyers. This connection may have suggested the idea of compiling a directory ' for the easy finding out of every inhabitant of the least consequence ', as she says in the preface. *See also* p. 5 above. A reprint of this directory was published for R. H. Sutton in 1889.

Manchester.

1773

488. THE MANCHESTER DIRECTORY . . . BY ELIZABETH RAFFALD . . . MANCHESTER : PRINTED FOR & SOLD BY THE AUTHOR & J. HARROP, OPPOSITE THE EXCHANGE. 1773.

2 + 78. [Gen. country tradesmen.]

$7\frac{3}{8} \times 4\frac{3}{8}''$.

Reprinted in facsimile, R. H. Sutton, 1889.

B.M. Manchester.

1781

489. THE MANCHESTER & SALFORD DIRECTORY . . . BY ELIZABETH RAFFALD . . . AT THE EXCHANGE COFFEE HOUSE . . . [imprint as above]. 1781.

iv + 106. [Gen. country tradesmen.]

$7 \times 4''$.

Advertised, ' Shortly will be Published ', in the *Manchester Mercury* on 5 September 1780.

Bod. B.M. Manchester.

1788

490. A DIRECTORY FOR . . . MANCHESTER & SALFORD FOR . . . 1788. MANCHESTER : PRINTED BY J. RADFORD, IN MILLER'S STREET.

132 pp. [Gen.]
$7\frac{1}{4} \times 4''$.

The author's name, Edmond Holme, is on p. [3]. He is entered as 'gentleman' in the 1794 directory. A list on p. 129 is dated 24 March 1788. A reprint, with a history of the town taken from *A Description of Manchester. By A Native*, (1783), was published in 1888, with the title, *Lewis's Directory of Manchester & Salford. 1788.*

B.M. Manchester. Warrington.

1794

491. SCHOLES'S MANCHESTER & SALFORD DIRECTORY . . . MANCHESTER : PRINTED BY SOWLER & RUSSELL. 1794.

xvi + 200. [Gen.]

$6\frac{3}{4} \times 4\frac{1}{4}''$. Printed wrappers, label. Price 2s. 6d.

Published ' at the latter end of 1794 ' according to the label but it was advertised ' just published ' in the *Manchester Mercury* on 26 August of that year. One copy (Chetham) has a variant title page with ' 1794 ' instead of ' MDCCXCIV '. The contents, with the names re-arranged, the additional names on p. 200 incorporated and additions to the descriptive part were published in *The Universal British Directory* (*see* No. 15 above). The same version appears in later editions of the *U.B.D.*, though Scholes himself published a new edition. John Scholes, who signs himself John Scholes Jun. in his 1797 directory, was apparently the son of John Scholes, tea-dealer. He is entered at his father's address, with no occupation. In 1797 he is entered as appraiser and auctioneer.

B.M. (2 copies one (579.b.34) with wrapper bound in). Guildhall. Manchester. Wigan.

1797

492. SCHOLES'S MANCHESTER & SALFORD DIRECTORY . . . SECOND EDITION. MANCHESTER : PRINTED BY SOWLER & RUSSELL, DEANSGATE. 1797.

4 + 196 ; adverts, 2. [Gen.]

$7\frac{1}{2} \times 4\frac{1}{4}''$. Blue wrappers.

Preface dated 7 April 1797. A list of alterations up to 24 June (2 pp.), promised free to purchasers of the directory, can be found bound up at the end of the Chetham copy.

B.M. Manchester. Wigan.

1800

493. BANCKS'S MANCHESTER & SALFORD DIRECTORY . . . MANCHESTER : PRINTED & SOLD BY G. BANCKS, CORNER OF ST. ANN'S SQUARE. 1800.

4 + 248. [Gen.]

6½ × 4″. Blue wrappers, label.

Preface dated 22 April 1800. A list of alterations is promised for July. Gerard Bancks, who carried on a well-respected business as a printer and stationer, died in 1804.

B.M. Manchester.

1802

494. [As above but dated 1802.]

Re-issue of 1800 edition with additions for 1802, pp. iii–xviii.

Manchester.

1804

495. DEANS & CO.'S MANCHESTER & SALFORD DIRECTORY . . . MANCHESTER: PRINTED & SOLD BY R. & W. DEAN & CO. MARKET STREET LANE. 1804.

viii + 260; plan. [Gen.]

6⅝ × 3¾″.

Preface dated 1 September 1804. The plan is engraved by J. Pigot.

B.M. Manchester. Rochdale.

1808

496. DEANS' MANCHESTER & SALFORD DIRECTORY; FOR 1808 & 1809 . . . MANCHESTER: PRINTED & SOLD BY R. & W. DEAN, 33 MARKET STREET LANE . . .

4 + 288; plan. [Gen.]

6¾ × 3¾″. Price 5s. sewed, 6s. bound.

Preface, dated 1 December 1807, says a great many copies of the last edition were left on hand, so not many more of this were printed than were subscribed for. The plan is by Pigot.

Blackburn. B.M. Manchester.

1811

497. DEANS' MANCHESTER & SALFORD DIRECTORY FOR 1811 . . . [imprint as 1808].

4 + 290; plan. [Gen.]

6⅞ × 4″. Grey wrappers.

The plan is unsigned.

B.M. Manchester.

498. PIGOT'S MANCHESTER & SALFORD DIRECTORY FOR 1811 . . . MANCHESTER: PRINTED BY M. WARDLE, CORNER OF NEW CANNON STREET, FOR J. PIGOT, ENGRAVER . . . 11 FOUNTAIN STREET.

4 + 220 + 40 ; plan. [Gen.]
    $8\frac{1}{4} \times 4\frac{7}{8}''$. Price 5s. sewed.
Preface dated 1 October 1810. Contains rather more names than Dean, 1811.
B.M. C.U.L. Manchester.

Pigot, who had hitherto co-operated with Dean & Co., at any rate to the extent of supplying the map for their directories and perhaps by helping with the compilation, now broke away and published his 1811 directory in competition with them. He calls attention in the preface to the superiority of his type and paper and announces a map, larger than that accompanying his directory which was to measure an inch more either way than the plan in Deans' 1811 directory, the dimensions of which are specially mentioned on Deans' title page. This declaration of war was, however, followed by an agreement, for in 1813 a directory was published, jointly by them both and from 1815 to 1821, Pigot & Deans' directory was published regularly every two years. Their last joint production appeared, a little late, in 1824. *See* p. 43 above for a further account of James Pigot.

1813

499. PIGOT'S MANCHESTER & SALFORD DIRECTORY FOR 1813 . . . MANCHESTER : PRINTED & SOLD BY R. & W. DEAN, 80 MARKET STREET ; SOLD ALSO BY J. PIGOT . . . 11 FOUNTAIN STREET. [Also issued with title DEANS' MANCHESTER & SALFORD DIRECTORY, etc. as above.]
    vi + 362 ; plan. [Gen.]
      $6\frac{1}{2} \times 3\frac{3}{4}''$. Price 5s. sewed.
This is the same format as Deans' 1811 directory. The plan is by Pigot.
B.M. (with ' Dean ' title). Guildhall. Manchester.

1815

500. PIGOT & DEANS' MANCHESTER & SALFORD DIRECTORY FOR 1815 . . . [imprint as 1813]. [Also issued with title NEW MANCHESTER & SALFORD DIRECTORY FOR 1815, etc. imprint as above.]
    4 + 308 ; map. [Gen. Tr.]
      $8\frac{1}{4} \times 4\frac{5}{8}''$. Blue wrappers, label. Price 6s. sewed.
The format is the same as Pigot's 1811 directory.
Guildhall (with second form of title). Manchester. Rochdale.

1817

501. [Title as 1815 but] FOR 1817.
    4 + 332 ; map. [Gen.]
      $8\frac{1}{2} \times 5''$. Price 6s. sewed, 7s. 6d. bound.
Manchester. A.R.W. Warrington.

1819

502. [Title as above but] FOR 1819–20 . . . PRINTED BY R. & W. DEAN . . . PUBLISHED BY THEM & J. PIGOT . . .
    4 + (adverts), 4 + 240 ; plan. [Gen. Tr.]
        Format, price as 1817.
    One of the adverts is dated 5 March 1819.
    Manchester. A.R.W.

1821

503. PIGOT & DEANS' NEW DIRECTORY OF MANCHESTER . . . ETC. FOR 1821–2 . . . [with places] TWELVE MILES ROUND . . . [imprint as 1819].
        vi + (adverts), 2 + 335 ; adverts, 15 ; plan, map. [Gen ; Tr. also for Manchester.]
        Format as 1817. Price 9s. 6d. bound.
    Bury. Guildhall. Manchester. Rochdale.

1822

503a. J. Butterworth, *Antiquities . . . and Complete History . . . of Manchester* (1822), has no formal directory but in the course of describing the streets, the author mentions and comments on a number of the principal tradesmen. (Copies : B.M., Manchester.)

1824

504. PIGOT & DEAN'S DIRECTORY FOR MANCHESTER . . . ETC. FOR 1824–5 . . . [with places] WITHIN TWENTY-FOUR MILES . . . MANCHESTER : PRINTED BY W. DEAN . . . & PUBLISHED BY HIM & J. PIGOT, AT THE DIRECTORY OFFICE, 16 FOUNTAIN STREET.
        2 + v–xx + 506 + 24 ; plan, with explanation, 2 pp.: map. [Gen ; Tr. also for Manchester.]
        Format as 1817. Calf with label. Price 10s.
    Bury. Guildhall. Manchester. Rochdale. Warrington.

1828

505. THE MANCHESTER & SALFORD DIRECTOR & MEMORANDUM BOOK FOR 1828. MANCHESTER : PUBLISHED BY M. WARDLE, 29 BACK KING STREET & T. WILKINSON, 19 RIDGFIELD.
        6 + 172 + xxiv + 12 + 54 ; adverts, 4 & 3 eng. [Gen. country manufacturers.]
        8 × 4¾″. Price, subsc. 5s. 6d.
    The title was engraved by G. Bradshaw, the originator of *Bradshaw's Railway Guide*. There is another form of it in which the publisher's names are in reverse order. The last 54 pp. are blank ruled memoranda pages.
    Guildhall. Manchester. A.R.W.

1829

506. THE MANCHESTER & SALFORD DIRECTOR FOR 1829. [Imprint as 1828.]

viii + 224 + 66 + 42 ; adverts, 2 & 1 eng. [Gen. Tr.] $7\frac{3}{4} \times 4\frac{1}{4}''$.

The correspondence on pp. iii–iv with the Stamp Office, about whether the inclusion of a tide-table rendered the book liable to stamp duty as an almanach, is dated September and October 1828.

Manchester (the P.L. copy is bound at the end of *The Bolton Director*. 1829).

507. PIGOT & SON'S GENERAL DIRECTORY OF MANCHESTER . . . &C. FOR 1829 . . . MANCHESTER : PRINTED & PUBLISHED BY J. PIGOT & SON, FOUNTAIN STREET . . .

22 + 2 + 23–328 + 98 + xxx ; adverts, 10 ; slip between 98/9 ; plan. [Gen. St. Tr.]

$7\frac{1}{4} \times 4\frac{5}{8}''$. Price, subsc. 7s. 6d. cloth, 8s. 6d. bound.

The inserted slip, which announces a list of the new coach regulations, is dated 12 January 1829. The street directory is intended to facilitate the delivery of business circulars and only includes addresses suitable for this purpose.

I.H.R. Manchester. A.R.W. (with slip). Wigan.

1830

508. [Title as above but] FOR 1830.

ix + 39 (beginning on verso of p. ix, last page numbered 22) + 23–328 + 9–22 + 108 + 36 ; adverts, 8. [Gen. St. Tr.]

Format as above. Price, subsc. as above, non-subsc. 8s. and 9s.

This is not the same as 1829 though the pagination of the general list is the same. The 39 pp. of additions are said to be for 1830 and ' collected and arranged up to the commencement of the present year '. Perhaps this indicates that this is an 1831 issue of an 1830 directory, with additions collected during the year.

Manchester.

1832

509. PIGOT & SON'S GENERAL & CLASSIFIED DIRECTORY OF MANCHESTER . . . &C. FOR 1832 . . . ALSO [places] WITHIN TWELVE MILES . . . [imprint as above].

24 + 17–510 + xvi + 6 ; adverts, 4 ; map. [Gen ; Tr. also for Manchester.]

$8 \times 5\frac{1}{4}''$. Price, 10s. 6d. cloth, 12s. bound ; non-subsc. 1s. extra.

The Manchester P.L. copy has a title not mentioning the places round and priced 8s. 6d. or 9s. 6d. This title has

presumably been taken from an issue containing Manchester and Salford only. No copy of such an issue has
been found.
Manchester. Guildhall. Wigan.

1833

510. [Title as above but] WITH AN ADDENDA FOR 1833.
Re-issue of 1832 with two more pp. of P.O. information
and 28 pp. additions instead of the 2 pp. in 1832. After
p. xvi are 8 pp. & adverts, 8. Prices as 1832.
511. [Another issue.] Places round not mentioned on title and
without pp. 393–510, the local directories. Price 8s. 6d. or
9s. 6d.
I.H.R. Chetham (without local directories).

1836

512. [Title as above but dated 1836.]
6 + 9–512 + 144 + xxvi ; adverts, 24 ; plan, map. [Gen ;
St. Tr. also for Manchester.]
Format as 1832. Price 11s. 6d. cloth, 13s. bound ; non-
subsc. 1s. extra.
The two copies in Manchester P.L. have differing lists of
additions.
I.H.R. Manchester. A.R.W.

1838

513. PIGOT & SON'S GENERAL, CLASSIFIED & STREET DIRECTORY
OF MANCHESTER . . . [with places] WITHIN TWELVE MILES
. . . & SOME OTHERS . . . MORE DISTANT . . . [imprint as
above]. 1838.
2 + 5–370 + 152 + 192 + xxxii ; adverts, 2, 38, 10 ;
plan, map. [Gen. etc. as 1836.]
Format, price as 1836.
Preface dated August 1838. *See also* p. 18 above.
Guildhall. Manchester. Warrington.

1840

514. PIGOT & SLATER'S GENERAL, CLASSIFIED & STREET DIRECTORY
OF MANCHESTER . . . PRINTED & PUBLISHED BY PIGOT &
SLATER . . . 1840.
22 + 9–342 + 2, 9–110 + 28 ; adverts ; plan. [Gen. St.
Tr.]
$9\frac{3}{8} \times 5\frac{1}{8}$". Price 8s. cloth, 9s. bound ; non-subsc. 1s.
extra.
Preface, dated April 1840, says there may be a few dis-
crepancies as information for the suburbs was collected
mostly from domestics. The new format has been adopted

in order that the book may be bound with Pigot's London directory. Manchester P.L. has the two bound together, with a slightly different title, priced 21s. or 25s. calf, non-subsc, 2s. 6d. extra.

I.H.R. Manchester. Rochdale.

1841

515. [Title as above but with places] WITHIN TWELVE MILES AND SOME OTHERS . . . 1841.

Re-issue of 1840, with a new preface dated January 1841 and two new pages, 343–4. After p. 110 (second pagination) is 2, 174 + 28 ; adverts, 40 pp. ; plan, map (1838). [Gen. etc. as above with Gen. for places round.]

Format as 1840. Price, subsc. 12s. 6d. cloth, 14s. bound.

Manchester.

516. PIGOT & SLATER'S CLASSIFIED COMMERCIAL DIRECTORY OF MANCHESTER . . . [etc. as above]. 1841.

158 + 2, 174 + 28 ; adverts, 42 ; plan, map (1841). [Tr. for Manchester ; Gen. for places round.]

Format as 1840. Price 7s. 6d. cloth, 8s. 6d. bound. Preface dated May 1841. A new directory for Manchester, with pp. 2, 174 (places round) as in January issue.

Manchester.

B.M. and A.R.W. have copies containing combinations of the above issues, as follows :

516a. B.M. . . . GENERAL & CLASSIFIED DIRECTORY OF MANCHESTER . . . *Contents.* 18 + 7–10 + 17–280 (Gen, part of first pagination of January issue) + 11–156 (Tr, part of first pagination of May issue) + 28 ; adverts, plan. *Price* 8s. 6d. or 9s. 6d., non-subsc. 1s. extra.

516b. A.R.W. Title as January issue. *Contents.* 8 + 17–280 (as above) + 2, 9–84 (St, part of second pagination of January issue) + 41–154 (Tr, part of first pagination of May issue) + 2, 174 as in both issues ; plan, map. *Price* 12s. 6d. or 14s. There are also copies of the 1841 edition at Bury and Warrington which have not been examined.

1843

517. PIGOT & SLATER'S GENERAL & CLASSIFIED DIRECTORY & STREET REGISTER OF MANCHESTER . . . 1843.

22 + 5–340 + 2, 108 + 2, 98 + 28 ; plan. [Gen. Tr. St.]

Format as above. Price 9s., non-subsc. 1s. extra.

Preface dated May 1843.

I.H.R. Chetham.

518. [Another issue] . . . GENERAL & CLASSIFIED DIRECTORIES & STREET REGISTERS OF MANCHESTER & LIVERPOOL . . . [with] ISLE OF MAN . . . 1843.

> 6 + Manchester as above + Pigot's *Liverpool*, 1843 (No. 484) + 2, 26 (Isle of Man. [Gen]) ; plans, map.
>> Price 15s., non-subsc. 16s. 6d.

Chetham. A.R.W.

519. A DIRECTORY OF MANCHESTER . . . [with] MANUFACTURING DISTRICT ROUND . . . BY I. SLATER, LATE PIGOT & SLATER . . . 1843.

> 6 + Manchester, as above + 2, 194 + 12 ; adverts, plan, map. [Gen. for places round.]
>> Format as above. Price, leather 14s., non-subsc. 15s. 6d.

Preface dated October 1843. *See also* No. 77 above.

Manchester P.L.

520. [Another issue.] A DIRECTORY OF . . . AN EXTENSIVE MANUFACTURING DISTRICT ROUND MANCHESTER . . . OCTOBER, 1843.

> 8 + 194 (as above) ; map.

Chetham.

1845

521. I. SLATER'S GENERAL & CLASSIFIED DIRECTORY & STREET REGISTER OF MANCHESTER & SALFORD & THEIR VICINITIES . . . PRINTED & PUBLISHED BY ISAAC SLATER . . . 1845.

> 24 + 9–464 + 88 + 14 ; plan. [Gen. Tr. St.]
>> Format as above. Price 9s., non-subsc. 10s. 6d.

Preface dated July 1845.

B.M. Manchester P.L.

522. [Another issue.] [Title as above but] TO WHICH ARE APPENDED . . . DIRECTORIES OF [places] . . . ROUND MANCHESTER . . .

> As above with pp. 1–194 (local directories, as 1843) ; map.
>> Price 14s. leather, non-subsc. 15s. 6d.

B.M. Chetham.

1848

523. SLATER'S GENERAL & CLASSIFIED DIRECTORY & STREET REGISTER OF MANCHESTER . . . [imprint as 1845]. 1848.

> 30 + 17–290 + 4, 142 + 2, 102 + 14 ; plan. [Gen. Tr. St.]
>> Format as above. Price 9s., non-subsc. 10s. 6d.

Preface dated July 1848.

B.M. Manchester.

1850

524. [Title as above.] 1850.

> 30 + 9–396 + 4, 118 + 2, 110 + 18 ; plan. [Gen. Tr. St.]
>> Format, price as above.

Preface dated October 1850. The 2 pp. of additions differ in different copies.
B.M. Guildhall. Manchester.

1851

525. SLATER'S ALPHABETICAL & CLASSIFIED DIRECTORY OF MAN-CHESTER . . . [with places] WITHIN TWELVE MILES & SOME OTHERS . . . 1851.

Re-issue of 1850 edition to p. 118, second pagination but with a new list of additions, 3 pp. + 4, 9–176 ; plan, map. [Gen. Tr. for Manchester ; Tr. for places round.]
Price 15s., non-subsc. 17s. 6d.
The local directories are the same as in Slater's *Lancashire, etc.* (1851), (No. 92 above), which also includes a slightly different directory of Manchester. The list of additions differs in different copies.
B.M. Manchester P.L.

526. [Another issue] SLATER'S CLASSIFIED COMMERCIAL DIRECTORY . . . OF THE . . . MANUFACTURING DISTRICT ROUND MAN-CHESTER . . . 1851.

Re-issue of pp. 9–176 above.
Price 6s. 6d.
B.M. Chetham.

1852

527. [Title as 1848.] 1852.

32 + 474 + 4, 122 + 14 ; plan. [Gen. Tr. St.]
Format as above. Price 9s., non-subsc, 10s. 6d.
Preface dated 20 July 1852.
Manchester P.L.

1855

528. [Title as 1848.] 1855.

38 + 522 + 4, 136 + 2, 120 + 14. [Gen. Tr. St.]
Format, price as above.
Preface dated May 1855. Also issued with 6 pp. additions in Slater's *Northern Counties*, Vol. II, 1855 (No. 99 above).
Guildhall. Manchester P.L.

529. THE MANCHESTER MERCANTILE & MANUFACTURING ANNUAL DIRECTORY . . . FOR 1854–55 . . . PUBLISHED BY COLLIN-SON & CO. 28 BROWN STREET . . . & PRINTED BY ALEXANDER IRELAND & CO. PALL MALL, MANCHESTER. 1855.

adverts, 8 + xvi + 292 + 12 + 6 + 10 ; adverts, 226 ; adds. slip. [Cm. (textile trades), Tr. St.]
8¾ × 5⅛". Green cloth.
Preface dated January 1855.
B.M. Manchester P.L.

OLDHAM
1817

530. AN HISTORICAL & DESCRIPTIVE ACCOUNT OF . . . OLDHAM . . . WITH A DIRECTORY . . . BY J. BUTTERWORTH . . . OLDHAM : PRINTED & SOLD BY J. CLARKE, MARKET PLACE . . . 1817.

    4 + xii + 212 ; adverts, 2 ; plan, map, 2 tables. [Cm.] $7\frac{3}{8} \times 4\frac{1}{8}''$. Printed boards. Price 5s.

Dedication dated April 1817. James Butterworth (1771–1837) began his career as a pupil teacher and later set up as a schoolmaster. He wrote poetry and a number of local histories, as well as two books on weaving, which he also practised. In 1798 he published *The Manchester Political & Literary Repository* in thirteen numbers at $\frac{1}{2}d$. each. He was postmaster at Oldham, where he had resided for thirteen years at the time of publishing this directory. (G. Shaw, ' James Butterworth,' *Lancs. & Chesh. Antiq. Soc. Trans.*, xxvi (1908), 124 ff.)

Bod. B.M. (10358.d.37). Rochdale.

PRESTON

1818. *See* LANCASHIRE, 1818 (No. 419c).

1821

531. A TOPOGRAPHICAL STATISTICAL & HISTORICAL ACCOUNT OF . . . PRESTON . . . INCLUDING . . . A DIRECTORY FOR 1821 . . . BY MARMADUKE TULKET. O.S.B. . . . . PRESTON : PRINTED FOR & SOLD BY P. WHITTLE . . . 1821. [Printer, I. Wilcockson, Chronicle Office, Preston.]

    348 pp. ; 6 plates. [Tr.]
      $7 \times 4''$.

' Tulket ' was a pseudonym for Peter Whittle (1789–1866). He was born in Lancashire and after an apprenticeship to Wm. Addison, a Preston bookseller, set up business there himself in 1810. By his own account he was an omnivorous reader. He wrote for a number of periodicals and produced several guides and local histories. He was awarded a pension for literary services in 1858. He is said to have been intelligent but ill-educated and his books, though not without value, are full of errors. (Vol. II of the above, published in 1837, pp. 336–48 ; *D.N.B.*)

B.M. (10352.aaa.7). Blackburn. Guildhall. Rochdale.

1845. *See* CHESHIRE, 1845.

1851

532. HISTORY, TOPOGRAPHY & DIRECTORY OF . . . PRESTON & SEVEN MILES ROUND WITH . . . CHORLEY. BY MANNEX &

Co. Beverley : Printed . . . by W. B. Johnson, Market Place . . . 1851.
> 182 pp. ; map. [Misc. Tr. for Preston & Chorley ; Gen. for places round.]
> 6¼ × 4⅝". Price 5s. 6d.
> Preface, dated February 1851, acknowledges use made of E. Baines's *History of Lancashire*.
> Guildhall. A.R.W.

ROCHDALE
1820

533. A Description & Directory of . . . Rochdale . . . by James Butterworth . . . Manchester : Printed by T. J. Evans, Market Street. 1820.
> 34 pp. [Tr.]
> 5⅝ × 3⅜".
> 'Humbly inscribed to John Walmsley, Esq. . . . as a token of respect and gratitude justly due from the author to him.'
> Oldham.

SOUTHPORT

For an account of early Southport directories, *see* F. H. Cheetham. 'Some Old Books on Southport', *Hist. Soc. of Lancs. & Chesh. Trans.*, lx (1908), 105 ff.

1826

534. A Guide to Southport . . . by Thomas Kirkland Glazebrook . . . Second Edition . . . London : Printed for C. & J. Rivington [etc.] by J. & J. Haddock, Market Gate, Warrington. 1826.
> 2 + 176 ; plates. [Misc. Tr.]
> 8⅜ × 5". Price 5s. 6d.
> Preface dated 29 May 1826. The first edition, 1809, has no directory.
> Bod. Southport (2 copies, one with cover dated 1845).

1831

535. Marina, or an Historical Account of Southport, Lytham & Blackpool . . . by P. Whittle . . . Preston : Printed & Published by Peter & Henry Whittle, Fishergate. 1831.
> viii + (Southport), 160 + (Lytham), 88 + (Blackpool), 72 ; plan, 3 plates. [Gen.]
> 8⅜ × 5". Price 10s. 6d.
> The sections were also issued separately.
> Bod. B.M. (578.c.8. Also Southport alone, 10349.cc.11/1). L.L. (Blackpool alone). Southport.

1832

536. A Concise History of Southport . . . Southport: Printed & Sold by William Alsop, 5, Gore's Terrace.
2 + 118 ; plate. [Gen.]
$5\frac{7}{8} \times 3\frac{5}{8}''$. Green printed boards.
Preface dated March 1832. There is also an issue without the directory, 104 pp.
Southport.

1836

537. An Historical & Descriptive Account of Blackpool, Lytham & Southport by a Popular Writer. London: Whittaker & Co.
Another edition of P. Whittle's *Marina*, with new plates but the same directories as in 1831. Published 1836 (*see* Cheetham, *op. cit.*, p. 117).
Southport.

1848

538. A Descriptive History of . . . Southport . . . by Frank Robinson. London: Arthur Hall & Co. Paternoster Row. 1848. [Printer, R. Johnson, Visiter Office, Lords' Street, Southport.]
124 pp. ; plates. [Gen.]
$6\frac{3}{8} \times 4\frac{3}{8}''$. Green cloth, gilt.
Preface dated May 1848.
B.M. (10358.aaa.45). Southport.

1849

539. A Guide to Southport . . . by J. S. . . . Liverpool: Printed & Published by J. Poore, 42 Castle Street.
53 pp. ; adverts, 7 ; plan. [Ct. Cm.]
$6\frac{5}{8} \times 4\frac{1}{4}''$. Stiff wrappers, label.
Preface dated 1 June 1849.
B.M. (10351.b.17 dated 1852 in catalogue). Southport.

WARRINGTON
(*See* Cheshire, 1846.)

WIGAN
(*See* Cheshire, 1845, also issued in Cheshire, 1846.)

LEICESTERSHIRE

1842

540. The Leicestershire Almanack, Directory & Advertiser for . . . 1842 . . . Leicester: Compiled & Published by T. Cook . . . 1 King Street.

4 + 120 ; adverts, 20 ; plate. [Ct. Tr.]
6⅝ × 3⅝".
Preface dated 1 January 1842.
Leicester.

1846

541. HISTORY, GAZETTEER & DIRECTORY OF LEICESTERSHIRE &
. . . RUTLAND . . . [with] GRANTHAM & STAMFORD . . . BY
WILLIAM WHITE . . . PRINTED BY ROBERT LEADER . . .
SHEFFIELD . . . 1846.
704 pp. ; adverts, 4 ; map. [Misc. Tr.]
7½ × 4⅝". Price, subsc. 12s. boards, 13s. 6d. calf.
Preface dated 25 July 1846.
Bod. B.M. C.U.L. Leicester. Salt.

1849

542. HAGAR & CO.'S COMMERCIAL DIRECTORY OF THE COUNTY OF
LEICESTER . . . NOTTINGHAM : PRINTED . . . BY STEVEN-
SONS, MIDDLE PAVEMENT. 1849.
2 + viii + 368 ; adverts, 36. [Ct. Cm ; Tr. also for
Leicester.]
8⅜ × 5⅛". Red cloth.
The text, though slightly altered and brought up to date,
is taken from White's 1846 directory. The piracy was
ignored by White, but when E. S. Drake copied Hagar,
word for word, in his 1861 directory he was prosecuted by
White and an injunction obtained against him. (*See* p. 23
above.)
Gen. Soc. Leicester. A.R.W.

1854

543. MELVILLE & CO.'S DIRECTORY & GAZETTEER OF LEICESTER-
SHIRE . . . WORCESTER : PRINTED BY . . . J. STANLEY,
SIDBURY & WYLD'S LANE.
4 + 240 ; map. [Ct. Cm ; Tr. also for Leicester.]
8¼ × 4⅞". Price, subsc. 10s.
Preface dated December 1853.
Leicester.

LEICESTER
1794

544. THE LEICESTER DIRECTORY . . . BY RICHARD WESTON . . .
PRINTED . . . BY — ADAMS, JUNR. LOUGHBOROUGH . . .
1794.
x + 56 ; small cuts in text. [Tr.]
6½ × 3⅝". Marbled wrappers. Price 1s. each or 10s. 6d.
per dozen.

Dedication dated September 1794. The adds. complete the directory to December 1794. The preface says this is intended as a commercial directory, not a general list of inhabitants. The Leicester section of *The Universal British Directory* is also for this year. There is no obvious connection between these two, but Weston may have supplied Wilkes with information. Richard Weston (1733–1806) was secretary to the Agricultural Society. He wrote a number of books on botanical subjects and was a regular contributor to *The Gentleman's Magazine* (*Gents. Mag.*, lxxvi (1806), 1080). He intended to produce a county directory and asks here for names to be sent in. The *U.B.D.* gives a William Adams, bookseller at Loughborough, who may be the printer.

Leicester.

1815

545. THE LEICESTER DIRECTORY . . . LEICESTER : PRINTED & SOLD BY J. FOWLER, GALLOW-TREE GATE. 1815.
  104 pp. [Cm. Tr.]
    $6\frac{5}{8} \times 3\frac{3}{4}''$.

The author seems ignorant of Weston for he says there is no previous directory of Leicester except a ' very inaccurate one ', recently published in London. It is not clear to what this refers unless it is to one of Holden's directories.

Leicester.

1827

546. THE LEICESTER DIRECTORY . . . LEICESTER : PRINTED & PUBLISHED BY T. COMBE & SON, GALLOWTREE GATE.
  2 + 84 + xxxii + 2 ; adverts interspersed. [Gen. Tr.]
    $6\frac{7}{8} \times 4''$.

Undated, but the town officials are those for 1827. Thomas Combe (1797–1872), probably ' Son ' above, became connected with the Clarendon Press about 1837 and subsequently was made a director. He founded the paper mills at Wolvercote, near Oxford and was made an honorary M.A. of the University (*D.N.B.*).

Leicester.

1843

547. A GUIDE TO LEICESTER CONTAINING . . . A DIRECTORY . . . WITH AN ALMANACK FOR 1843 . . . COMPILED, PRINTED & PUBLISHED BY T. COOK . . . 1 KING STREET, LEICESTER.
  8 + 5–96 + iv + 97–121 ; adverts, 122–148 ; almanach, etc. 20 pp. [Gen. Tr.]
    $6\frac{7}{8} \times 4\frac{1}{8}''$. Price, 1s. wrappers, 1s. 6d. boards, 2s. half bound.

Preface, dated 1 January 1843, says that of 3,000 circulars sent to those whose names ought to appear, many were

treated with indifference, others with contempt and ' in not
a few cases, the parties applied to would neither give their
names verbally nor in writing '.
Leicester.

LINCOLNSHIRE

For parts of Lincolnshire near Hull, *see also* Yorkshire directories,
1831, 1851.

1826

548. The History & Directory of . . . the County of Lincoln,
including . . . Kingston-upon-Hull . . . by   William
White & Co.   Edited by William Parson.   Leeds :
Printed by Edward Baines . . . 1826.
   xii + 13–204 + lxxviii + 2. [Misc. Tr. for larger places ;
Ct. Cm. for smaller.]
      $6\frac{3}{8} \times 4''$. Price, subsc. 6s. 6d. calf.
   The Hull section (pp. i–lxxviii) includes only annals, guide,
etc., and no directory. It is the same as in White's Hull
directory, 1826, which also includes some places in Lincolnshire, reprinted from this directory.
I.H.R.

549. [Another issue.] Same title but including after p. 204,
White's Hull directory, 1826 (*q.v.*) as far as p. 217 (218,
blank), with fly-title instead of title, and the 2 pp. corrections at the end reprinted to form pp. iii–iv with beginning
of index. It has not the 2 pp. adds. which are at the end of
the first issue.
Guildhall. Lincoln. A.R.W.

1842

550. History, Gazetteer & Directory of Lincolnshire . . .
by William White . . . Printed . . . by R. Leader . . .
Sheffield . . . 1842.
   780 pp. [Misc. Tr.]
      $7 \times 4\frac{1}{4}''$. Price, subsc. 12s. boards, 13s. 6d. calf with
   map.
   Preface dated 21 March 1842.
Guildhall. Lincoln.

1849

551. Hagar & Co.'s Commercial Directory of the Market
Towns in Lincolnshire . . . Nottingham : Printed . . .
by Stevensons, Middle Pavement. 1849.
   4 + lxxvi + 352 ; adverts, 42 ; map. [Gen. Tr.]
      $8\frac{3}{8} \times 5\frac{1}{8}''$. Red cloth.
   Map dated 22 March 1849.
B.M. Lincoln.

For Kelly's directory, 1849, *see* National Section, No. 115.

GAINSBOROUGH

(See NOTTINGHAMSHIRE, 1844.)

GRANTHAM

(See LEICESTERSHIRE, 1846.)

GRIMSBY

1852

552. TESSEYMAN'S DIRECTORY & HANDBOOK TO . . . GRIMSBY
. . . LONDON : HOULSTON & STONEMAN . . . GRIMSBY,
WILLIAM TESSEYMAN. 1852.
　　98 pp. ; adverts, 42. [St. Misc. Tr.]
　　$7\frac{1}{4} \times 4\frac{1}{8}''$. Stiff printed wrappers.
　Preface dated September 1852.
　B.M.

LINCOLN

1843

553. THE LINCOLN COMMERCIAL DIRECTORY & PRIVATE RESIDENTS'
GUIDE. LINCOLN : PRINTED & PUBLISHED BY VICTOR &
BAKER . . . NEWLAND STREET. 1843.
　　4 + 18–51 ; adverts, 9 ; plan, map. [Tr. Gen.]
　　$8\frac{1}{8} \times 5\frac{5}{8}''$. Printed boards.
　Preface dated 10 May, 1843.
　Lincoln. A.R.W.

STAMFORD

(See LEICESTERSHIRE, 1846.)

ISLE OF MAN

(See ISLANDS.)

MIDDLESEX

1853

554. MASON'S COURT GUIDE & GENERAL DIRECTORY FOR BRENT-
FORD, KEW [& neighbouring places in Middlesex & Surrey]
. . . 1853.
　　4 + 13–187 ; adverts, 3. [Ct. Cm. Tr.]
　　$7\frac{1}{8} \times 4\frac{1}{8}''$. Green cloth.
　Preface signed R. H. Mason, Observer Office, Greenwich,
　July 1853.
　Bod. Guildhall.

HAMPTON

(See SURREY, 1851.)

HARROW
1850

555. HANDBOOK FOR . . . VISITORS TO HARROW ON THE HILL . . . WITH A DIRECTORY . . . EDITED BY THOMAS SMITH . . . LONDON : W. N. WRIGHT . . . 60 PALL MALL. J. S. CROSSLEY. HARROW. 1850.
  4 + 120 ; adverts, 8 ; plate. [Ct. Cm.]
    6¼ × 4". Blue cloth, gilt. Price 2s. 6d.
B.M. (10350.a.27). Guildhall.

STAINES
(*See* BERKSHIRE, 1846 ; SURREY, 1851.)

TWICKENHAM
(*See* SURREY, 1851.)

MONMOUTHSHIRE

1848. *See* WALES, 1848, 1849.

1852

556. LASCELLES & CO.'S DIRECTORY & GAZETTEER OF MONMOUTH . . . BIRMINGHAM : LASCELLES & CO. PRINTERS. 1852.
  238 pp. ; adverts 50 ; map. [Ct. Cm. Tr. for larger, Gen. for smaller places.]
    8¼ × 5½". Red cloth. Price, subsc. 12s. 6d.
Preface dated August 1852. The second edition. No copy of the first edition has been found.
Cardiff. Newport.

NEWPORT
1847

557. THE ANCIENT & MODERN HISTORY OF NEWPORT, MONMOUTH- SHIRE. WITH A GUIDE & DIRECTORY. 1847. PRINTED BY W. CHRISTOPHERS AT THE MERLIN OFFICE, NEWPORT FOR J. M. SCOTT & D. D. MORRIS.
  4 + 9–116 ; slip (adds) between 112/3 ; plan, map, 3 plates. [Tr.]
    7½ × 4⅝". Blue cloth.
Dedication dated September 1847, signed 'the Author, J. M. Scott'. Scott was a printer and reporter on the staff of the *Monmouthshire Merlin*. David Morris was a litho- grapher. Christophers was an insurance agent as well as a printer.
Newport. A.R.W.

1848

558. KELLY'S NEWPORT DIRECTORY & TIDE TABLE FOR 1848.
NEWPORT : PRINTED & PUBLISHED BY W. L. KELLY, BRANCH
POST OFFICE, COMMERCIAL STREET.
    2 + 158 (including *37–*48) + (adverts), 78 + 14 + 257–
    268 ; adverts interspersed. [Cm. Tr.]
    $7\frac{1}{4} \times 4\frac{1}{4}''$. Printed boards.
    Wm. L. Kelly, besides keeping the branch post office, was
    a bookseller and insurance agent. A second edition was
    advertised in the *Monmouth, Glamorgan & Brecon Herald*
    on 10 December 1852 but no copy has been found.

NORFOLK
1836

559. HISTORY, GAZETTEER & DIRECTORY OF NORFOLK . . . BY
WILLIAM WHITE . . . PRINTED BY ROBERT LEADER . . .
SHEFFIELD . . . 1836.
    816 pp. [Misc. Tr.]
    $7 \times 4\frac{1}{4}''$. Price 12s. boards, 13s. 6d. calf ; non-subsc,
    3s. extra.
    Preface dated 29 February 1836. According to White's
    Suffolk directory, 1844, p. 755, this edition was sold out
    before the end of the year.
    Bod. Guildhall. Norwich. Yarmouth.

1844. *See* SUFFOLK, 1844.

1845

560. HISTORY, GAZETTEER & DIRECTORY OF NORFOLK . . . SECOND
EDITION . . . BY WILLIAM WHITE . . . [imprint as 1836].
1845.
    816 pp. ; map. [Misc. Tr.]
    Format, price as 1836.
    Preface dated 21 April 1845.
    Guildhall. Norwich. Yarmouth.

1850

561. HUNT & CO.'S DIRECTORY OF EAST NORFOLK WITH PART OF
SUFFOLK . . . 1850. PRINTED FOR E. HUNT & CO. . . . BY
B. W. GARDINER . . . LONDON.
    x + 292 + 38 ; adverts, 70. [Misc. Tr. for Norwich ;
    Gen. for other places.]
    $7 \times 4\frac{1}{8}''$. Cloth. Price 5s., non-subsc. 5s. 6d.
    Preface dated August 1850.
    Guildhall. Norwich. Yarmouth.

1854

562. HISTORY, GAZETTEER & DIRECTORY OF NORFOLK . . . BY
FRANCIS WHITE & CO. . . . PRINTED BY THE TRUSTEES OF

E. Blurton at the Britannia Offices, Castle Street &
King Street, Sheffield. 1854.
 882 pp. ; map. [Gen. Tr.]
  $7 \times 4\frac{1}{4}''$. Price 13s. 6d., non-subsc, 3s. 6d. extra.
 Preface dated March 1854. *See* p. 67 above.
Bod. B.M. Guildhall. Norwich.

NORWICH
1783

563. The Norwich Directory . . . Norwich : Printed & Sold
by W. Chase & Co, March 22, 1783.
 $2 + vi + 5-52 + 2 + 59-73 + 7$; plan. [Gen.]
  $7\frac{3}{4} \times 4\frac{1}{2}''$. Price 1s. 6d.
B.M. (impf.). Chetham.

1784

564. Re-issue of above with same title and contents + Appendix,
Jan. 3, 1784 [adds], viii pp.
 All copies of either issue have the gap in pagination after
p. 52.
Bod. Norwich.

1802

565. The Norwich Directory . . . by Thomas Peck. Nor-
wich : Printed & Sold by J. Payne, 22 Market Place.
 $xii + 60 + 24 + 2$ (blank) $+ 16$; plan. [Gen.]
  $8\frac{1}{8} \times 4\frac{7}{8}''$. Blue wrappers.
 Plan dated 10 February 1802. The dedication is to the
Mayor, Jeremiah Ives, Jun., who was mayor, 1801–2. The
A.R.W. copy has not the 16 pp. addenda at the end. It
may be an earlier issue or perhaps the addenda were issued
separately and have been bound up with the other copies.
Bod. Guildhall (impf). Norwich. A.R.W.

1803

566. The Norwich Directory . . . by T. Peck. Norwich :
Printed by Bacon, Cockey Lane.
 $6 + 58 + 26$. [Gen.]
  $7\frac{3}{4} \times 4\frac{5}{8}''$.
 Dedicated to the Mayor, Sir Roger Kerrison, who was mayor
1802–3. The title mentions a plan of the city.
I.H.R.

1810

567. A Concise History & Directory of . . . Norwich for
1811 . . . Norwich : Printed by & for C. Berry, Jun.
Dove Lane. 1810.
 $iv + 156$. [Gen.]
  $7\frac{1}{4} \times 4\frac{1}{8}''$.

Preface, dated 19 October 1810, says nine years have expired
since the last Norwich directory ' which was out of print
almost as soon as in '. This seems to ignore the second
edition of Peck's directory.
C.U.L.   Norwich.

1842

568. THE NORWICH GUIDE & DIRECTORY . . . BY G. K. BLYTH.
LONDON : R. HASTINGS . . . LINCOLNS INN FIELDS. NOR-
WICH : JOSIAH FLETCHER. 1842.
  2 + xii + 248 + 268 (numbered by columns, 2 to a page)
  + 269–316 ; adverts, 20 ; plate. [Ct. Tr. Misc.]
  $7\frac{3}{4} \times 4\frac{1}{4}''$. Green cloth, white label. Price 5s., non-
subsc. 6s.
The court section is dated April 1842, the trades, July 1842
and the preface, August 1842. Some copies have a slip
with two additional names pasted at foot of p. 266. Nearly
every house in the town was personally visited, some of
them twice. The guide, xii + 248, was also issued without
the directory and with a cancel title.
B.M. (796.d.23). C.U.L. Norwich.

1843

569. Re-issue of above with cancel title, imprint NORWICH :
JARROLD & SONS, LONDON STREET & J. FLETCHER, HAY-
MARKET. 1843.
A.R.W.

1852

570. MASON'S NORWICH GENERAL & COMMERCIAL DIRECTORY &
HANDBOOK . . . LONDON : PUBLISHED BY THE PROPRIETOR.
1852. [Printers, Adlard & Palmer, Ludgate Hill.]
  96 + 24 ; adverts, 28. [Gen. Tr.]
  $8\frac{3}{4} \times 5\frac{1}{2}''$. Printed boards. Price 2s. 6d., non-subsc. 3s.
Preface dated April 1852.
Bod. Norwich.

NORTHAMPTONSHIRE

1849

571. HISTORY, GAZETTEER & DIRECTORY OF NORTHAMPTONSHIRE
. . . BY WILLIAM WHELLAN & CO. LONDON : WHITTAKER
& CO. AVE MARIA LANE. PETERBOROUGH : ROBERT GARD-
NER . . . 1849.
  xvi + 11–962. [Misc. Tr. for larger, Ct. Cm. for smaller
places.]
  $8\frac{1}{2} \times 5\frac{3}{8}''$. Boards. Price 20s. with map.
Preface dated Goole, 30 October 1849. An imitation of
W. White's directories.
B.M. Manchester.

NORTHAMPTON

1853

572. DIRECTORY OF . . . NORTHAMPTON . . . NORTHAMPTON :
PRINTED BY THOMAS PHILLIPS. [Sheep Street.] 1853.
Title on wrapper ; 120 pp. ; table. [Ct. Tr.]
$7\frac{1}{4} \times 4''$. Blue printed wrappers.
Northampton.

NORTHUMBERLAND

1827. *See* DURHAMSHIRE, 1827.

1847

573. A GENERAL DIRECTORY OF . . . NEWCASTLE-ON-TYNE &
GATESHEAD [with Durham and other towns and villages]
. . . BY FRANCIS WHITE & CO. PRINTED . . . BY JOHN
BLURTON, BRITANNIA OFFICES . . . SHEFFIELD . . . MARCH,
1847.
616 ; adverts, 14. [Gen. for villages ; Misc. Tr. for towns.
Also St. for largest towns.]
$7 \times 4\frac{1}{4}''$. Cloth, gilt. Price in calf, 10s., non-subsc.
12s. 6d.
Preface dated 19 March 1847.
B.M.

574. [Another issue.] [Title as above but] WITH GUISBOROUGH
[and other places] . . . IN THE NORTH RIDING OF YORKSHIRE
. . . JULY, 1847.
Re-issue of above with a new title, preface and index,
without the errata leaf (pp. [615–6]) and with additional
directories, 615–63. The errata are not incorporated.
Guildhall. I.H.R.

575. [Another issue.] [Title as first issue as far as YARM and then
a number of other places in Northumberland and with
Berwick-on-Tweed . . .] DECEMBER. 1847.
As first issue to 614, then 615–742.
Newcastle.

1850

576. WARD'S NORTHUMBERLAND & DURHAM DIRECTORY . . . 1850
. . . NEWCASTLE-ON-TYNE. ROBERT WARD, PRINTER &
PUBLISHER. ST NICHOLAS CHURCH YARD.
viii + 88 + [diary, unpaged] + 2, 3b–360b ; adverts, 102.
[Gen. Tr.]
$7\frac{3}{8} \times 4\frac{3}{4}''$.
All the towns are in Northumberland except South Shields
and Sunderland.
B.M. (lacks 227/8). Manchester. Newcastle.

1851

577. WARD'S NORTH OF ENGLAND DIRECTORY . . . 1851 . . . [imprint as above].

> 112 + 4 + 6*–386*. [Misc. Tr ; St. also for Newcastle & Gateshead.]
>> Format as above. Cloth.
>
> Preface dated 20 January 1851. Contains places in Dur, Cumb and Yorks as well as in Northumberland.

Carlisle. Guildhall. Newcastle. A.R.W.

1852

578. [Title as above but] 1852.

> 96 + 1*–72* ; adverts, 60. [Misc. Tr.]
>> Format as above. Stiff wrappers, red label. Price 1s.
>
> Preface dated 31 December 1851. A supplement to 1851, containing adds. for Carlisle and seven additional towns, all in Northumberland except Penrith.

Newcastle. A.R.W.

1853

579. [Title as above but] 1853.

> 96 + 3 + 4*–439* ; adverts, 120. [Misc. Tr.]
>> Format as above. Cloth.
>
> Preface dated 20 January 1853. Contains some of the same towns as 1851 and three others.

Newcastle. A.R.W.

1854

580. [Title as above but] SUPPLEMENTARY EDITION. 1854.

> 6 + 11–92 + 6 + 7*–64* ; adverts, 84. [adds.]
>> Format as above. Stiff wrappers. Price 1s. 6d.
>
> Contains a list of adds. for some of the directories previously issued.

Newcastle. A.R.W.

1855

581. [Title as 1851 but] 1855.

> 68 + 3 + 4*–564* ; adverts, 128. [Misc. Tr ; St. also for Newcastle.]
>> Format as above. Cloth.
>
> Preface dated 14 March 1855. Contains directories for most of the towns in the 1851 edition.

Newcastle. A.R.W.

582. HISTORY, TOPOGRAPHY & DIRECTORY OF NORTHUMBERLAND . . . BY WILLIAM WHELLAN & CO. LONDON : WHITTAKER

& Co, Ave Maria Lane. Manchester : Galt & Co. . . .
1855. [Printers, Galt, Kerruish & Gent, Manchester.]
  xviii + 17–1010 ; map. [Gen ; Tr. also for towns.]
    $8\frac{3}{8} \times 5\frac{3}{8}''$. Price, subsc. 20s. or with map on rollers,
    24s. 6d.
  Preface dated Pontefract, February 1855.
B.M. Newcastle.

BERWICK-ON-TWEED
1806

583. A Directory & Concise History of Berwick-on-Tweed
 . . . likewise Farmsteads Twelve Miles Round . . .
Printed by W. Lockhead.
  192 pp. ; map. [Gen ; St. Tr. also for Berwick.]
    $6\frac{3}{4} \times 3\frac{7}{8}''$. Wrappers, label. Price 3s.
  The label is dated 1806 and on p. 188 is the date May 1806
  but the preface says the book was ready for the press ' last
  year '. An unsystematic and amateurish production but
  the compiler ' candidly acknowledges this undertaking to
  be too great for him '. The following verse appears on
  p. 72.

  Long may Britannia boast of her noble commanders
  And always rule the roast, like the great Alexanders.
  May Berwick once more give a ticket to brave Strachan
  Who I hope will soon moor Jerome's flying Squadron.

B.M. (lacking first 7 pp.). I.H.R. (lacking index, pp. 189–92).

1827. *See* Durhamshire, 1827.

NEWCASTLE-ON-TYNE
1778

584. Whitehead's Newcastle Directory for 1778 . . . Newcastle : Printed by Tho. Angus ; St Nicholas Church-
yard. 1778.
  60 pp. ; table. [Tr.]
    $5 \times 3\frac{1}{8}''$.
  The only known copy lacks title, pp. 59–60 and the table.
  These details are here taken from the reprint, *The First
  Newcastle Directory*, ed. J. R. Boyle (1889), which contains
  a useful account of Newcastle directories by the editor.
  The reprint must have been made from a perfect copy but
  its present whereabouts has not been discovered. William
  Whitehead was a turner and musical instrument maker.
  He also published *Whitehead's Historian's Pocket Com-
  panion* (1777). The cut on the title of the directory is said
  to be by Bewick. There are copies of the reprint in Bod,
  Guildhall and Newcastle P.L.
Soc. of Antiquaries of Newcastle-on-Tyne.

1782

585. THE NEWCASTLE & GATESHEAD DIRECTORY FOR 1782, 83 &
84 . . . PRINTED BY T. LAWSON, VINE ENTRY, FLESH-
MARKET . . .
> eng. title + 62 ; advert, 2 ; 2 tables. [Cm.]
> $5\frac{1}{8} \times 3\frac{1}{8}''$. Price 8d.
> Also by Whitehead. Pp. 59–60 contain information on
> what innkeepers might give soldiers quartered on them to
> eat instead of meat and the rates paid for soldiers' quarters.
> B.M.

1787

586. AN ACCOUNT OF NEWCASTLE-ON-TYNE . . . NEWCASTLE ;
PRINTED BY T. ANGUS FOR THE AUTHOR & SOLD BY HIM ON
THE MIDDLE OF HIGH BRIDGE. 1787.
> 108 pp. ; table. [Cm.]
> $5\frac{1}{8} \times 3\frac{1}{8}''$. Price 1s.
> Whitehead's third directory. Preface dated 1 May 1787.
> The fly-title (p. 51) runs THE NEWCASTLE & GATESHEAD
> DIRECTORY FOR 1787–89 . . . CORRECTED FROM JUNE,
> 1787. The title has the same Bewick cut as the 1778
> edition.
> B.M. Newcastle.

1790

587. WHITEHEAD'S NEWCASTLE & GATESHEAD DIRECTORY FOR
1790 . . . CORRECTED TO MAY, 1790. NEWCASTLE : PRINTED
BY D. AKENHEAD FOR THE AUTHOR [etc. as 1787].
> 132 pp. ; table. [Tr. for Newcastle ; Cm. for Gateshead.]
> $5\frac{1}{8} \times 3\frac{1}{8}''$. Price 1s.
> The cut on p. 101 is said to be by Bewick. Reprinted in
> 1902 by R. Ward & Sons of Newcastle-on-Tyne and presented
> free to subscribers to Ward's directory. I.H.R. has a
> copy of the reprint.
> Gateshead. Newcastle.

1795

588. THE NEWCASTLE & GATESHEAD DIRECTORY FOR 1795 . . .
COLLECTED . . . BY WILLIAM HILTON & ASSISTANTS. NEW-
CASTLE : PRINTED & SOLD BY M. ANGUS. SIDE.
> 78 pp. ; table. [Cm.]
> $5 \times 3\frac{1}{8}''$. Marbled wrappers. Price 1s.
> Preface, dated 12 January 1795, acknowledges the com-
> piler's debt to ' the late ingenious Mr William Whitehead '.
> Any mistakes or omissions which may probably occur must
> be attributed to the inattention of those who ignored the
> handbills issued on the previous 5th of November ' and to
> no other cause whatsoever '. ' No false delicacy, no super-

cilious distinction, will even be thought of in the Work ;
but all Tradesmen & Mechanics of every denomination be
impartially treated . . .'. (pp. [77–8]). *See also* p. 20
above.

William Hilton was a native of Stockton and a mercer at
Gateshead. He is here entered as a letter writer and he
was known as Hilton, the poet. He published two volumes
of poetry in 1775–6. He died in 1798. (*See* W. H. D.
Longstaffe, *History of Darlington* (1854), pp. xxxviii ff.)

B.M. Newcastle.

1801

589. THE DIRECTORY FOR . . . 1801 OF . . . NEWCASTLE-UPON-
TYNE, GATESHEAD & PLACES ADJACENT . . . NEWCASTLE-
ON-TYNE. PRINTED BY J. MITCHELL. DEAN STREET.

xx + 62 ; adverts, 2. [Tr. Cm.]
$6\frac{1}{2} \times 3\frac{7}{8}''$. Price 2s.

A feature of this directory is the classified list of those
connected with the import and export trade, which was ' for
the convenience of foreigners and strangers, who have
generally occasion for reference to such men '. The compiler says he was concerned in trade himself and ' if the
following sheets can facilitate business or unite our interests
. . . by a more certain and enlarged knowledge of our respective concerns, the object of such a work is obtained '. *See
also* p. 19 above.

B.M. Guildhall. Newcastle.

1811

590. MACKENZIE & DENT'S TRIENNIAL DIRECTORY FOR NEWCASTLE-
UPON-TYNE, GATESHEAD & PLACES ADJACENT . . . NEW-
CASTLE-UPON-TYNE : PRINTED & PUBLISHED BY MACKENZIE
& DENT, ST NICHOLAS CHURCH YARD.

104 pp. [Tr. Pr.]
$6\frac{1}{2} \times 3\frac{3}{4}''$. Price 2s.

Dedication dated April 1811. The special commercial
section is again a feature of this directory.

B.M. (2 copies, one extensively corrected and added to in
ink). Newcastle.

1824

591. A GENERAL DIRECTORY FOR NEWCASTLE UPON TYNE, GATES-
HEAD & PLACES ADJACENT . . . NEWCASTLE : PRINTED FOR
THE PUBLISHER . . . 1824. [Printer, Francis Humble, Dur-
ham.]

88 pp. ; adverts, 6 and interspersed. [Gen.]
$7 \times 4\frac{1}{8}''$. Marbled boards. Price 2s. boards, 2s. 6d. half
bound.

There is an entry for Stephen Humble, bookseller and publisher, who perhaps published this directory.
I.H.R. Newcastle. Gateshead. A.R.W.

1833

592. A DIRECTORY OF . . . NEWCASTLE & GATESHEAD & THEIR SUBURBS . . . COMPILED & ARRANGED BY ALEXANDER IHLER. NEWCASTLE : PRINTED . . . BY T. & J. HODGSON, CHRONICLE OFFICE, UNION STREET. 1833.
xvi + 196 ; adverts, 4 ; plan. [Gen. Tr.]
$7\frac{3}{4} \times 4\frac{1}{8}''$.
B.M. Newcastle.

1838

593. DIRECTORY OF . . . NEWCASTLE-UPON-TYNE & GATESHEAD FOR . . . 1838. BY M. A. RICHARDSON. NEWCASTLE : PRINTED & PUBLISHED BY M. A. RICHARDSON, 101 PILGRIM STREET.
viii + 278 ; adverts, 68 and interspersed. [Gen. Tr.]
$7\frac{1}{4} \times 4\frac{3}{8}''$. Red or green cloth, label.
The additions (vi–viii) were collected in December 1837. Moses Aaron Richardson (1793–1871) was the son of a schoolmaster. He was a keen antiquarian, genealogist and local historian and wrote a number of works on these subjects. In 1850 he emigrated to Australia. (D.N.B.)
B.M. Guildhall. Gateshead. Manchester. Newcastle.

1839

594. SUPPLEMENT TO RICHARDSON'S DIRECTORY FOR . . . NEWCASTLE & GATESHEAD. MAY 1839.
Title on wrapper ; (adverts), 20 + 40 ; slip. [Adds.]
$7\frac{1}{4} \times 4\frac{3}{8}''$. Grey printed wrappers.
Newcastle (bound with 1838 directory).

1844

595. WILLIAMS'S COMMERCIAL DIRECTORY OF NEWCASTLE-UPON-TYNE & GATESHEAD . . . NEWCASTLE : PRINTED AT THE COURANT OFFICE BY MESSRS BLACKWELL & CO. FOR J. WILLIAMS . . . 1844.
6 + 228 ; adverts, 8 pp. & some eng. [St. Gen. Tr. for Newcastle ; Ct. Tr. for Gateshead ; Gen. for villages.]
$8\frac{7}{8} \times 5\frac{1}{2}''$. Blue cloth.
A.R.W.

NOTTINGHAMSHIRE

1832

596. HISTORY, GAZETTEER & DIRECTORY OF NOTTINGHAMSHIRE . . . BY WILLIAM WHITE. SHEFFIELD : PRINTED BY ROBERT LEADER . . . 1832.

704 pp. [Misc. Tr. for larger places ; Gen. for smaller.]
7 × 4". Price 10s. 6d. boards, 12s. 6d. calf, non-subsc.
3s. extra.
Preface dated 1 August 1832.
Guildhall. Nottingham.

1844

597. HISTORY, DIRECTORY & GAZETTEER OF THE COUNTY . . . OF
NOTTINGHAM . . . [with] GAINSBOROUGH . . . BY FRANCIS
& JOHN WHITE. PRINTED . . . BY JOHN BLURTON . . . &
SOLD BY F. WHITE & CO. 43 REGENT STREET, SHEFFIELD.
1844.
xii + 13–768 ; adverts, 10 ; map. [Gen. Tr. for larger
places ; Misc. Tr. for smaller.]
7 × 4¼". Price, subsc. 12s. boards, 13s. 6d. calf.
Preface dated December 1844. William White called this
' a pirated edition . . . by an unprincipled man in a very
blundering manner '. (*See* p. 23 above.)
Birmingham. B.M. Guildhall. Nottingham. Salt.

1853

598. HISTORY, DIRECTORY & GAZETTEER FOR THE COUNTY OF
. . . NOTTINGHAM . . . BY FRANCIS WHITE & CO. . . .
PRINTED . . . BY JOHN BLURTON . . . SHEFFIELD . . . 1853.
xii + 13–744 ; adverts, 22. [Gen. etc. as 1844.]
7 × 4¼". Calf. Price 8s. 6d., non-subsc. 3s. 6d. extra.
Preface dated January 1853.
Guildhall. Nottingham.

BINGHAM
1851

599. BINGHAM, WITH SOME ACCOUNT OF EAST BRIDGFORD. BY
ANDREW ESDAILE. 1851.
Said to contain names of farmers, cottagers and about
ninety freeholders. (*See Notts & Derby N. & Q.*, (1897), v,
105–8.) Unfortunately no copy of this book has been
traced.

NOTTINGHAM
1799

600. THE NOTTINGHAM DIRECTORY . . . COMPILED & ARRANGED
BY E. WILLOUGHBY. NOTTINGHAM : PRINTED . . . BY C.
SUTTON & SOLD . . . BY MR WILLOUGHBY, CASTLE GATE,
NOTTINGHAM. 1799.
viii + 108. [Gen. Tr.]
6¾ × 4". Price 2s.
Preface dated 12 September 1799. Edward Willoughby
was an auctioneer.
B.M. Guildhall. Nottingham. A.R.W.

1814

601. The Nottingham Directory . . . Nottingham : Printed & Sold by E. Hodson, St. Peter's Gate . . . 1814.
    88 pp. [Gen.]
    $6\frac{7}{8} \times 3\frac{7}{8}''$. Price 1s. 6d.
Preface, dated 10 November 1814, announces a list of additions to be presented free to purchasers of the directory.
Nottingham (lacks 33–6).

1815

602. The Nottingham Directory . . . Nottingham : Printed at the Review Office by Sutton & Son. 1815.
    viii + 124. [Gen. Tr.]
    $6\frac{3}{4} \times 3\frac{7}{8}''$.
B.M. Nottingham (lacks 69–72).

1818

603. 1818. The Nottingham Directory . . . Printed by Sutton & Son, Bridlesmith Gate.
    iv + 104. [Cm. Tr.]
    $6\frac{3}{4} \times 4''$.
Nottingham.

1825

604. Glover's Nottingham Directory for 1825 . . . Nottingham : Printed & Published by S. Glover, Carlton Street.
    iv + 5–157 ; adverts, 3 and interspersed ; slips containing adds. between 64/5, 70/1, 84/5, 148/9 (a leaf) and pasted at foot of 82, also a note between ii/iii ; plan. [Tr. Cm.]
    $7\frac{3}{8} \times 4\frac{1}{8}''$. Blue printed wrappers.
Preface, dated 12 April 1825, apologises for delay in delivering the plan, owing to three members of the engraver's family having been bitten by a mad dog. For Stephen Glover, *see* Derbyshire, 1829, above.
B.M. (578.b.61, lacking 95–98 & 2 slips). Guildhall. A.R.W.

1834

605. History, Topography & Directory of . . . Nottingham & the Adjacent Villages . . . Nottingham : Printed & Published by W. Dearden, Carlton Street, 1834.
    vi + 3–96 + 174 ; adverts, 6 ; plan. [Misc. Tr. with Gen. or Tr. for villages.]
    $7\frac{1}{4} \times 4\frac{1}{8}''$. Green cloth.
B.M. (10358.bb.51). Gen. Soc (corrected in ink). A.R.W.

1840

606. The Nottingham Annual Register . . . 1840. By James Orange . . . London : Hamilton, Adams & Co.: J. Howitt, Nottingham. [Printed by J. Howitt.]
    8 + 154 ; adverts, 26. [Tr.]

$7\frac{1}{4} \times 4\frac{1}{4}''$. Purple cloth, green end papers. Price, subsc. 3s.

Orange also wrote a *History of Nottingham*, published in numbers and parts by Howitt, 1839–40. It was originally intended that the directory should be bound with it but in fact the two are not the same size. (*See* J. P. Briscoe in *Notts & Derby N. & Q.*, v (1897), 62–3.)

Bod. Guildhall. A.R.W.

1844

607. THE HISTORY & DIRECTORY OF . . . NOTTINGHAM . . . BY STEPHEN GLOVER . . . NOTTINGHAM : PRINTED & PUBLISHED . . . BY J. HOWITT, CLUMBER STREET.' 1844.

4 + 128 + 206 ; adverts, 36 & interspersed. [Gen. Tr.]
$8\frac{7}{8} \times 5\frac{1}{4}''$. Cloth, printed label. Price 7s. 6d.

The directory is headed 'Taken 1843'. In some copies the list of deaths on p. 204 is on a strip pasted on instead of printed on the page. This contains more names than the Nottingham directory in F. White's *Nottinghamshire*, 1844 (No. 597).

Chetham. Guildhall. I.H.R. Salt.

1848

608. LASCELLES & HAGAR'S COMMERCIAL DIRECTORY OF . . . NOTTINGHAM . . . NOTTINGHAM : PRINTED . . . BY STEVENSON & CO. MIDDLE PAVEMENT. 1848.

adverts, 30 + 230. [Gen. Tr. ; Gen. for suburbs.]
$8\frac{1}{2} \times 5\frac{1}{4}''$. Price 5s. 6d., non-subsc. 8s.

Guildhall. A.R.W.

1854

609. WRIGHT'S NOTTINGHAM DIRECTORY . . . FOR 1854. NOTTINGHAM : C. N. WRIGHT, LONG ROW, 1854.

adverts, 8 + 378 ; adverts, 40 ; slip (adds) between 8/9. [Gen. St. Tr. ; Gen. for suburbs.]
$7\frac{1}{4} \times 4\frac{3}{4}''$. Green cloth.

Christopher Norton Wright, whose first directory this seems to be, is described in various directories as shorthand writer and directory publisher. He also lived and had a printing works for a time in Birmingham. About 1875 he moved to Leicester where he published a large number of directories. His business was taken over by Kelly's Directories Ltd. in 1900. He was still living in Leicester in 1902 and seems to have died in 1909.

Manchester. A.R.W.

OXFORDSHIRE

1846

610. HUNT & CO.'S . . . OXFORD DIRECTORY . . . [with] ABING
DON, BANBURY [and other places in Oxfordshire] . . . 1846.
PRINTED FOR E. HUNT & CO. BY B. W. GARDINER . . .
CAVENDISH SQUARE.
  8 + 218 + 12 : adverts, 76. [Ct. Tr ; St. also for Oxford.]
  7⅛ × 4¼". Blue cloth. Price 6s.
  Preface dated August 1846.
  Bod. Oxford.

1852

611. HISTORY, GAZETTEER & DIRECTORY OF THE COUNTY OF
OXFORD . . . PETERBOROUGH : PRINTED & PUBLISHED BY
ROBERT GARDNER FOR SUBSCRIBERS ONLY . . . 1852.
  x + 864 ; map. [Misc. Tr.]
  8½ × 5½". Half calf. Price 17s. 6d. or with map on
  rollers, £1.
  Preface dated July 1852.
  Bod. Guildhall. Oxford.

1854. *See* BERKSHIRE, 1854.

BANBURY

1832–1889

612. [*Rusher's Banbury List & Directory.*]
  Rusher's Banbury Directory was preceded for twenty years
  by *Rusher's Banbury List*, which has no directory proper.
  The *List* was first published in 1812 and thereafter annually,
  with the same number of pages (12). The first edition cost
  2d. In 1826, a larger size of paper was adopted and the
  price was raised to 3d. In 1827 the title was changed to
  Rusher's Banbury List & Directory but the contents remained
  the same. In 1832, the first edition to contain a court list
  and trades directory was published. Until 1881 the *List*
  and *Directory* were issued both separately and together, in
  coloured wrappers, with the appropriate title printed on
  them, thus : RUSHER'S ORIGINAL BANBURY LIST. PRICE
  3d ; RUSHER'S ORIGINAL BANBURY DIRECTORY. PRICE
  6d ; RUSHER'S ORIGINAL BANBURY LIST & DIRECTORY.
  PRICE 9d. Either *List* or *Directory* or both were also issued
  in combination with *Moore's Almanach*. Extra pages,
  varying from two to sixteen, on the same paper as the
  wrappers and containing advertisements and miscellaneous
  information, were sometimes included. From 1881 the
  List and the *Directory* were issued together as one volume,
  paged continuously.
  Neither *List* nor *Directory* have title pages. The 1832
  edition of the *Directory* is paged 15–26. There are two

issues, one ending with an advertisement of prints of Banbury churches and the other with an advertisement of
Reports of Charities.   New editions, of the *Directory* were
published annually, except in 1836, '38 and '40.   They
were paged 15–22 in 1833, 15–23 in 1834, 17–25 in 1835,
17–26 in 1837 and 39.   From 1841 to 1880 the *Directory*
was paged 1–12 until 1877, 1–15 in 1878 and 79 and 1–19
in 1880.   From 1881 to 1889 the combined volume contained 356 pp.   The editor, J. G. Rusher was one of a large
family of printers of which James Rusher of Reading was
also a member.   He also edited the *Banbury Chapbooks*.   He
died in 1877, aged 93, having taken a prominent part in
public affairs.   He was mayor of Banbury in 1833, Chamber-
lain of the Corporation in 1834 and Justice of the Peace for
the Borough in 1842.   After his death, the directory was
continued by his daughter.

Copies. Bod. (a complete set of both list and directory, with
many duplicates, distributed among seven volumes, most
of them presentation copies from J. G. Rusher.   One volume
has a cutting from *The Banbury Guardian* for 8 March 1877,
giving an obituary notice of Rusher).   B.M. (1812, 15, 21,
23–74).   Guildhall (1834–72).

OXFORD

1835

613. THE OXFORD UNIVERSITY, CITY & COUNTY DIRECTORY FOR
1835 . . . OXFORD.   PRINTED & PUBLISHED BY J. VINCENT.
1835.
    70 pp.   [Tr. for Oxford.]
    4¾ × 3⅝″.   Purple wrappers, label.   Price 1s.
Bod.

RUTLANDSHIRE

1846.   *See* LEICESTERSHIRE, 1846.

SHROPSHIRE

1828

614. THE SALOP DIRECTORY . . . [for] EACH OF THE MARKET
TOWNS IN THE COUNTY . . . SHREWSBURY : PUBLISHED BY
TIBNAM & CO. . . . 1828.
    4 + 142 ; 2 plates.   [Misc. Tr.]
    6½ × 4″.   Grey cloth.
Gen. Soc.   Shrewsbury.

1851

615. HISTORY, GAZETTEER & DIRECTORY OF SHROPSHIRE . . . BY
SAMUEL   BAGSHAW . . . SHEFFIELD :   PRINTED . . . BY

SAMUEL HARRISON, 5 HIGH STREET & SOLD BY SAMUEL
BAGSHAW, WENTWORTH TERRACE, SHEFFIELD. 1851.
4 + 716. [Gen; Tr. also for larger places.]
$8\frac{1}{2} \times 5\frac{3}{8}''$. Purple cloth. Price, subsc. 14s. 6d.
Preface dated 25 October 1851.
Guildhall. Shrewsbury. Salt.

1854. *See* LANCASHIRE (Whellan), 1854.

SHREWSBURY

Minshull's directories of Shrewsbury present a problem which the
present author does not claim to have solved. The preface to the
fourth edition, 1803, gives 1784 as the date of Minshull's first
directory. Copies have been seen of a 1786 and a 1797 edition, and
in *Shropshire N. & Q.*, N.S., vi (1897), 69, an edition of 1793 is
mentioned of which no copy has been found. Whether the reference
in the 1803 directory is a mistake for 1786, which seems possible
as Minshull only arrived in Shrewsbury in 1784, or whether
the 1797 edition, which has no date on the title but is here dated
from the name of the mayor, is wrongly attributed to 1793 in
Shropshire N. & Q., it seems impossible to determine. The absence
of any copy of a 1793 edition is some argument in favour of the
latter alternative. We can, at any rate, be sure of the existence of
five editions, of one of which, either 1784 or 1793, no copy has
been found. The others are as follows.

1786

616. THE SHREWSBURY GUIDE & SALOPIAN DIRECTORY . . . FOR
1786 . . . BY T. MINSHULL . . . SHREWSBURY, PRINTED &
SOLD BY A. PRYSE, HIGH STREET.
4 + 9–56 + xix + 20–22 ; plan. [Gen.]
$6\frac{1}{4} \times 3\frac{5}{8}''$.
The Minshulls were Chester printers. Thomas Minshull
(*c.* 1760–1810) settled in Shrewsbury in 1784. It is thought
that he was a journeyman printer, employed by firms in
the town. He was the author of a number of poems.
(R. S. Brown, ' Stationers & Printers of Chester ', *Hist. Soc.
of Lancs & Chesh Trans*, lxxxiii (1932), 101–52 ; L. C. Lloyd,
' The Book Trade in Shropshire ', *Shrops. Arch. Soc., Trans*,
xlviii (1935–6). *See also* p. 6 above).
Bod. Shrewsbury.

1797

617. THE SHREWSBURY VISITOR'S POCKET COMPANION OR SALOPIAN
GUIDE & DIRECTORY . . . BY T. MINSHULL. SHREWSBURY :
PRINTED & SOLD BY THE BOOKSELLERS.
Title + 9–60 ; plate. [Gen.]
$5\frac{7}{8} \times 3\frac{3}{4}''$.
Dated from the name of the mayor, Henry Bevan, who was

mayor 1796/7. Compiled about the same time as the Shrewsbury directory in *The Universal British Directory* (No. 18) ; there seems no obvious connection but no doubt Wilkes made use of this directory for the *U.B.D.* Only one copy has been seen and it is possible that there should be some pages between the title and p. 9.
Guildhall.

1803

618. [Title as above but] FOURTH EDITION. SHREWSBURY : PRINTED FOR THE AUTHOR BY J. HODGES, MARDOL-HEAD . . . 1803.

92 pp. ; plate, plan, map. [Gen.]
$6\frac{1}{4} \times 3\frac{5}{8}$".
Preface dated February 1803.
B.M. (2 copies, 10351.aa.44 & 10347.aa.16/2).

1804

619. [Title as above but] FIFTH EDITION . . . J. HODGES, OPPOSITE TO THE COUNTY HALL. 1804.
Re-issue of above, with a cancel title.
Shrewsbury.

1846. *See* CHESHIRE, 1846.

SOMERSET

1840

621. A GENERAL DIRECTORY FOR . . . SOMERSET . . . TAUNTON : PRINTED & PUBLISHED BY WILLIAM BRAGG. 1840.

2 + ii + 410 ; adverts, 2. [Ct. Tr.]
$7\frac{3}{8} \times 4\frac{1}{4}$". Printed boards. Presented free to subscribers to the *Somerset County Gazette*.
Preface dated 20 February 1840. Pt. I (ii + 25–270 ; adverts, 12), was also issued separately, with a note on the cover to say that Pt. II would be delivered as soon as possible. *See also* pp. 14, 17 above.
Bristol. I.H.R. (Pt. I). Taunton. A.R.W. (Pt. I).

1848. *See* DEVONSHIRE, 1848 ; WILTSHIRE, 1848.

1850

622. HUNT & CO.'S DIRECTORY & TOPOGRAPHY OF AXBRIDGE, BRUTON [and other towns in Somerset] . . . [and] BRISTOL . . . PRINTED FOR E. HUNT & CO. BY B. W. GARDINER . . . PRINCES STREET . . . LONDON. 1850.

iv + 122 + 232 ; adverts, 20 pp. [Ct. Tr. for larger places ; Ct. Cm. for smaller places and Bristol.]
7×4". Green cloth. Price, non-subsc. 6s.
Preface dated July 1850. The Bristol section is a re-issue of parts of Hunt's Bristol directory for 1848.
A.R.W.

1854

623. A DIRECTORY FOR . . . BATH . . . WELLS . . . [also Frome, Keynsham and places in Glos & Wilts] . . . BATH : SAMUEL VIVIAN, 41 BROAD STREET. 1854.

    xii + 428 ; adverts, 429–506. [Gen. Tr. ; St. also for Bath.]

    7 × 4¼″. Green printed boards. Price 3s., non-subsc. 3s. 6d.

    Preface dated 21 January 1854.

    Bath. Bod. B.M. Taunton.

BATH

1787

See BRISTOL, 1787. Bath guides as early as 1773 contain lists of medical men and lodging houses but this seems to be the first regular directory.

1792

624. THE NEW BATH DIRECTORY FOR . . . 1792 . . . BATH : PRINTED BY & FOR W. GYE, 4 WESTGATE BUILDINGS & 14 MARKET PLACE . . .

    4 + 32 ; adverts, 4 ; adds (one leaf) inserted between 26/7. [Pr. Tr.]

    8½ × 5⅜″. Price 1s.

Dedication dated 2 January 1792. Advertised in the *Bath Chronicle* on 2 February. This is an offprint of the Bath section of *The Universal British Directory* (*see* No. 13, above), with new title, dedication, two pages of additions and a roughly printed strip containing a list of the corporation pasted over the corresponding list on p. 11. In spite of the imprint, this was printed by the printers of the *U.B.D.* and the advertisements are of publications by Champante & Whitrow who were its London agents. William Gye was a philanthropist and a much-respected citizen of Bath. When he died in 1806 he was buried in Bath Abbey and 4,000 people are said to have attended his funeral. He had thirteen children, of whom one, Henry Gye, published a directory of Bath in 1819. (*See* W. Longman, *Tokens of the Eighteenth Century*, 1916, pp. 57–9.)

Bod.

1800

625. ROBBINS'S BATH DIRECTORY . . . PRINTED & SOLD BY ROBBINS, 9 BRIDGE STREET . . . 1800.

    2 + 150 ; adverts, 2 pp. at beginning & 2 at end. [Gen.]

    6½ × 3⅞″. Price 1s. 6d.

Preface dated 28 May 1800. The compiler says he collected the information himself and it took him a long time.

Bath.

E. Green, *Bibliotheca Somersetensis* (1902), mentions a Robbins directory for 1801. No copy has been found, but a statement in the preface to the 1805 directory that it is three years since the last Bath directory was published seems to show that there was at least one edition between 1800 and 1805.

1805

626. The New Bath Directory for . . . 1805 . . . Bath : Printed & Sold by J. Browne . . . George Street. 1805.

> 2 + 150 ; plan. [Gen. Pr.]
> $6\frac{3}{8} \times 3\frac{1}{4}''$.
> Preface dated 7 January 1805. Perhaps, from the similarity of wording and arrangement, compiled by the same person as the 1800 directory.

Bath (lacking 45–52).

1809

627. The New Bath Directory for . . . 1809 . . . Bath : Printed & Sold by J. Browne . . . 6 Bridge Street.

> xii + 13–130 + 2. [Pr. Gen.]
> $6\frac{3}{4} \times 4\frac{1}{8}''$. Buff printed wrappers, printed on inner sides & included in the pagination.
> Preface dated 12 June 1809. P. 13 is headed ' Corrected to April 1809 '.

Bath (with plan dated 1805).

1812

628. The New Bath Directory corrected to May, 1812 . . . Bath : Printed, Published & Sold by Wood & Cunningham at the City Printing Office, 9 Union Street.

> 136 pp. ; plan, map. [Pr. Gen.]
> $6\frac{5}{8} \times 4''$. Yellow printed wrappers. Price 2s. 6d. sewed, 3s. boards.

Bath. B.M.

1819

629. Gye's Bath Directory, corrected to January, 1819 . . . Printed by & for H. Gye, Market Place, Bath.

> 4 + 130 ; adverts, 40 eng ; plan. [Pr. Gen.]
> $8\frac{1}{4} \times 5''$. Grey printed wrappers. Price 3s.
> Preface dated January 1819. For Henry Gye, *see above*, Bath, 1792.

Bath. B.M. C.U.L. A.R.W.

1824

630. KEENES' IMPROVED BATH DIRECTORY CORRECTED TO JANUARY, 1824. BATH: PRINTED & PUBLISHED BY JOHN & JAMES KEENE, AT THE BATH JOURNAL & GENERAL PRINTING OFFICE, 7 KINGSMEAD STREET.

2 + iv + 106 ; adverts, 6 & 38 eng. [Gen. Pr.]
$8\frac{5}{8} \times 5\frac{1}{4}''$. Green wrappers, pink label.

Compiled from the rate books, a method on which the publishers here pride themselves but which they later regretted and abandoned in the second edition, finding that personal application at every house was the only reliable way. *See also* p. 18 above.

Bath.

1826

631. THE BATH DIRECTORY CORRECTED TO JANUARY, 1826. [Imprint as 1824.]

vi + 156 ; adverts, 2 pp. at beginning & 14 at end, 4 eng. [Gen. Pr.]
$7 \times 4\frac{1}{8}''$. Price 3s. stitched, 3s. 6d. boards. *See* p. 18 above.

Bath. B.M.

1827

632. ADDENDA COMPLETING THE BATH DIRECTORY UP TO JANUARY, 1827. [Imprint as 1824.]

8 pp. [Adds.]
Format as 1826.

Compiled from entries made by the public in books left at the publishers' office and at the public libraries for nearly three months before printing. Announces an edition for 1828 of which no copy has been found.

B.M. (bound with the 1826 edition).

1829

633. KEENES' BATH DIRECTORY, CORRECTED TO JANUARY, 1829. [Imprint as 1824.]

iv + 164 ; adverts, 12. [Ct. Pr. Cm.]
$7 \times 4\frac{1}{8}''$. Price 4s. 6d.

Bath. B.M. Manchester.

1833

634. BATH DIRECTORY, CORRECTED TO APRIL 1833 BY H. SILVERTHORNE. BATH: PRINTED & PUBLISHED BY A. E. BINNS, 19 CHEAP STREET . . .

iv + 166 ; adverts, 48 & 10 eng. [Gen. Pr.]
$6\frac{7}{8} \times 4''$. Price 4s. 6d.

Henry Silverthorne is not entered in this edition but by 1837 he was librarian and assistant secretary to the Bath

Literary & Scientific Institution, a literary club, with reading room, lectures and museum, founded in 1824. He was also for a time sub-secretary to the S.P.C.K. By 1841 he had set up a bookselling and stationery business, as well as a printing office at which his 1841 and 1846 directories were printed.
Bath.

1837

635. THE BATH DIRECTORY . . . BATH: PUBLISHED BY H. SILVERTHORNE . . . 10 ARGYLE BUILDINGS . . . 1837. [Printer, George Wood, Parsonage Lane, Bath.]
    viii + 244 ; adverts, 36 & 14 eng. [Gen. St. Pr.]
    6⅞ × 4". Price 5s.
Preface, dated May 1837, refers to the positive refusal of very many inhabitants to supply information.
Bath. Guildhall.

1841

636. [As 1837 but] 17 WALCOT BUILDINGS . . . 1841.
    viii + 250 + 5 ; adverts, 1, 24, 16 & 7 eng. [Gen. St. Pr.]
    6⅞ × 4". Price 5s.
Preface dated March 1841.
Bath.

1846

637. [As 1841 but] 1846.
    viii + 16 + 13–274 ; adverts, 50 pp. & some interspersed. [Gen. St. Pr.]
    6¾ × 4". Price 5s.
Preface dated February 1846.
Bath. Gen. Soc. A.R.W.

1848. *See* WILTSHIRE, 1848.

1849

638. THE BATH ANNUAL DIRECTORY & ALMANACH. 1849. BATH: PRINTED & PUBLISHED BY CHARLES CLARK, 5 BRIDGE STREET . . .
    118 pp. ; adverts, 4, 3–106. [Ct. Tr. St.]
    6¾ × 4". Price 1s. 6d.
Preface dated December 1848.
Bath.

1850

639. BATH ANNUAL DIRECTORY . . . EDITED BY FRANCIS NORTON ERITH . . . 1850. [Imprint as 1849.]
    228 pp. ; adverts, 74. [Gen. Tr. St.]
    6¾ × 3⅞". Price 2s.
Preface dated 13 April 1850. Erith was an accountant and commission agent. Mrs Erith kept a preparatory school.
Bath. A.R.W.

1852

640. A Directory for . . . Bath & its Environs . . . Bath :
Printed & Published by Samuel Vivian, 41 Broad Street,
1852.
  6 + 306 ; adverts, 307–352 ; addenda slip. [St. Gen. Tr.]
  $6\frac{7}{8} \times 3\frac{7}{8}''$. Pink printed boards.
  Preface dated 11 March 1852.
Bath. A.R.W.

PORTISHEAD

1855

641. The Portishead Guide & Visitor's Handbook . . . also
a Useful Village Directory . . . by Bond & Fardon.
Portishead : J. & S. Wedmore ; H. Bond, Chemist . . .
1855.
  $7\frac{1}{8} \times 4\frac{3}{8}''$. Light green cloth, gilt. [Tr.] Map & Plates.
Somerset Arch. Soc., Taunton (Tite Collection).

STAFFORDSHIRE

(For places near Birmingham, *see also* Warwickshire and Birmingham
directories.)

1802

642. The Staffordshire Pottery Directory . . . Hanley :
Printed by J. Allbut & Son . . . 1802.
  iv + 146 (including 137*–138*) ; map, 3 tables. [Gen.]
  $8\frac{1}{4} \times 4\frac{3}{8}''$.
Birmingham.

1810

643. The Staffordshire Pottery Directory . . . Printed &
Sold by Chester & Mort, Hanley & Newcastle.
  64 pp. [Cm.]
  $7\frac{1}{8} \times 4\frac{1}{4}''$.
Undated. The Salt copy is dated 1810 in pencil. John
Mort was a bookseller in Newcastle-under-Lyme. He is
mentioned in *On the Road a Hundred Years Ago* (1830) ;
see p. 9, n. 2 above.
Salt.

1818

644. Staffordshire General & Commercial Directory for
1818 . . . Compiled by Messrs W. Parson & T. Bradshaw.
Manchester : Printed by J. Leigh, Market Place . . .
  Published in three parts.

[Pt. I] . . . CONTAINING . . . NEWCASTLE-UNDER-LINE, THE
POTTERIES & THE TOWN OF LEEK . . .
  6 + c + 130 ; map. [Gen. Tr.]
  Preface dated 30 March 1818.
[Pt. II] . . . CONTAINING LICHFIELD . . . STAFFORD & TAM-
WORTH [& a number of other towns] . . . WITH THE NEIGH-
BOURING VILLAGES . . .
  4 + ci–clxxii + 131–274 + 20. [Gen. Also Tr. for towns.]
[Pt. III] . . . CONTAINING . . . BILSTON, WALSALL [etc.]
. . . AND THE WHOLE OF . . . THE SOUTH OF THE COUNTY
OF STAFFORD . . .
  4 + clxxiii–ccxl + 275–398 + 21–48 + xxxii + 4 ; map.
  [Gen ; Tr. also for towns.]
  Preface dated 21 October 1818.
  $6\frac{3}{4} \times 3\frac{7}{8}''$. Price per vol., 5s. sewed, 6s. bound.
This directory is uniform with the *Lancashire General
Directory for 1818–19–20*, which formed Vol. II of the
Directory of English Counties and no doubt the two were
part of a project to cover all the counties in the Kingdom
to which the compilers refer in the preface to Pt. III. The
plan seems to have been abandoned in face of opposition,
perhaps from James Pigot. *See* p. 65 above for further
comment on both these directories.
Guildhall. I.H.R. (impf). Salt. A.R.W. (Pts. I & III).

645. [Another issue.] STAFFORDSHIRE GENERAL & COMMERCIAL
DIRECTORY . . . OF THE PRINCIPAL TOWNS & VILLAGES OF
THE COUNTY. COMPILED & PUBLISHED BY THE PROPRIETORS,
W. PARSON & T. BRADSHAW. [Imprint as first issue.]
  A re-issue in one volume, with the three parts bound up
  in order of the various paginations, without the separate
  title pages and contents tables or the preface to Pt. I but
  with a new title and index and the address and map from
  Pt. III, thus :
    4 + ccxl + 398 + 48 + xxxii + 4 ; map. Price 16s. 6d.
    bound.
Birmingham. Bod. Salt.

1822

646. THE NEWCASTLE & POTTERY GENERAL & COMMERCIAL
DIRECTORY FOR 1822–23 . . . HANLEY : PRINTED & SOLD
BY T. ALLBUT . . .
  4 + 150. [Gen.]
    $6\frac{3}{4} \times 3\frac{7}{8}''$. Price 2s. 6d.
  Covers the same places as Pt. I of the 1818 directory,
  excluding Leek. R. Simms, *Bibliotheca Staffordiensis* (1894),
  mentions an 1823 edition. No copy has been found ;
  perhaps it is the same as the above.
I.H.R. Salt. A.R.W.

1834

647. HISTORY, GAZETTEER & DIRECTORY OF STAFFORDSHIRE . . .
BY WILLIAM WHITE . . . PRINTED . . . BY ROBERT LEADER
. . . SHEFFIELD . . . 1834.
  12 + 3–772. [Misc. Tr. ; for smallest places, Gen.]
    $7 \times 3\frac{7}{8}''$. Price, with map, 12s. boards, 13s. 6d. calf,
    non-subsc. 3s. extra.
  Preface dated 12 May 1834.
Birmingham. Guildhall. A.R.W.

1844

648. A DIRECTORY OF BURTON-ON-TRENT, UTTOXETER, TAMWORTH,
LICHFIELD, & ASHBY-DE-LA-ZOUCHE . . . COMPILED BY W.
WESLEY, OFFICE OF THE MONTHLY ADVERTISER. 1844.
  adverts, 2 + 2 + 46 ; adverts, 8. [Gen.]
    $8\frac{3}{4} \times 5\frac{1}{8}''$. Wrappers. Free to subscribers to *The
    Monthly Advertiser* for 1844.
  Preface dated January 1844. A sketchy affair including
  only the principal inhabitants. It was compiled in order
  to make *The Monthly Advertiser* better known, according
  to the preface.
Salt.

1846

649. WILLIAMS'S COMMERCIAL DIRECTORY FOR STAFFORD & THE
POTTERIES . . . MANCHESTER : PUBLISHED BY J. WILLIAMS,
SEN . . . MAY, 1846.
  8 + (adverts), 28 + (Stockport), 62 + (Macclesfield), 48 +
  (Congleton), 18 + (Leek), 16 + (Stafford), 16 + (Hanley),
  8 + (Burslem), 20 + (Shelton), 12 + (Stoke & Longton),
  16 + (Newcastle, Stone & Tunstall), 24 + (Blackburn), 36.
  [Cm.]
    $7\frac{1}{8} \times 4\frac{1}{8}''$. Orange leather. Price 10s. cloth, 12s. leather ;
    non-subsc. 2s. extra.
  All of this directory, except Blackburn, appears in other
  Williams' directories ; Stockport–Leek in *Stockport, etc.*,
  1845 (*see* CHESHIRE, 1845), with some additional pages for
  Leek and Stafford–Newcastle in *Chester, etc.*, 1846 (*see*
  CHESHIRE, 1846).
Guildhall. Salt.

1851

650. HISTORY, GAZETTEER & DIRECTORY OF STAFFORDSHIRE . . .
BY WILLIAM WHITE . . . PRINTED . . . BY ROBERT LEADER
. . . SHEFFIELD . . . 1851.
  809 pp. ; adverts, 810–864 & interspersed ; map. [Misc.
  Tr. ; for smallest places, Gen.]
    $7\frac{1}{8} \times 4\frac{3}{8}''$. Price 12s. 6d. boards, 14s. calf ; non-subsc.
    3s. extra.

Preface dated 28 July 1851. The Staffordshire directories end on p. 798, followed by a list of Birmingham merchants and directories for Dudley, Stourbridge and Halesowen in Worcestershire. There was probably an issue containing pp. 1–798 only, though no copy has been found.
Birmingham. B.M. Guildhall. Manchester. Salt.

BURTON-ON-TRENT
(*See* DERBYSHIRE, 1846, 1852.)

LEEK
(*See* LANCASHIRE, (Whellan), 1854.)

NEWCASTLE-UNDER-LYME

1836

651. COTTRILL'S POLICE DIRECTORY OF . . . NEWCASTLE-UNDER-LYME FOR 1836 . . . NEWCASTLE-UNDER-LYME : PRINTED BY J. BAYLEY.

10 + 74 ; adverts, viii, 16. [Ct. Cm. Tr.]
$7\frac{1}{8} \times 4\frac{3}{8}''$. Blue boards, label.
Preface dated January 1836. Includes a commercial list for part of Stoke-on-Trent. Isaac Cottrill was a police officer. He persuaded the local authorities to repaint the names of the streets and to fix a number to every house. He made a list of inhabitants for his own use as a police officer, from which he compiled this directory. It is an exceptionally full one, including many labourers.
B.M. Salt. A.R.W.

1839

652. [As above but] FOR 1839 . . . PRINTED BY HYDE & CREWE, HIGH STREET. 1839.

xx + 69 ; adverts, 70–74 ; plate, with reference, 2 pp. [Ct. Cm. Tr.]
$7\frac{1}{8} \times 4\frac{3}{8}''$. Green cloth wrappers, label.
Includes part of Stoke-on-Trent.
Guildhall. Salt. A.R.W.

STOKE-ON-TRENT
(*See* NEWCASTLE-UNDER-LYME, 1836, 1839.)

WALSALL
1813

653. THE HISTORY & DIRECTORY OF WALSALL . . . BY THOS. PEARCE. BIRMINGHAM : PRINTED BY THOMSON & WRIGHTSON, NEW STREET . . . 1813.

x + 234 ; plate. [Gen. Tr.]

7¾ × 4⅞″. Printed boards.

On p. 231 is the date 16 January 1813. Pearce was church-warden, constable from 1804–1812, vestry clerk and agent for the Birmingham Fire Office. He says he had twice taken the population of the town for the Census and as there were more than 11,000 inhabitants, he felt encouraged to publish a directory. The book contains some interesting particulars about the arrangements for a police force in Walsall.

B.M. (10360.ee.19). A.R.W.

WEST BROMWICH

1836

654. THE HISTORY & TOPOGRAPHY OF WESTBROMWICH [*sic*] & ITS VICINITY. BY JOSEPH REEVES . . . LONDON : BALDWIN & CRADOCK, PATERNOSTER ROW : PRINTED BY T. DAVIES, WESTBROMWICH.

6 + 176 ; 3 plates. [Gen.]

6⅞ × 4½″. Cloth.

Preface dated 1 December 1836.

B.M. (10350.c.2). A.R.W.

WOLVERHAMPTON

1827

655. DIRECTORY OF WOLVERHAMPTON . . . ALSO . . . BILSTON, WILLENHALL & WEDNESFIELD . . . WOLVERHAMPTON : PRINTED & PUBLISHED BY J. SMART, CHRONICLE OFFICE, HIGH STREET. 1827.

lxviii + 112 ; adverts interspersed ; plan. [Gen ; Tr. also for Wolverhampton.]

6¼ × 4″. Printed boards.

Preface dated March 1827. Joseph Smart was proprietor and publisher of the *Wolverhampton Chronicle*. For an account of him and of his father, *see* G. Mander, *Early Wolverhampton Books & Printers* (1922).

Birmingham. Guildhall. Salt.

1833

656. BRIDGEN'S DIRECTORY OF . . . WOLVERHAMPTON, INCLUDING BILSTON, [etc.] . . . WOLVERHAMPTON : JOSEPH BRIDGEN, DARLINGTON STREET. 1833.

200 pp. [Gen ; Tr. also for Wolverhampton.]

7 × 4⅛″. Green cloth, label.

Guildhall. Salt. A.R.W. Wolverhampton.

1838

657. [Title as 1833 but] 1838.
104 + 78; adverts interspersed. [Gen. Tr. for Wolverhampton; Ct. Tr. for other places.]
7 × 4⅛″. Green cloth, label.
Wolverhampton.

1846. *See* CHESHIRE, 1846.

1847

658. WOLVERHAMPTON POST OFFICE DIRECTORY FOR 1847, INCLUDING BILSTON [etc.] . . . WOLVERHAMPTON: PRINTED FOR THE PROPRIETORS BY J. BRIDGEN.
4 + 146; adverts, 24. [Gen. Also Tr. for all places together.]
7¼ × 4¼″. Green cloth.
This is arranged in the same way as Kelly's Post Office directories. It seems just possible that Kelly & Co. were the unnamed proprietors.
Guildhall. A.R.W.

1849

659. WOLVERHAMPTON DIRECTORY FOR 1849 INCLUDING BILSTON [etc.] . . . WOLVERHAMPTON: PRINTED FOR THE PROPRIETORS BY G. WILLIAMS, TEMPLE STREET.
4 + 194; adverts, 68 & interspersed; plate. [Gen; St. Tr. also for Wolverhampton.]
7¼ × 4¼″. Mauve or green cloth.
Salt. A.R.W.

1851

660. MELVILLE & CO.'S DIRECTORY OF WOLVERHAMPTON, WITH BILSTON [etc.] . . . WORCESTER: PRINTED FOR THE PUBLISHERS BY J. STANLEY, SIDBURY & WYLD'S LANE.
4 + 150; adverts, 160. [Gen; Tr. also for Wolverhampton.]
8¼ × 5⅛″. Price, with map, 10s. 6d.
Preface dated September 1851.
A.R.W.

SUFFOLK

1844

661. HISTORY, GAZETTEER & DIRECTORY OF SUFFOLK & THE TOWNS NEAR ITS BORDERS . . . BY WILLIAM WHITE . . . PRINTED . . . BY R. LEADER . . . SHEFFIELD . . . 1844.
766 pp. [Misc. Tr. for larger, Gen. for smaller places.]
7 × 4″. Price, subsc. 12s. boards, 13s. 6d. calf.

Preface dated 1 February 1844 ; the latest date in the list of additions is 12 December 1843. Includes a few places in Norfolk.

B.M.   Guildhall.

1850.   *See* NORFOLK, 1850.

1855

662. HISTORY, GAZETTEER & DIRECTORY OF SUFFOLK . . . BY WILLIAM WHITE . . . PRINTED . . . BY R. LEADER . . . SHEFFIELD . . . 1855.

    4 + 13–284.   [Misc. Tr. for larger, Gen. for smaller places.] $7\frac{1}{8} \times 4\frac{1}{8}''$.   Price, subsc. 12s. 6d. boards, 14s. calf ; with map mounted, 2s. 6d. extra.

Preface dated 3 January 1855.

Guildhall.   Ipswich.

SURREY

1851

663. W. ARCHDEACON'S DIRECTORY FOR RICHMOND, KEW, TWICKENHAM, KINGSTON, HAMPTON, STAINES, WINDSOR, ETON, EGHAM, WINGFIELD, MAIDENHEAD, COOKHAM, SLOUGH, ETC. . . . LONDON : PRINTED BY CHARLES WRIGHT & CO. ALBION BUILDINGS, BARTHOLOMEW CLOSE, FOR W. ARCH- DEACON. 1851.

    iv + (Richmond),   24 + (Twickenham),   12 + (Kingston), 18 + (blank), 2 + (Hampton, etc. as title), 160 ;   adverts, 42 ;   map.   [Ct. Pr. Cm. ;   St. also for Windsor.] $7\frac{1}{8} \times 4\frac{3}{8}''$.   Red cloth.   Price 4s.

Mr J. L. Douthwaite.

1853.   *See* MIDDLESEX, 1853.

CROYDON

1851

664. A NEW COMMERCIAL & GENERAL DIRECTORY OF . . . CROYDON . . . 1851.   CROYDON : PUBLISHED BY JOHN GRAY, 131 HIGH STREET.

    2 + xxii + 156 ;   adverts, 157–204.   [St. Gen. Tr. Also Ct. for places near.] $7\frac{1}{8} \times 4\frac{1}{8}''$.   Blue cloth.   Price 3s. 6d.

Preface dated 16 June 1851.   John Gray was printer, bookseller and insurance agent and kept a circulating library.   *See also* p. 19 above.

Croydon.   Guildhall.

1853

665. THE COMMERCIAL & GENERAL DIRECTORY OF . . . CROYDON
. . . 1853. [Imprint as 1851.]
xxviii + 192 ; adverts, 193–242. [St. Gen. Tr.   Also Gen.
for places near.]
    Format, price as 1851.   Buff cloth.
    Preface dated 14 March 1853.
Croydon.

1855

666. [Title as 1853 but] 1855.   CROYDON :   PUBLISHED BY GRAY·
& WARREN, 131 HIGH STREET.
xl + 176 ; adverts, 177–242. [St. etc. as 1853.]
    Format, price as 1851.   Red cloth.
    Preface, dated July 1855, says that ' even the three or
four months which have elapsed during the compilation '
have caused a few inaccuracies.
Croydon.

DORKING

1855

667. A HANDBOOK OF DORKING . . . DORKING :   PRINTED &
PUBLISHED BY JOHN ROWE.   LONDON :   G. WILLIS . . .
COVENT GARDEN.   1855.
8 + 156 + 20 ; adverts, 42, 8, 4 ;   map & plates. [Ct.
Cm.]
    7 × 4¾″.   Maroon cloth.
C.U.L.   Guildhall.

EGHAM

(*See* BERKSHIRE, 1846.)

RICHMOND

1824

668. RICHMOND & ITS VICINITY . . . BY JOHN EVANS, LL.D. . . .
RICHMOND :   PRINTED FOR JAMES DARNILL, HILL STREET.
xiv + 2 + 280 ;   3 plates. [Ct. for Ham & Petersham,
135–8.   Pr. St. for Richmond, 152–8, 206–11].
    6 × 3⅝″.
Preface dated 2 August 1824.   Principal private residents
only.   John Evans (1767–1827) was a Baptist minister, an
educationalist and the author of a large number of books,
one of which, *A Sketch of the Denominations of the Christian
World,* went through fourteen editions in his lifetime.   He
also wrote *An Attempt to Account for the Infidelity of Edward
Gibbon,* published in 1797.
B.M. (579.a.30).

1825

669. [Title as above but] Second Edition, Corrected . . .
xxiv + 196 ; map, plate. [Ct. etc. as above.]
6 × 3⅝″. Cloth. Price 4s.
Dedication dated 16 August 1825. In this edition the
directories are collected .together in an Appendix at the
end instead of being scattered through the text.
B.M. (10350.aa.23). Guildhall.

SUSSEX

1831–1833. *See* Kent, 1831–1833.

BRIGHTON

1799

670. The Brighthelmston Directory for 1799. By Edward
Cobby . . . Brighton : Printed by W. & A. Lee.
Published by the Compiler, No. 2, Prince's Place.
viii + 52 ; plan. [Ct. Pr.(alph). Tr.]
8⅛ × 4⅞″. Pink wrappers. Price 2s. 6d.
Plan dated 11 July 1799 ; preface dated 28 August 1799.
This is the second edition ; no copy of the first seems to
be extant. Cobby was a hatter, hosier and undertaker.
W. & A. Lee were printers at Lewes.
Brighton (2 copies).

1800

671. [Title as above but] for 1800.
viii + 52. [Ct. Pr.(alph). Tr.]
Format, price as 1799.
Only pp. 1–8 of the directory, including the court and
professional lists and the first page of the commercial list,
are new. The rest, except for the tide tables, pp. 49–52,
are merely re-issues of the corresponding pages of the 1799
directory. This edition was reprinted in J. G. Bishop,
A Peep into the Past (1880).
Brighton.

1822

672. Brighton Annual Directory & Fashionable Guide. By
T. H. Boore . . . Brighton : Printed for the Publisher
by R. Sicklemore, Jun. Gleaner Office . . .
6 + iv + 120 ; adverts, 2. [Ct. Cm. Tr.]
7 × 4⅛″. Printed wrappers. Price 2s. 6d.
Boore was a law stationer, accountant and debt collector.
Richard Sicklemore's office was at 63 Cavendish St.
Brighton.

673. The Stranger in Brighton & Baxter's New Brighton
Directory . . . Brighton : Printed & Published by
J. Baxter & Co. Directory Office, 21 North Street . . .
Sold also by . . . J. Baxter, High Street, Lewes.
   10 + iii–lxxviii + 6 + 54 ; errata slip paged 53* ; map,
3 plates. [Ct. Tr. St.]
   7¼ × 4¼″. Printed boards. Price 3s., non-subsc. 4s.
Plates dated 20 October 1822. John Baxter (1781–1858)
invented an inking roller for use on printing presses. He
was the father of George Baxter, the colour printer.
Brighton. Guildhall. A.R.W.

1824

674. Baxter's Stranger in Brighton & Directory . . .
Brighton : Printed & Published by the Proprietor &
Sold by . . . J. Baxter, High Street, Lewes . . . 1824.
   10 + iii–lxxxiv + 75–159 + 3 ; plan with index, 2 pp. ;
plate. [Gen. Tr.]
   7¼ × 4⅛″. Printed boards. Price 4s.
The next edition, 1826, has no directory because, according
to the preface, Brighton was changing so fast.
Birmingham. Brighton. B.M. (10347.b.11/1). Guildhall.

1832

675. A New Directory for Brighton for 1832 . . . By T. A.
Swaysland . . . & J. Gill . . . Brighton : Printed
by C. Christopherson, Cavendish Street.
   4 + 104. [Cm. Pr.]
   7⅛ × 4¼″. Printed boards.
Preface dated 13 July 1832. Swaysland was a rate
collector. Gill was an accountant.
Brighton.

1833

676. The Brighton Directory for 1833 . . . Burn, Printer
. . . 23 North Street.
   Re-issue of 1832 with a cancel title.
Brighton.

1839

677. Leppard & Co.'s Brighton Directory for 1839–40 . . .
Brighton : Printed & Sold by William Leppard . . .
   eng. title + 4 + iv + 128 (including 25*–28*) ; adverts,
50. [Ct. Tr.]
   7¾ × 4⅜″. Green cloth.
Preface dated 3 August 1839.
Brighton. Guildhall. A.R.W.

1843

678. LEPPARD & CO.'S BRIGHTON & HOVE DIRECTORY. 1843. [Imprint as 1839 but] EAST STREET.
10 + 20 + 107·; adverts, 108 & 50 pp. [Cm. Ct. Tr.]
7¾ × 4⅜". Blue cloth.
Preface dated 12 May 1843.
Guildhall. A.R.W.

679. [Title as above but] REVISED EDITION.
eng. title + 24 + 118 ; adverts, 72. [Cm. Ct. Tr.]
7¾ × 4⅜". Green cloth.
The adverts are dated July 1843.
Brighton.

1845

680. [Title as 1843 but] 1845–6.
eng. title + 4 + xliv + 150 ; adverts, 50. [Gen. St. Ct. Tr.]
7¾ × 4⅜". Red cloth, gilt, pink end papers.
Preface dated 16 August 1845. The general list gives no occupations. The engraved title, title, address and index are printed in blue and successive sections in black, red, yellow, green and brown. This remarkable harlequin production was no doubt specially designed to attract attention. If so it was unsuccessful for no further editions were published until Leppard's successor tried to revive it in 1854.
Brighton. A.R.W.

1846

681. POST OFFICE BRIGHTON DIRECTORY. 1846. PRINTED & PUBLISHED BY KELLY & CO. . . . LONDON.
190 ; adverts, 191–218. [St. Ct. Cm. Tr.]
6½ × 4½". Red cloth. Price 3s., non-subsc. 4s.
This is not a reprint of the Brighton directory in Kelly's Six Home Counties directory of the previous year. It is an isolated effort on his part for he printed no more separate town directories (except one for Sheffield, 1854) or provincial directories in this format until much later in the century.
Bod. Brighton. B.M. Guildhall.

1848

682. THE COURT GUIDE & GENERAL DIRECTORY FOR BRIGHTON. PUBLISHED BY ROBERT FOLTHORP, 170 NORTH STREET. 1848. [Printers, Stewart & Murray, Old Bailey.]
xxxii + 352 ; adverts, 24. [Ct. Cm. St. Tr.]
6⅜ × 4⅛". Yellow cloth. Price 3s.
This is the first of a remarkable series of directories which, under successive publishers, continued to be published until

1908. Folthorp was a bookseller, printer and insurance agent.
Brighton. A.R.W.

1850

683. [Title as 1848 but] 1850.
title + v–xlviii + 354 ; adverts, 30. [Ct. St. Cm. Tr.]
Format as above.   Red cloth or red leather, yellow edges, yellow end papers.
Brighton. Guildhall. A.R.W.

1852

684. [Title as 1848 but] INCLUDING HOVE . . . 1852.
4 + xl + 378 ; adverts, 30, 8. [Ct. St. Cm. Tr.]
Format, binding as above.   Price, leather, 4s. 6d.
Brighton. A.R.W.

1854

685. FOLTHORP'S COURT DIRECTORY FOR BRIGHTON, INCLUDING HOVE & CLIFTONVILLE. CORRECTED TO APRIL, 1854. PUBLISHED BY R. FOLTHORP, ROYAL LIBRARY, BRIGHTON.
xxiv + 118 ; adverts, 119–36. [Ct. St. (private addresses only).]
Format as above.   Red cloth.
Brighton.

686. THE ORIGINAL BRIGHTON & HOVE DIRECTORY, INCLUDING CLIFTONVILLE. FOURTH ISSUE, JULY, 1854. BRIGHTON : W. J. TAYLOR (LATE LEPPARD), 16 & 17 EAST STREET.
12 + 5–423 ; adverts, 1, 60 ; plan. [St. Ct. Cm. Tr.]
$6\frac{1}{2} \times 3\frac{7}{8}''$.   Green cloth.
The reference in the preface to 1836 as the date of the first edition of Leppard's directory, is evidently a mistake for 1839.
A.R.W.

CHICHESTER
1804

687. THE CHICHESTER GUIDE & DIRECTORY . . . A NEW EDITION. CHICHESTER : PRINTED & PUBLISHED BY J. SEAGRAVE . . .
2 + 70 + 6 ; plate. [St.]
$8\frac{1}{8} \times 4\frac{7}{8}''$.
This is a new edition of *The Chichester Guide* by Alexander Hay, published first in 1783, and in a number of subsequent editions. Hay's *History of Chichester* was published in 1804, which may have suggested the republication of the *Guide*, which also contains an announcement of Hayley's *Triumphs of Music*, published in 1804. There is nothing,

however, to indicate the date of the directory section and
it is possible that there was more than one issue of this
edition of the *Guide* with different editions of the directory.
Bod. Brighton.

HASTINGS

1820

688. HASTINGS GUIDE. SECOND EDITION . . . PUBLISHED BY
P. M. POWELL, LIBRARY, MARINE PARADE, HASTINGS &
LONGMAN, HURST . . . LONDON.
> 94 pp. ; plan, map, plates.
> $7\frac{1}{2} \times 4\frac{1}{4}''$. Blue boards, label.
> The plan is dated 1819, but a reference on p. 79 to ' our
> late beloved sovereign ' indicates that this was published
> after the death of George III. It contains very little
> directory information, but the lists of lodgings on pp. 67–88
> give the occupations of some of the owners (*see* especially
> the list for the High Street on p. 81). The first edition has
> not been found. The third and fourth, n.d. and 1825,
> contain similar information. The fifth edition does not.
> B.M. (10347.b.12/1, also 3rd. & 4th. eds). Guildhall.

1852

689. OSBORNE'S STRANGER'S GUIDE & COMMERCIAL DIRECTORY
TO HASTINGS & ST LEONARD'S FOR 1852. HASTINGS:
PRINTED & SOLD BY H. OSBORNE 55 GEORGE STREET.
> 86 + 2 + 18 ; adverts, 30 ; plan. [Ct. Tr.]
> $6\frac{1}{2} \times 4\frac{1}{4}''$. Blue cloth.
> The next edition, 1854, has only a court & clergy list.
> A.R.W.

WORTHING

1811

690. A SKETCH OF WORTHING . . . TO WHICH IS ADDED A SELEC-
TION OF LUDICROUS POETICAL EFFUSIONS . . . WORTHING:
PRINTED FOR J. MACKCOULL, AT THE APOLLO MUSIC &
CLASSICAL LIBRARY, CHAPEL STREET, WORTHING : & SOLD
BY M. JONES, NEWGATE STREET LONDON. 1811. [Printer,
N. W. Jones. Old Bailey.]
> title + 5–106. [St.]
> $7\frac{1}{8} \times 4\frac{1}{4}''$.
> The directory contains only the principal tradesmen and
> was intended to provide visitors with a choice of whom to
> deal with. The association with Newgate Street and the
> Old Bailey is not fortuitous. John Mackcoull came of a
> poor but disreputable family. His mother, who was known
> as ' Gunpowder ' to her intimates, was particularly adept

at stealing pewter pots from inns.   His three sisters were
also thieves.   His brother Benjamin was hanged for
stealing a watch.   His brother James, also a petty thief
and suspected of murder, was tried for robbing the Paisley
Bank at Glasgow of £20,000.   He was condemned to
death but reprieved and died in gaol shortly after.   John
Mackcoull, who added a talent for forging to the family
accomplishments, kept a disreputable lodging-house in
London.   He retired about 1810 to Worthing, where he
asserted that suspicion and police persecution followed him
and nearly brought him to ruin.   (J. Mackcoull. *Abuses
of Justice*, 1809. *Memoirs of James Mackcoull*, 1822.
Prefaces to later editions of the *Sketch of Worthing*.)   Other
editions of this book have no directory.
B.M. (291.c.12).   Worthing.

1849

691. PHILLIPS HANDBOOK & DIRECTORY OF WORTHING . . .
WORTHING :   JOHN PHILLIPS.   LONDON :   WHITTAKER & CO.
    4 + 84 ;   adverts, 34.   [Gen. St.]
    6¾ × 4¼".   Pink boards.   Price 1s.   Also red leather,
    elaborately gilt, gilt edges.
Undated but adverts dated 1849 and a reference to 1849
in text.   Only the best streets are included.
B.M. (1303.a.24).   Worthing.   A.R.W. (leather bound.)

1850

692. [Title as 1849 but] SECOND EDITION . . . 1850.
    4 + 90 ;   adverts, 40.
    Format as 1849.
Worthing.

WARWICKSHIRE
1830

693. THE HISTORY, TOPOGRAPHY & DIRECTORY OF WARWICKSHIRE
    . . . BY WM. WEST . . . BIRMINGHAM, PRINTED & PUB-
LISHED BY R. WRIGHTSON, ATHENAEUM, NEW STREET . . .
1830.
    xiv + 800 ;   adverts interspersed ;   2 plans, 6 plates.
    [Gen. ; Tr. also for Birmingham.]
    8⅞ × 5½".   Red cloth, label.   Price 30s. ;   L. P. £2 2s.
Pp. 301–488 are a re-issue of Wrightsons's *Annual Directory
of Birmingham*, 1829–30, repaginated.   William West
(1770–1854) was for many years assistant to a London
bookseller.   He then went to Cork, of which place he
compiled a directory which was published in 1810.   He was
still living in Cork when he wrote this history of Warwickshire.   West returned to London in 1837 and became editor
of the *Aldine Magazine* in 1839.   He also wrote *Fifty Years*

Recollections of an Old Bookseller (1830). He died in the Charterhouse.

Birmingham. Bod. B.M. (577.h.29). Warrington.

1850

694. History, Gazetteer & Directory of Warwickshire . . . by Francis White & Co. . . . Printed . . . by John Blurton . . . Sheffield . . . 1850.

xii + 912; adverts, 913–6, 54. [Gen. Tr.]

$8\frac{3}{8} \times 5\frac{3}{8}''$. Price 17s. 6d. cloth, 20s. calf; non-subsc. 3s. 6d. extra.

Preface dated February 1850. The Birmingham section (pp. 1–404) was first issued in 1849 (*see* Birmingham, 1849). It is here brought up to date by eight pages of additions (905–12). Most of the preliminary general history is copied from Bagshaw's directory of Kent, 1847.

Birmingham. Gen. Soc. I.H.R.

1852

695. Slater's Classified Directory of the Manufacturing District Fifteen Miles round Birmingham, including Worcester & The Potteries . . . Manchester: Printed & Published by Isaac Slater . . . & Sold by J. H. Beilby . . . Birmingham.

4 + 9–474; adverts, 2, 50. [Ct. Tr.; Cm. also for Wolverhampton & Potteries.]

$7\frac{1}{8} \times 4\frac{1}{2}''$. Price 8s. 6d. cloth, non-subsc. 11s.

Uniform with Slater's *Birmingham*, 1852. N.d. but Isaac Beck, who is advertised on p. 30 of the adverts as at 19 Paradise St., was living at that address from 1852 to 1854.

Birmingham. B.M. (dated 1850 in catalogue and 1858 in pencil on title).

1855

696. General & Commercial Directory & Topography of . . . Birmingham, including Aston [etc.] . . . with Wolverhampton [etc.] . . . & Dudley & Oldbury . . . by Francis White & Co . . . Printed . . . by S. Harrison, 'The Sheffield Times' Office . . . Sheffield . . . 1855.

4 + 68 + 680; adverts, 116. [Gen. Tr. St. for Birmingham; Misc. Tr. for other places.]

$8\frac{3}{8} \times 5\frac{1}{8}''$. Price 14s. 6d., non-subsc. 3s. 6d. extra.

Preface dated June 1855. Re-issued in 1856 with Coventry and Warwick added.

Birmingham. B.M. Guildhall.

BIRMINGHAM

A full account of Birmingham directories is to be found in B. Walker, 'Birmingham Directories' (*Birm. Arch. Soc. Trans.*,

lviii for 1934, pub. 1937), from which much of the information below
is derived.

1763 and 1764

697, 698. Unfortunately no copies are known of either of these
directories. They were both by James Sketchley, who
began his career as a printer and publisher at Tamworth.
He moved in 1759 to Birmingham, where he carried on
business as a printer, bookseller, state lottery and estate
agent and auctioneer. He also ran a pawnbroking business
and a servants' registry office. For some years he lived in
Bristol, where his chief work was as an auctioneer. He
published a directory of this town in 1775. He returned
to Birmingham in 1780 and died in America in 1801. He
seems to have been the pioneer of provincial directories,
his being, so far as we know, the first directory of any
place in England outside London. He was apparently
inspired by T. Mortimer's *Universal Director*, a directory
of London for 1763, for the introduction to his 1767 directory
(which no doubt is much the same as that to the 1763
edition) contains phrases taken straight from the introduction to Mortimer's book. He was evidently impressed
by the need for providing commercial information about
Birmingham in London for he advertised his first directory
in the *London Chronicle* for 14–16 July 1763. Samuel
Sketchley, who was concerned in James Sketchley's 1770
directory and who was then living in Birmingham, also
published a directory of Sheffield in 1774 with T. Sketchley
of Hull. He is there described as ' of Bristol ', to which
town James Sketchley had also gone. Both Samuel and
T. Sketchley, like James, were auctioneers. They must all
have been one family, perhaps father and sons.

1767

699. SKETCHLEY'S BIRMINGHAM, WOLVERHAMPTON & WALSALL
DIRECTORY . . . THIRD EDITION . . . PRINTED BY & FOR
J. SKETCHLEY . . . MD, DCC, LXVII [*sic*].
2 + ii + 116. [Pr. Tr.]
5¾ × 3½″. Price 1s. 6d.
Pp. 113–14 are misnumbered 11 and 106. *See also* p. 7
above.
Birmingham.

1770

700. SKETCHLEY & ADAMS'S TRADESMAN'S TRUE GUIDE : OR AN
UNIVERSAL DIRECTORY FOR . . . BIRMINGHAM, WOLVER-
HAMPTON, WALSALL, DUDLEY & THE VILLAGES IN THE
NEIGHBOURHOOD . . . BIRMINGHAM : PRINTED BY & FOR
J. SKETCHLEY, AT No. 61, O. ADAMS, No. 83 IN HIGH STREET ;
& S. SKETCHLEY, No. 74 IN BULL STREET. 1770.

122 pp. [Pr. Tr. for Birmingham ; Cm. for other places.]
$7\frac{7}{8} \times 4\frac{7}{8}''$.

Pagination 75–6 is repeated. The Wolverhampton section
was reprinted as a supplement to *The Wolverhampton
Antiquary*, 1925. The preface to this reprint says there
are notable omissions. The whole was reprinted in an
adapted and re-arranged form as *The Streets & Inhabitants
of Birmingham* ; ed. R. B. Prosser ; preface by S. Timmins,
1886. There is a copy of this reprint in the B.M.
(10352.d.24).

Birmingham. Birm. Assay Office.

1773

701. THE NEW BIRMINGHAM DIRECTORY & GENTLEMAN & TRADES-
MAN'S COMPLEAT MEMORANDUM BOOK . . . PRINTED BY &
FOR M. SWINNEY, AT No. 76 IN HIGH STREET . . .

h.t., title + 84 (unnumbered) + 50 (blank ruled pp.) ;
plate. [Cm.]
$6\frac{5}{8} \times 4''$. Red leather. Price 2s.

The date 1772 is mentioned in the preface and the book
was advertised in *Aris's Birmingham Gazette* on 15 March
1773. It is printed in Baskerville type. Swinney, who
was a type founder, is said to have acquired some of
Baskerville's matrices. He died in 1812, aged seventy-
four. *See* J. Hill, *Bookmakers of Old Birmingham* (1907).

Birmingham (2 copies, one without h.t., the other lacking
title and some pages). Bod. (without blank pages).

1776

702. SWINNEY'S BIRMINGHAM DIRECTORY : OR GENTLEMAN'S &
TRADESMAN'S COMPLETE GUIDE . . . BIRMINGHAM : PRINTED
BY M. SWINNEY AT No. 76 IN HIGH STREET . . .

10 + 13–20 + 76 (unnumbered) ; plate. [Cm.]
$6\frac{1}{4} \times 3\frac{3}{4}''$.

The list of names is dated 1775–6. The Birmingham copy,
the only one known, is made up partly of leaves from the
1773 edition and partly of new leaves with revised entries.
It may be a made-up copy but it is quite likely that this
is how the book was published. It is not mentioned by
Walker.

Birmingham.

1777

703. THE BIRMINGHAM DIRECTORY : OR MERCHANT & TRADES-
MAN'S USEFUL COMPANION ; BIRMINGHAM : PRINTED &
SOLD BY PEARSON & ROLLASON . . . 1777.

xxxvi + 64 ; plate. [Cm.]

704. [Another issue.] xxviii + 64 (with addenda on p. 55);
plate.
>   6 × 4". Price 1s. 6d.
>   This was advertised in *Aris's Gazette* on 8 September 1777.
>   Three weeks later it was re-advertised, with a request for
>   corrections and the book was then re-issued with the
>   addenda. The second issue was reprinted in 1896 with
>   the title *Birmingham 120 Years Ago*, ed. C. E. Scarse.
>   There was also a reprint in 1890 of which the Birmingham
>   P.L. has a copy bound with some interesting newspaper
>   cuttings.
>   Birmingham (both issues). Bod. (2nd issue).

1780

705. THE BIRMINGHAM, WOLVERHAMPTON, WALSALL, DUDLEY,
BILSTON & WILLENHALL DIRECTORY . . . BIRMINGHAM:
PRINTED & SOLD BY PEARSON & ROLLASON . . . 1780.
>   xxxvi + 128; plate. [Cm; Tr. also for Birmingham.]
>   6¼ × 3¾". Wrappers. Price 1s. 6d.
>   Advertised in *Aris's Gazette* on 2 October 1780 but may
>   have been published earlier in the year. Pp. xix/xx are
>   a cancel.
>   Birmingham. Bod. Guildhall. Salt (2 copies, one in
>   wrappers, uncut, with the original pp. xix/xx).

1781

706. [Re-issue of 1780, with cancel title dated 1781.]
Birmingham. B.M. Salt.

1783

707. [Swinney's directory. No copy known. Advertised in *Aris's
Gazette* on 26 May 1783.]

1785

708. A NEW DIRECTORY FOR . . . BIRMINGHAM & . . . DERITEND
. . . BY CHARLES PYE, BIRMINGHAM: PRINTED . . . BY
PEARSON & ROLLASON. 1785.
>   iv + 100; plan. [Cm.]
>   6½ × 3¾".
>   Survey taken by personal application according to the title.
>   Charles Pye worked successively as watchmaker, wine
>   merchant and collector of taxes, besides being a printer
>   and engraver. He filled in time between these occupations
>   by compiling directories. Though dogged, according to
>   his own account, by piracies, he continued to publish them
>   till 1800 but his attitude about entries became more and
>   more casual. In 1791 he took ' the liberty of abridging
>   the titles of a great many who informed me that the

directory was of no use ' and proposed to charge for more
than one insertion.   In 1800 he gave up a personal canvass
and advertised by handbill and in the newspapers, asking
for entries, for which he charged 6*d*. each.   ' If this directory
be incomplete ', he said in the handbill, ' the fault must
remain with the inhabitants.'   This method of proceeding
not proving a success, he published no more directories.
He also wrote *Provincial Copper Coins & Tokens* (1795), a
Dictionary of Ancient Geography (1820) and *A Description
of Modern Birmingham* (1820), republished in 1825 as *The
Stranger's Guide to Modern Birmingham*.   He had two sons,
John and Charles, both engravers. (Walker, *op. cit.*;
W. Longman, *Tokens of the Eighteenth Century* (1916);
prefaces to Pye's directories; and *D.N.B.*, under John
Pye.)
Birmingham.

1787

709. THE BIRMINGHAM DIRECTORY FOR . . . 1787. CORRECTED
TO THE FIRST OF AUGUST. BY CHARLES PYE. BIRMINGHAM :
PRINTED BY PEARSON & ROLLASON FOR THE COMPILER &
SOLD BY HIM IN CHEAPSIDE . . .
iv + 108.   [Cm. Tr.]
$6\frac{1}{2} \times 4''$.   Price 2*s*., with plan 2*s*. 6*d*.
Pye says in his 1791 directory that the sale of his last
publication was injured by a ' spurious directory, published
immediately after '.   There is no directory extant to which
this can refer but perhaps he meant a Birmingham section
of Bailey's *General Directory of England & Wales*, of which
the only surviving part is that for Bristol & Bath (*see*
BRISTOL, 1787.)
Birmingham.

1788

710. [Re-issue of 1787 with new title, dated 1788 and 13 additional
names on p. iv.]
Birmingham.

1791

711. PYE'S BIRMINGHAM DIRECTORY.   1791.
vi + 102.   [Cm. Tr.]
$6\frac{3}{4} \times 3\frac{7}{8}''$.   Price 2*s*., with plan 2*s*. 6*d*.
Engraved title with no imprint.
Birmingham.   A.R.W.

1792

712. [The New Birmingham Directory for 1792.   John Ward.]
No copy known but re-issued in 1798, *q.v.*   Not mentioned
by Walker.   It is a reprint from the same setting of type,

repaged, of the Birmingham section of *The Universal British Directory* (*see* No. 13, above), with the corrections on p. 250 incorporated. Pye complained that the Birmingham directory in the *U.B.D.* was a copy of his 1791 directory and quite out of date (*see* p. 34 above).

1797

713. PYE'S BIRMINGHAM DIRECTORY FOR . . . 1797 . . . SOLD BY ALL THE BOOKSELLERS IN THE TOWN & BY W. RICHARDSON . . . LONDON.

viii + 100. [Cm. Tr.]
6 × 4″. Price 2s. ; with plan, 2s. 6d.
See p. 19 above.
Birmingham. Bod.

1798

714. THE NEW BIRMINGHAM DIRECTORY FOR 1798 . . . BIRMINGHAM : PRINTED FOR & SOLD BY J. WARD, No. 13 HILL STREET.

2 + 5–54 ; adverts, 4. [Ct. Tr.]
8½ × 5″. Price 1s.
This is Ward's 1792 directory (No. 712), re-issued with an '8' stamped over the original '2'. Not mentioned by Walker. In the only known copy, the pagination of gatherings F and G (37–44 and 45–52) are transposed but the text follows consecutively.
Birmingham.

1800

715. THE BIRMINGHAM DIRECTORY FOR . . . 1800 . . . ARRANGED BY CHARLES PYE. BIRMINGHAM : PRINTED AT T. A. PEARSON'S PRINTING OFFICE, HIGH STREET . . .

16 pp. [Cm.]
6 × 4″. Price 2s. ; with plan, 2s. 6d.
Preface dated 17 March 1800. The handbill in which Pye asked for entries (quoted in full above, p. 17) is dated 4 March 1800. *See also* No. 708 above.
Bod. Walker mentions a copy, with plan dated 1795.

716. A POETIC SURVEY ROUND BIRMINGHAM . . . BY J. BISSET . . . ACCOMPANIED BY A MAGNIFICENT DIRECTORY . . . ENGRAVED IN EMBLEMATIC PLATES. PRINTED . . . BY SWINNEY & HAWKINS, HIGH STREET.

viii + 9–40 + 4 ; 24 plates, lettered A–X & 3 numbered 1–3 ; 45–62 + 2 ; plan. [Cm.]
8¾ × 5⅜″. Price 6s. ; with proof plates, 10s. 6d. ; coloured 21s. ; printed in colours £2 2s.
Fly-title to plates dated 1 January 1800. The directories consist of lists of names engraved against views of parts of

Birmingham or emblematic backgrounds. There are a few plates for single firms. The Birmingham P.L. has a note of an order for a copy in colours, but no coloured copy has been found and perhaps none was ever really issued ; even the presentation copy to the King is in black and white. Bisset says that he advertised for entries by advertisements and handbills. He seems to have at first charged 10s. 6d. for entries, or free insertion if the plate was ordered. Later entries seem to have been free. The first advertisement he mentions is one dated 16 July 1799 and entries were accepted up to the end of November. The Birmingham Assay Office has a letter, dated 30 July 1799, from Bisset to Matthew Boulton, enclosing a handbill and prospectus of this directory. *See also* No. 20 (Bisset's *Grand National Directory*) in the National section above, where there is a further note on Bisset.

Birmingham (5 copies). Birm. Assay Office (presentation copy to Matthew Boulton). Bod. B.M. (992.i.5/2 and 289.i.24, presentation copy to the King, large paper, specially bound in red morocco with black calf inlaid panel, pink silk end papers, accompanied by a letter from Bisset, dated 22 April 1800). A.R.W.

717. CHAPMAN'S BIRMINGHAM DIRECTORY . . . BIRMINGHAM : PRINTED BY T. CHAPMAN, No. 76 IN BULL STREET.
   4 + 134 (including 110*–113*). [Gen. Tr.]
   7 × 4¾". Price 2s. 6d.

Advertised, ' now published ', in *Aris's Gazette* on 23 June 1800. Chapman said in an announcement in *Aris's* on 24 March, that every householder would be personally visited, no charge would be made for entries and no self-interested motive would induce him ' to spurn at or leave out the poorest Artist or Mechanic '.

Birmingham. Birm. Assay Office (in orig. wrappers). Guildhall.

Other editions, with similar title but with relevant date, as follows :

1801. **718.** Re-issue of above, with new title, list of officials, etc., viii pp., without pp. 110*–113*, and with an Appendix (adds), 10 pp. Birmingham. B.M. (without Appendix).

1803. **719.** 4 + 140. [Gen. Tr.] Birmingham. Guildhall.

1805. **720.** Re-issue of 1803, with new title and six additional names instead of nine on p. 4 of first sheet, which has been reset. A.R.W.

1808. **721.** CHAPMAN'S ANNUAL DIRECTORY OF BIRMINGHAM & ITS VICINITY. 4 + 132. [Gen.] A plan could be had, bound with the book or separately, for 6d. Birmingham (without plan).

722. BISSET'S MAGNIFICENT GUIDE OR GRAND COPPERPLATE
DIRECTORY FOR . . . BIRMINGHAM . . . IN ELEGANT &
EMBLEMATIC ENGRAVINGS . . . BY J. BISSET . . . PRINTED
. . . BY R. JABET, HERALD OFFICE . . . 1808.

> eng. title + viii + 8 + 8 plates numbered I–VIII, 24
> numbered A–X & 19 numbered 1–14, XV, 16, xvii, 18, 19 ;
> plan. [Cm.]
>> $8\frac{3}{4} \times 5\frac{3}{8}''$. Printed boards or cloth. Price 5s., with
>> proof plates 10s. 6d.
>
> Publication announced in *Aris's Gazette* on 25 April 1808.
> Eng. title dated 1 May 1808. Plates A–X and 1–3 are the
> same as in Bisset's 1800 directory. The others are new
> and include changes bringing some of the 1800 information
> up to date.
> Birmingham (3 copies). Birm. Assay Office. B.M.
> (10352.h.32).

723. NEW TRIENNIAL DIRECTORY OF BIRMINGHAM . . . BIRMING-
HAM : PRINTED & PUBLISHED BY THOMSON & WRIGHTSON
. . . NEW STREET . . . 1808.

> 2 + iv + 160 ; slip (adds) pasted at foot of p. 159 ; adverts
> interspersed. [Gen. Tr.]
>> $6\frac{3}{4} \times 4\frac{1}{4}''$. Green wrappers. Price 3s.
>
> Preface dated 14 November 1808. Apologies for delay in
> publication, with a slighting reference to Chapman's
> directory, were published in *Aris's Gazette* on 31 October.
> The contents were apparently confined to merchants,
> tradesmen and *respectable* inhabitants. The 'superb plates'
> mentioned on the title are engraved advertisements, of
> which there are a number of particularly fine ones in all
> Wrightson's directories.
> Birmingham (2 copies, one impf). B.M.

Robert Wrightson's directory continued to appear every two or
three years. His partnership with Lewis Thomson was dissolved
in 1813 and he carried on the directory alone. A rival issue in
1823, published by several Birmingham booksellers, among them
his old partner, Thomson, only made one appearance, but in 1829
and 1830, Henry Beilby, another Birmingham bookseller, in conjunction with James Pigot, made a raid on his territory and the
directory was at a low ebb until in 1831, or soon after, Wrightson
was joined by Wareing Webb. They continued to publish the
directory until 1847. In that year the business was taken over by
James Bell, under the name of Wrightson & Bell. He sponsored
a directory by Henry Shalders in 1854. Wrightson's directories
will now be listed in a summarised form, with changes in title,
contents or format from the 1808 edition noted. The trades
directory continued to cover only selected trades. The interleaved
engraved advertisements are a feature of all editions until 1831.
Some of the gaps in the series may be due to no copy for that
year having survived. Other Birmingham directories, including
Shalders' will be listed after the Wrightson series.

1812. **724.** 6 (including 3 blanks) + iv + 170 + 2 (blank).

1815. **725.** iv + 196 ; plate.

1818. **726.** iv + 198 ; plan.   4s. sewed, 5s. half bound, 6s. with plan.

1821. **727.** iv + 230.

1823. **728.** 6 (2 leaves adverts) + x + 184 + 64 (selected trades for places round) ; plan. Published in August.

1825. **729.** 2 + xii + 194 + 68.

1829. **730.** WRIGHTSON'S ANNUAL DIRECTORY . . . 2 + 188. No directories for places round. $8\frac{5}{8} \times 5\frac{1}{8}''$. Also issued in West's *History . . . of Warwickshire* (1830), pp. 301–488 (*see* WARWICKSHIRE, 1830) and, with the same pagination, a new title and one less name in the adds. list, as WRIGHTSON'S ANNUAL DIRECTORY . . . 1831.

1831. **730a.** *See* above.

1833. **731.** THE DIRECTORY OF BIRMINGHAM . . . WRIGHTSON & WEBB . . . viii + 142.

1835. **732.** 196 pp. (unnumbered) ; map. Tr. very brief. Said to be compiled by Robert Lunn (*see Birmingham Daily Post*, 9 November 1870).

1839. **733.** 228 ; adverts, 8 ; plan. 6s. or 6s. 6d. with plan.

1842. **734.** 162 ; adverts, 163–70. N.d. but advertised in *Aris's Gazette* on 26 December 1842.

1847. **735.** xii + 3–190 ; plan. N.d. but advertised in the *Midland Counties Herald* on 25 March 1847.

Copies may be found as follows ; Birmingham (1812–1847). B.M. (1815). Guildhall (1815, 21, 35, 39, 47). A.R.W. (1815, 21 (impf), 23, 35, 39, 47 (2 copies, one dated 1842 in ink on cover)).

1823

736. WARD & PRICE'S NEW BIRMINGHAM DIRECTORY . . . BIRMINGHAM : PRINTED BY WARD & PRICE, 61 & 62 LOVE-DAY STREET & PUBLISHED BY J. BUTTERWORTH, T. WOOD & J. BELCHER, HIGH STREET, W. HODGETTS, SPICEAL STREET ; L. THOMPSON, TEMPLE ROW & W. COOPER, UNION STREET. 1823.

vi + 188 + 72 ; adverts interspersed. [Cm. Tr. Also manufacturers in towns round.]
$6\frac{3}{8} \times 3\frac{5}{8}''$.

Advertised in *Aris's Gazette* on 7 July 1823. It was violently attacked by Wrightson in the same paper, in an advertisement of his own directory. The names in the two directories do not precisely correspond.

Birmingham. A.R.W.

1829

737. PIGOT & CO.'S COMMERCIAL DIRECTORY OF BIRMINGHAM & ITS ENVIRONS . . . PUBLISHED NOVEMBER, 1829 BY J. PIGOT

& Co . . . & Sold by them & Messrs Beilby, Knott &
Beilby, Birmingham.
    iv + 130 (including 23½ & 24½) + 14 ; adverts. [Cm. Ct.
Tr. Also Tr. for places round.]
    9¼ × 5½″. Pink cloth, green label. Price 6s. 6d.
The contents vary from those in the corresponding
directories in Pigot's *National Commercial Directory For
1828–9* (No. 47 above). The binding is also quite unlike
the usual binding of Pigot's directories, though the size is
the same.
Birmingham. Salt.

1830

738. Pigot & Co.'s Commercial Directories of Birmingham,
Worcester & their Environs . . . Published May, 1830
. . . [imprint as 1829].
    iv + 142 + 24 ; adverts. Re-issue of 1829 with Upton-
on-Severn and Worcester added. Price 7s. 6d.
The additional section contains more names than the
corresponding directories in Pigot's *National Commercial
Directory for 1828–9* (No. 47 above).
Birmingham. A.R.W.

1839

739. Robson's Birmingham & Sheffield Directory . . .
[Birmingham, Coventry, Dudley, Wolverhampton & environs,
Sheffield & environs]. William Robson & Co., 4 Cloak
Lane, Cheapside . . .
    6 + viii + 66 + 201–294 + 395–834 ; adverts, 12 + 117–
156 ; map. [Cm. Tr ; St. also for Birmingham & Sheffield.]
    9⅜ × 5¾″. Red cloth, green label. Price 12s. 6d., non-
subsc. 15s.
Dated 1839 on label.
Birmingham. Gen. Soc. (with Robson's London directory,
1839). Manchester. A.R.W.

1842

740. Pigot's New & Complete Directory of Birmingham &
its Environs . . . Birmingham : James Henry Beilby,
64 New Street. London : J. Pigot & Co . . .
    4 + 16 + 9–220 + 26 ; adverts, 8, 70 ; map. [Ct. Cm.
Tr. for Birmingham ; Misc. Tr. for places round.]
    9¼ × 5½″. Price 7s. 6d.
This was advertised in the *Midland Counties Herald* on
15 December 1842 but it is a re-issue, repaged, of the
corresponding directories in Pigot's *Royal National Commercial Directory of Warwickshire, etc.*, December 1841
(No. 71 above).
Birmingham.

1849

741. HISTORY & GENERAL DIRECTORY OF . . . BIRMINGHAM . . .
BY FRANCIS WHITE & CO. . . . PRINTED FOR THE AUTHORS
BY JOHN BLURTON . . . SHEFFIELD . . . 1849.
  2 + v–viii + 2 + 404 ; adverts, 54. [Gen ; Tr. also for
Birmingham.]
  $8\frac{3}{8} \times 5\frac{3}{8}''$.   Price 9s. boards, 11s. calf, non-subsc. 2s. 6d.
extra.
Preface dated 20 April, 1849.   Includes villages round.
Birmingham.   Guildhall.

1852

742. SLATER'S GENERAL & CLASSIFIED DIRECTORY OF BIRMINGHAM
& ITS VICINITIES FOR 1852–3 . . . MANCHESTER : PRINTED
& PUBLISHED BY ISAAC SLATER . . . AND SOLD BY J. H.
BEILBY, BIRMINGHAM.
  420 + 218 ; adverts, 4, 112 & interspersed.   [Ct. Tr.]
  $7\frac{1}{2} \times 4\frac{1}{2}''$.   Price 7s. 6d., non-subsc. 9s.
Preface dated September 1852.   The format is different
from that of Slater's national directories.   For another
Slater-Beilby directory *see* WARWICKSHIRE, 1852.
Birmingham.   Guildhall.

1853

743. THE EDGBASTON DIRECTORY & GUIDE FOR 1853 . . .
BIRMINGHAM : PUBLISHED BY WM. JOESBURY, ASTON STREET
& W. H. HOWE, NEW STREET.   1853.
  (adverts), 12 + 36 ; adverts, 13–36 & interspersed.   [St.
Gen.   No occupations in either list.]
  $8 \times 5\frac{1}{4}''$.   Bright blue wrappers, gilt.
Birmingham.

1854

744. SHALDERS' BIRMINGHAM DIRECTORY.   1854 . . . BIRMING-
HAM : WRIGHTSON & BELL, 8 NEW STREET & MAY BE HAD
OF THE PROPRIETORS, 110 VYSE STREET.
  20 + 5–68 + 340 (unpaged).   [Ct. Tr.]
  $7\frac{1}{4} \times 4\frac{1}{2}''$.   Price 2s. 6d.
Dedication signed Henry Shalders.   A shoddy production
on bad paper, largely taken up with advertisements, some
whole-page and included in pagination, some inserted
among text.
Birmingham.   A.R.W.

COVENTRY

1850

745. LASCELLES & CO.'S DIRECTORY & GAZETTEER OF . . .
COVENTRY & NEIGHBOURHOOD . . . COVENTRY : PRINTED

FOR THE PUBLISHERS BY DAVID LEWIN, HERTFORD STREET.
1850.
    150 ; adverts, 58 ; map. [Ct. Tr.]
      8¼ × 5½″. Red cloth. Price, subsc. 4s. 6d., with map 6s.
    Preface dated May 1850.
Birmingham. B.M.

EDGBASTON
(See BIRMINGHAM, 1853.)

KENILWORTH
(See LEAMINGTON, 1846.)

LEAMINGTON
1829

746. MONCRIEFF'S GUIDE TO LEAMINGTON SPA . . . FOURTH
EDITION, REVISED & CORRECTED TO THE SUMMER OF 1829.
LEAMINGTON : PUBLISHED BY J. MERRIDEW AT HIS LIBRARY,
29 BATH STREET . . . 1829.
    90 ; adverts, 8 ; 14 plates. [Tr.]
      6¾ × 4⅛″. Green cloth, label. Price 4s. or without
plates, stitched, 2s.
Preface dated July 1829. Earlier editions of *Moncrieff's
Guide* have no proper directory. In this edition the
directory is headed ' J. Merridew's Leamington Directory
(from Actual Survey) . . .'
Leamington. A.R.W.

1830

747. [title as above but] FIFTH EDITION . . . CORRECTED TO THE
SUMMER OF 1830 . . . 34 BATH STREET . . . 1830.
    94 ; adverts, 2 pp. & interspersed ; plates, map, plan.
[Tr.]
      7⅛ × 4⅛″. Green cloth, label.
Preface, dated September 1830, says the directory is
corrected to September and made from an actual survey.
B.M. (10352.aaa.40). Guildhall. Leamington.

1832

748. [*New Leamington Guide.* John Fairfax. 1832. First edition.
With a directory ? No copy found.]

1833

749. SECOND EDITION. FAIRFAX'S NEW GUIDE & DIRECTORY TO
LEAMINGTON SPA . . . LEAMINGTON : PRINTED & PUB-
LISHED BY JOHN FAIRFAX, GLOCESTER STREET . . . 1833.
    168 ; adverts, 12 & some eng. ; map. [Ct. Tr.]
      6½ × 3⅞″. Stiff printed wrappers. Price 2s.

Taken by actual survey in August 1833. John Fairfax
(1804–77) was a leading member of the Leamington Con-
gregationalists. He was bankrupted by the costs of a
libel suit (which he won) and in 1838 he emigrated to
Australia, where he prospered. In 1851 he re-visited
England and paid off all the debts which he had left in
Leamington on his departure. For three years before his
death he was a member of the New South Wales legislative
council. (*D.N.B.*)
Guildhall. Leamington.

750. MONCRIEFF'S GUIDE TO LEAMINGTON SPA . . . CORRECTED
TO JULY, 1833 . . . LEAMINGTON & WARWICK : PRINTED
& PUBLISHED BY JOHN MERRIDEW, HIGH STREET & CASTLE
STREET, WARWICK . . . 1833.
    112 ; adverts, 6 ; 11 plates, map, plan ; slip (addenda to
    guide). [Tr.]
        7¼ × 4¼″. Printed wrappers or printed boards or cloth
        with label. Price, cloth with plates, 4s. 6d.
    Also issued without plates ; also bound with other of
    Merridew's *Guides*.
Birmingham (wrappers, plates & slip). Bod. B.M.
(10352.bb.49, boards with plates). Leamington. A.R.W.
(cloth).

1835

751. THIRD EDITION. FAIRFAX'S NEW GUIDE [etc. as Fairfax,
1833] . . . JOHN FAIRFAX, BATH STREET . . . 1835.
    182 ; adverts, 4 ; map. [Ct. Tr.]
        6½ × 3¾″.
Preface dated May 1835. The directory survey was taken
in March.
Bod. Leamington.

1837

752. MERRIDEW'S IMPROVED EDITION OF MONCRIEFF'S . . . GUIDE
TO LEAMINGTON SPA . . . SEVENTH EDITION. [Imprint as
Merridew, 1833.] 1837.
    120 ; adverts, 10 ; plate, map. [Tr.]
        6¼ × 3¾″. Wrappers. Price 2s.
B.M. (10351.aaa.31). Leamington. A.R.W.

1838

753. FOURTH EDITION. FAIRFAX'S GUIDE, DIRECTORY &
ALMANACH TO LEAMINGTON SPA . . . FOR 1838 . . . [Imprint
as 1835.]
    viii + 8 + 196 ; adverts, 24 & some eng. ; map. [Ct. Tr.]
        6½ × 4″. Printed wrappers. Price 2s. 6d.
A.R.W.

Beck's *Leamington Guide*, editions from 1840 onwards, said on the title to contain a directory, only has brief professional lists.

1846

754. WILLIAMS'S GUIDE & DIRECTORY OF ROYAL LEAMINGTON SPA, WARWICK, [etc.] . . . BIRMINGHAM : PUBLISHED BY J. WILLIAMS . . . 1846.

4 + (adverts), 88 + (Leamington & villages), 48, 12 + (Warwick), 14 + (Kenilworth), 4 + (Liverpool), 52 + (Chester), 18, 54, 16 + (Wrexham), 16 + (Welshpool), 6 + (Llanidloes and Newtown), 12 + 4. [Gen ; Tr. also for Leamington & Chester ; St. for Chester. Tr. only for Liverpool.]

$7\frac{1}{8} \times 4\frac{1}{8}''$.

Chester & Wrexham were also published in Williams's *Chester, etc.*, (*see* CHESHIRE, 1846).

Leamington.

1849

755. A DIRECTORY OF ROYAL LEAMINGTON SPA. LEAMINGTON : PRINTED & PUBLISHED BY T. S. DEWHIRST, 27 LOWER UNION PARADE. 1849.

119 ; adverts, 9. [Gen. Tr.]

$6 \times 3\frac{3}{4}''$.

Leamington.

WARWICK

(*See* LEAMINGTON, 1846.)

WESTMORLAND

(*See also* CUMBERLAND, Lake District.)

1829. *See* CUMBERLAND, 1829.

1849

756. HISTORY, TOPOGRAPHY & DIRECTORY OF WESTMORLAND & LONSDALE BY P. J. MANNEX . . . BEVERLEY : PRINTED FOR THE AUTHOR BY W. B. JOHNSON, MARKET PLACE. 1849.

465 ; adverts, 3. [Gen ; Tr. also for larger places.]

$8\frac{1}{2} \times 5\frac{1}{8}''$. Price 15*s*. 6*d*., non-subsc. £1 ; maps 3*s*. 6*d*.

For Mannex *see* CUMBERLAND, 1847.

Carlisle. Chetham. A.R.W.

1851

757. [*History & Directory of Westmorland*. Mannex & Co. 1851.] No copy found.

WINDERMERE
(See also CUMBERLAND, Lake District.)

1854

758. GUIDE TO WINDERMERE . . . BY MISS HARRIET MARTINEAU
. . . WINDERMERE : JOHN GARNETT. LONDON : WHIT·
TAKER & CO. [Printer, John Garnett.]
2 + ii + 3–103 ; adverts, p. 104, xvi ; 7 plates, map.
[Gen. for places on or near Lake Windermere.]
6½ × 4″. Purple cloth. Price 1s.
Reviewed in the *Westmorland Gazette* on 15 July 1854.
For John Garnett, *see* CUMBERLAND, Lake District, 1855.
Bod. B.M. (10351.b.21). C.U.L.

759. [Title as above but] SECOND EDITION . . .
2 + ii + 3–110 ; 7 plates, map. [Gen.]
6⅜ × 4″. Blue printed wrappers. Price 1s.
The B.M. copy was acquired on 27 November 1854. It
contains a few more names than the first edition. There
was a third edition, *c.* 1856. The fourth, *c.* 1858, has no
directory.
Bod. B.M. (10351.b.28). C.U.L.

ISLE OF WIGHT
(See ISLANDS.)

WILTSHIRE
1848

760. HUNT & CO.'S DIRECTORY . . . FOR . . . BATH, BRISTOL &
WELLS [with Bradford, Chippenham & other places in Wilts
& Somerset] . . . MAY, 1848. PRINTED FOR E. HUNT &
CO. BY B. W. GARDINER . . . LONDON.
viii + 138 + 190 + 132 ; adverts, 30. [Ct. Tr ; Cm. also
for Bath.]
7 × 4″. Green cloth. Price 9s.
The Bristol section is parts of Hunt's Bristol directory
repaged (*see* BRISTOL, 1848). Wells is Bristol Hot Wells
and not Wells in Somerset.
Bath. Bristol.

1851. *See* DORSETSHIRE, 1851.
1854. *See* SOMERSET, 1854.

CRICKLADE
(See CIRENCESTER, 1847.)

SALISBURY
(*See* HAMPSHIRE, 1852.)

SWINDON
(*See* CIRENCESTER, 1847.)

WARMINSTER
1834

761. [*The Warminster Directory & Almanach.* Journal Office. Warminster.] The 1894 edition is said in E. H. Goddard, *Wiltshire Bibliography* (1929), to be the sixtieth issue. No early editions have been found.

WORCESTERSHIRE

(For places near Birmingham *see also* Warwickshire and Birmingham directories.)

1820

762. WORCESTERSHIRE GENERAL & COMMERCIAL DIRECTORY FOR 1820. PART FIRST . . . COMPILED BY S. LEWIS, LOWES-MOOR, WORCESTER. STOURBRIDGE : PRINTED FOR THE PROPRIETOR BY J. HEMING . . . [Pt. II] . . . WORCESTER : PRINTED & PUBLISHED . . . BY T. EATON.

[Pt. I] 200 ; advert, 2. [Gen. Tr.]

[Pt. II] 6 + 207–498 ; adverts, 499–500, 4 and interspersed ; map. [Gen. Tr.]

$6\frac{1}{8} \times 3\frac{3}{4}''$. Printed boards. Price per vol., 5*s*. boards, 6*s*. bound.

The trade directories are numbered by columns, two to a page.

Birmingham (boards, with map). Guildhall. Kidderminster. Worcester.

1840

[Bentley's History, etc. of Worcestershire.]

This directory was issued in seven parts, each complete in itself and bound separately. The Worcester volume, Pt. VI, of which the preface is dated January 1840, was issued first, followed by Pts. II and III, and the last part, Pt. VII, the history of Worcestershire, was issued some time after June 1841. Pts. II, III and VI were published in a collected volume and re-published with additions for 1841. The remaining parts were also published in one volume and sold in sets with Vol. I. Finally Pts. I and II were issued, with additions, as *Bentley's History, etc., of the Midland Mining District.* Each part is described separately below in the

order in which they are found in the bound volumes.
Different issues of the parts are to be found in different
copies of the bound volumes and the lists of copies will
indicate which issues each contains.

The size is $7\frac{1}{4} \times 4\frac{3}{8}''$ and the parts are uniformly bound in
patterned olive green cloth, with the title gilt on spine.
The collected volumes were bound in calf.

763. [Pt. II.] BENTLEY'S HISTORY & GUIDE TO DUDLEY . . .
SECOND VOLUME OF BENTLEY'S HISTORY, DIRECTORY &
STATISTICS OF WORCESTERSHIRE. BIRMINGHAM : PRINTED
. . . BY BULL & TURNER, 27 UPPER TEMPLE STREET . . .
   4 + (Dudley), 13–140 + (Tipton), 141–176 ; adverts, 229–
   240, 4 pp. & interspersed ; plan. [Gen. Tr.]
This was also issued without Tipton and, another issue,
with Dudley Port (no copy found). The I.H.R. copy is
peculiar. It contains an altogether remarkable quantity
of misprints and is inscribed ' Hubert Allen, Birmingham,
from Josiah, Feby. 1850 as a sample of printing '. *See
also Bentley's Midland & Mining District*, 1841, below.
I.H.R.   Salt.

764. [Pt. III.] [As above] OF EVESHAM . . . PERSHORE [& other
places] IN THE COUNTY SOUTH . . . OF WORCESTER . . .
VOL III OF BENTLEY'S HISTORY [etc. as above. Imprint
as above].
   viii + 13–164 ; adverts, 165–8. [Gen. Tr.]
765. [Another issue.] With 2 pp. after p. viii and 12 pp., adds.
for 1841.
Rev. Chas. Hutchinson (1st. issue). For 2nd issue *see* copies
of the collected Vol. I, below.

766. [Pt. VI.] [As above] OF . . . WORCESTER . . . [and] FOUR-
TEEN NEIGHBOURING PARISHES . . . VI VOL. OF BENTLEY'S
HISTORY [etc. as above. Imprint as above].
   xii + 13–228 ; adverts, 229–42, 10 & interspersed ; plan.
   [Gen ; Tr. also for Worcester.]
767. [Another issue] 2 + 12 (adds. to Pt. VII for 1841) + 13–192,
   as first issue + 28 (St. for Worcester & adds) + 193–228,
   as first issue ; adverts, 229–42.
No separate copies found. *See* copies of the collected Vol. I
below.

768. [Vol. I.] BENTLEY'S HISTORY, GAZETTEER, DIRECTORY &
STATISTICS OF WORCESTERSHIRE . . . VOL. I. BIRMINGHAM :
PRINTED FOR THE PROPRIETOR, JOSEPH BENTLEY . . . &

SOLD BY W. S. ORR & CO. LONDON.   [Printers, Bull & Turner, Birmingham.]
    Containing Pts. II, III, VI, each with separate title.
C.U.L. (no title, Pt. II to p. 140, Pt. III, 2nd issue, Pt. VI, 2nd issue).   I.H.R. (Pt. II to p. 140, Pts. III & VI, 1st issues).   A.R.W. (same as I.H.R.)

769. [Pt. I.] BENTLEY'S . . . DIRECTORY OF BROMSGROVE . . . [and other places] IN THE EASTERN PART OF THE COUNTY . . . VOL. I OF BENTLEY'S HISTORY [etc. as Pt. II.   Imprint as Pt. II].
    136 pp.   [Gen ; Tr. also for towns.]
770. [Another issue.]   With pp. 137–142 (adds. for 1841).
A.R.W. (with Pt. VI, both 1st issues).   For second issue *see* second collected volume below.

771. [Pt. IV.] [As above] OF KIDDERMINSTER . . . [and other places] IN THE WESTERN PART OF THE COUNTY, . . . VOL. IV OF BENTLEY'S HISTORY [etc. as Pt. II.   Imprint as Pt. II].
    140 pp.   [Gen ; Tr. also for towns.]
No separate copy found.   *See* second collected volume below.

772. [Pt. V.] [As above] OF STOURBRIDGE & [other places in] THE NORTH PART OF THE COUNTY . . . VOL. IV OF BENTLEY'S HISTORY [etc. as Pt. II.   Imprint as Pt. II].
    69 pp. ; adverts, 70–72.   [Gen ; Tr. also for towns.]
No separate copy found.   *See* second collected volume below.

773. [Pt. VII.] BENTLEY'S ANCIENT & MODERN HISTORY OF WORCESTERSHIRE . . . VOL. VII OF BENTLEY'S HISTORY [etc. as Pt. II.   Imprint as Pt. II].
    156 + 137–180 ; table.   [Ct. for the county.]
774. [Another issue.]   With 12 pp. adds to Pt. III as in Pt. III, second issue and 12 pp. adds. to Pt. VII + 28 pp., St. and adds. for Worcester as in Pt. VI, second issue.   With 12 pp. adverts.
B.M. (010358.n.29, 1st issue).   *See also* second collected volume below.

775. [Vol. II.] [Title as Vol. I but Vol. II and Bull & Turner's name in imprint].
    Containing Pts. I, IV, V, VII each with separate title.
C.U.L. (Pt. I 1st issue, Pt. VII 2nd issue).   A.R.W. (Pt. I, 2nd issue, Pt. VII, 1st issue).

Joseph Bentley wrote an account of his early life (J. Bentley, *Gems of Biography* (1856).   Copy ; B.M., C.O.c.1), according to which his parents were weavers and he was sent to work weaving at the age of seven.   He taught himself to read while at work and acquired the rest of his education in scraps and pieces.   He investigated the Manchester Sunday Schools in 1833 and becoming interested in the connection between education, or the lack of it, and crime, he collected a number of statistics about school attendances and the educational record of criminals. He was employed by Pigot & Son in compiling their National Commercial directories between 1832 and 1838 and this enabled him to travel over the country, collecting his own statistics as well as theirs. His results were published by Pigot & Son in 1838 under the title *The State of Education Contrasted with the State of Crime.* He hoped by the sale of his Worcestershire directory and other publications to finance further research on these lines. He published *Education as It Is, Ought To Be and Might Be,* in 1842 and a long list of other books on educational and financial topics. He also worked as a schoolmaster and used to describe himself as ' the oldest school inspector '. (*See* preface to his directory and his other works.)

1841

776. BENTLEY'S HISTORY, GAZETTEER & DIRECTORY OF THE MIDLAND MINING DISTRICT . . . [imprint as 1840].
　　4 + 142 + 4 + 13–260 ; adverts, 88 ; plan.
　　7¼ × 4⅛″. Olive green cloth. Price 6s.
A re-issue, with new title, of Bentley's *Worcestershire*, Pt. I, Bromsgrove, 2nd issue and Pt. II, Dudley, with pp. 177–260, West Bromwich and other places added.
A.R.W.

1847. *See* HEREFORDSHIRE, 1847.
1851. *See* STAFFORDSHIRE, 1851.

1855

777. M. BILLING'S DIRECTORY . . . OF THE COUNTY OF WORCESTER . . . BIRMINGHAM : M. BILLING'S STEAM-PRESS OFFICES, LIVERY STREET. 1855.
　　8 + iv + 420 ; adverts, iv, 120. [Gen ; Tr. also for larger places.]
　　8½ × 5¼″. Cloth.
Birmingham. B.M. Kidderminster. Worcester.

UPTON-ON-SEVERN
(*See* BIRMINGHAM, 1830.)

WORCESTER
1788

778. THE WORCESTER DIRECTORY. WORCESTER : PRINTED & SOLD BY JOHN GRUNDY, FRIAR'S STREET . . . 1788.
　　xxvi + 48. [Pr. Gen.]
　　7¼ × 4½″.
The professional list in all of Grundy's directories includes names for the county.
Bod. B.M. A.R.W.

1790

779. THE WORCESTER ROYAL DIRECTORY . . . [imprint as 1788]
. . . 1790.
    96 pp. [Pr. Gen.]
    $7\frac{1}{2} \times 4\frac{1}{8}''$. Boards, label.
Worcester.

1792

780. [Title, imprint as 1790] FOR 1792.
    88 pp. [Pr. Gen.] Size as 1790.
Bod. B.M. Worcester.

1794

781. [Title, imprint as 1790) FOR 1794.
    96 pp. ; plate. [Pr. Gen.] Size as 1790.
Birmingham. Gen. Soc. Worcester. A.R.W.

1797

782. THE WORCESTER GUIDE & WORCESTER ROYAL DIRECTORY
    . . . [imprint as 1790] . . . 1797.
    152 pp. [Pr. Gen.] Size as 1790.
    The contents of this directory were reprinted in *The
    Universal British Directory* (*see* No. 18 above), with the
    adds. on p. 48 incorporated and with some additional
    matter.
B.M. (10368.d.13). Worcester. A.R.W.

1830. *See* BIRMINGHAM, 1830.

1837

783. GUIDE & DIRECTORY TO . . . WORCESTER FOR 1837 . . .
WORCESTER : T. STRATFORD, PRINTER, THE CROSS.
    xii + 210 ; adverts, 14 & interspersed ; plate, map. [Tr.]
    $7\frac{1}{8} \times 4\frac{3}{8}''$. Blue or brown cloth, label. Price 4s.
Birmingham (2 copies, one without appendix). Guildhall.
Worcester. A.R.W.

1840

784. HAYWOOD'S DIRECTORY OF . . . WORCESTER . . . FOR . . .
1840 . . . R. HAYWOOD, PRINTER, 8 HIGH STREET,
WORCESTER.
    82 ; adverts, 22 & interspersed. [Pr. Tr.]
    $7\frac{1}{8} \times 4\frac{1}{8}''$.
    The printer reckoned to sell 500 copies and if he did, to
    continue annually.
Worcester.

1851

785. LASCELLES & CO.'S DIRECTORY . . . OF WORCESTER & NEIGHBOURHOOD . . . WORCESTER : PRINTED . . . BY J. STANLEY, SIDBURY PLACE & WYLD'S LANE. 1851.

4 + 152 ; adverts, 100. [Ct. Cm. Tr. for Worcester ; Gen. for villages.]

$8\frac{1}{2} \times 5\frac{1}{4}''$. Red cloth.

Preface dated January 1851.

Guildhall. A.R.W.

1852. *See* WARWICKSHIRE, 1852.

YORKSHIRE

1822–1823

786. HISTORY, DIRECTORY & GAZETTEER OF THE COUNTY OF YORK . . . BY EDWARD BAINES. THE DIRECTORY DEPARTMENT BY W. PARSON . . . VOL. I. WEST RIDING . . . PRINTED & PUBLISHED BY EDWARD BAINES AT THE LEEDS MERCURY OFFICE . . . 1822.

20 + xii + 13–654 (599 follows 588) + cxliv. [Gen ; Tr. also for most places. Short Tr. for London, Birmingham & other towns.]

$7 \times 3\frac{5}{8}''$. Price 7s. 6d. sheep, 8s. 6d. calf, non-subsc. 10s. 6d. or 11s. 6d.

Dedication dated 1 January 1822. The directories exclude labourers and those only connected with trades arising from the sale of their own produce. There are two issues of the 4 pp. adds. before p. i ; (*a*) having the mayors of Leeds, Doncaster, etc. for 1822 on p. [4] and (*b*) having the corporation of Leeds for 1822 on p. [4].

B.M. (579.c.34). I.H.R. (with adds. *b*). Liv. Ath. A.R.W.

[Vol. II.] [Title as above but] VOL. II. EAST & NORTH RIDINGS . . . 1823.

16 + 654 + 2. [Gen. etc. as Vol. I.]

Size, price as Vol. I.

There are two issues of the adds. pp. 1–4 : (*a*) ending with a correction of the note about Chantrey's birthplace on p. 288 of Vol. I and (*b*) ending with the Sheriffs of York for 1823 and a note on Pontefract sessions. The 2 pp., adds., at the end include the mayor of York for 1823–4, the High Sheriff, appointed 1 February 1823 and additions to Vol. I.

Birmingham (adds. *b*). B.M. (579.c.35). I.H.R. (adds. *b*). A.R.W. (2 copies, adds. *a* & *b*).

787. [Another edition.] [Vol. I. Title as above.]

16 + xii + 13–654 + cxliv.

Size, price as above.

The adds. in the first edition are here incorporated in the text (*e.g.* the corporation of Leeds is for 1822–3 instead of

for 1821–2) as well as most of those from pp. 1–4 of Vol. II,
issue (a) of the first edition.
Birmingham.   I.H.R. (lacking title).

787a. [Another issue.]   No prices printed on title and with
additional pages, 655–672, covering more places.
Liv. Ath.

787b. [Vol. II.]   [Title as above.]   Some of the information is
brought up to date (e.g. mayor of York is Thomas Smith,
who was mayor 1823–4).   There are no adds. at the end
and pp. 1–4 are adds. issue (a) of the first edition.
Liv. Ath.

There are a number of other copies of this directory available,
for instance at Halifax, Huddersfield, Leeds, Warrington and York,
but the precise issues have not been ascertained.   The variations
are confusing and it is possible that some copies differ slightly
from those described above.

1830

788. DIRECTORY OF . . . LEEDS . . . YORK & THE CLOTHING
DISTRICT OF YORKSHIRE [Wakefield, Dewsbury, Huddersfield,
etc. and villages] . . . BY WM. PARSON & WM. WHITE . . .
LEEDS: PRINTED . . . BY EDWARD BAINES & SON; &
SOLD AT THE DIRECTORY OFFICE, 44 HUNSLET LANE . . .
1830.
530 + xxiv; plan with slip (advert. of a larger plan).
[Tr. with Gen. for larger, Misc. for smaller places.]
$7\frac{1}{8} \times 4\frac{1}{8}''$. Red leather. Price 6s. 6d., non-subsc. 7s. 6d.
Preface dated 23 February. A second volume to contain
Annals and other historical matter was announced but it
was never published. See also p. 19 above.
Bod. B.M. Halifax. Huddersfield. Leeds. York.

1831

789. DIRECTORY, GUIDE & ANNALS OF KINGSTON-UPON-HULL,
SCARBOROUGH, [etc.] . . . & THE TOWNS & PORTS CONNECTED
WITH THE RIVERS HUMBER, OUSE & TRENT . . . BY WM.
WHITE . . . SHEFFIELD: PRINTED BY R. LEADER, ANGEL
STREET . . . 1831.
2 + vii–lxxii + 352. [Tr. with Gen. for Hull, Misc. for
other places.]
$7 \times 4''$. Price, subsc. 6s. sheep, 7s. calf.
I.H.R. Hull. Scarborough. A.R.W.

1837–1838

790. HISTORY, GAZETTEER & DIRECTORY OF THE WEST RIDING
OF YORKSHIRE, WITH . . . YORK & . . . HULL . . . BY

WILLIAM WHITE . . . VOL. I. PRINTED . . . BY ROBERT
LEADER . . . SHEFFIELD . . . 1837.

> xii + 732 ; adverts, 16. [Gen. or Misc ; Tr.]
> $7\frac{1}{8} \times 4\frac{1}{8}''$. Price 8s. 6d. cloth, 10s. calf, non-subsc. 1s. 6d.
> extra.
> Preface dated 14 August 1837.

[Vol. II.] [Title as above but] 1838.

> 860 ; adverts, 2. [Gen. etc. as Vol. I.]
> Size, price as Vol. I.
> On p. 10 is the date 24 October 1838.

791. There is also an issue which, instead of adds. for Leeds, etc.
pp. 853–9, has adds. for Sheffield, 853–5. These include
an alteration dated early in 1839.
Gen. Soc. (856 pp.). Guildhall (8 pp.). Huddersfield (860
pp.). I.H.R. (860 pp.). Salt (856 pp.). A.R.W. (860 pp.).
Also, issue unidentified, Halifax, Hull, Leeds.

The Sheffield and Hull, York sections were also issued
separately, as no doubt were the other parts though only
copies of the two former have been found.

792. *Sheffield.* HISTORY & GENERAL DIRECTORY OF SHEFFIELD
[with places round] . . . PART FIRST OF THE HISTORY [etc.]
OF THE WEST RIDING . . . [imprint as above]. 1837.

> iv + 322. Price 5s. 6d. cloth, 6s. 6d. calf, non-subsc.
> 1s. extra.

Sheffield.

793. *Hull.* HISTORY & GENERAL DIRECTORY OF . . . KINGSTON-
UPON-HULL & . . . YORK [etc. as above but] PART FOURTH
. . . 1838.

> 4 + 541–756. Price 5s. 6d. cloth, 6s. 6d. calf, with map
> 1s. extra.

Hull. A.R.W.

1840

794. HISTORY, GAZETTEER & DIRECTORY OF THE EAST & NORTH
RIDINGS OF YORKSHIRE . . . BY WILLIAM WHITE . . .
[imprint as 1837] . . . 1840.

> 720 pp. [Gen. or Misc ; Tr.]
> $7\frac{1}{8} \times 4\frac{1}{8}''$. Price, subsc. 10s. 6d. cloth, 12s. 6d. calf with
> map. With vols. for 1837–8, 30s.
> Preface dated 13 April 1840.

795. [Another issue.] [Title as above.]

> 804 ; adverts, 4. Directories for Hull & York added.

Guildhall (720 pp.). Huddersfield (720 pp.). Hull. I.H.R.
(804 pp.). Leeds. Salt (804 pp.). A.R.W. (804 pp.).

1842

796. DIRECTORY & TOPOGRAPHY OF . . . LEEDS & . . . THE
CLOTHING DISTRICT OF . . . YORKSHIRE [Bradford, Halifax,

etc.] . . . BY WILLIAM WHITE . . . PRINTED BY ROBERT
LEADER . . . PUBLISHED IN NOVEMBER 1842.
    514 ; adverts, 2. [Gen. or Misc ; Tr.]
    $7\frac{1}{8} \times 4\frac{1}{8}''$. Price 6s. 6d., non-subsc. 7s. 6d.
The adds. (pp. 513–14) correct the Leeds directory to
November 1842.
B.M. Guildhall. Halifax. Leeds.

1843

797. [Title as 1842 but with additional towns] . . . 1843.
    538 pp. Re-issue of 1842 with pp. 515–38 covering more
places.
Halifax. Leeds.

1844

798. WILLIAMS & CO.'S DIRECTORY OF THE TOWNS & VILLAGES
WITHIN 22 MILES OF . . . YORK. HULL : PRINTED BY
W. H. SMITH, 203 QUEEN STREET.
    4 + 9–220. [Ct. Tr.]
    $8\frac{1}{4} \times 5\frac{1}{4}''$. Leather, gilt.
The inscription on the cover says ' of York & towns within
22 miles ' but York is not included. There is a Williams'
directory of York, 1843, but it is not in the same format.
Guildhall. Halifax. A.R.W.

1846

799. GENERAL DIRECTORY OF KINGSTON-UPON-HULL & . . . YORK,
WITH . . . SCARBOROUGH [& other towns & villages] IN THE
EAST RIDING . . . BY F. WHITE & CO . . . PRINTED . . .
BY J. BLURTON . . . & SOLD BY F. WHITE & CO. 54 HERMIT-
AGE STREET, SHEFFIELD . . . 1846.
    540 ; adverts, 22. [Gen. St. Tr. for Hull ; Misc. Tr. for
other places.]
    $7 \times 4\frac{1}{4}''$. Price, subsc, 7s. 6d.
Preface dated 2 January 1846.
B.M. Grimsby. Guildhall. Hull. A.R.W. York.

1847

800. DIRECTORY & TOPOGRAPHY OF LEEDS, BRADFORD [etc.] &
THE . . . CLOTHING DISTRICTS OF THE WEST RIDING . . . BY
WILLIAM WHITE . . . PRINTED BY ROBERT LEADER . . .
1847.
    564 ; adverts, 144. [Gen. or Misc. Tr.]
    $7\frac{1}{4} \times 4\frac{1}{4}''$. Price 7s. 6d., non-subsc. 8s. 6d., map 1s.
Preface dated 1 July 1847.
B.M. Guildhall. Halifax. Huddersfield. Leeds. A.R.W.
See NORTHUMBERLAND, 1847.

1851

801. GENERAL DIRECTORY & TOPOGRAPY OF KINGSTON-UPON-
    HULL & . . . YORK [with Beverley, Bridlington, etc.] . . .
    BY FRANCIS WHITE & CO. . . . PRINTED . . . BY JOHN
    BLURTON . . . SHEFFIELD. 1851.
        6 + 3–808 ; adverts, 48. [Gen. or Misc ; Tr ; St. also for
    larger places.]
        7 × 4". Price 8s. 6d., non-subsc. 3s. 6d. extra.
    Preface dated April 1851.
802. [Another issue.] [Title as above but with LINCOLN, BOSTON,
    etc. added.]
        1001 ; adverts, 5.
        Price 12s. 6d., non-subsc. 3s. 6d. extra.
    Contains places in Lincolnshire, pp. 809–920 and more
    places in Yorkshire, 921–1001. Preface dated November
    1851.
    B.M. (Nov.). Hull A.R.W. (April). York.

1852

803. GAZETTEER & GENERAL DIRECTORY OF SHEFFIELD & . . .
    WITHIN . . . TWENTY MILES ROUND . . . BY WILLIAM
    WHITE . . . PRINTED BY ROBERT LEADER . . . SHEFFIELD.
    1852.
        603 ; adverts, 604–12, 144 & interspersed. [Gen. Tr ; St.
    also for Sheffield.]
        7⅛ × 4⅛". Price, subsc. 8s. 6d.
    Preface dated 1 May 1852.
    Guildhall. Halifax. Sheffield. A.R.W.

1853

804. DIRECTORY & GAZETTEER OF LEEDS . . . & THE . . .
    CLOTHING DISTRICTS OF . . . YORKSHIRE . . . BY WILLIAM
    WHITE . . . PRINTED BY ROBERT LEADER . . . 1853.
        4 + 2 + 5–8 + 2 + 9–720 ; adverts, 132. [Gen. Tr ; St.
    also for Sheffield.]
        7⅛ × 4⅛". Price, subsc, with map & plan, 10s.
    Preface dated 15 August 1853.
    Guildhall. Halifax. Huddersfield. Leeds. A.R.W.

805. [Separate issue of Leeds section] WHITE'S NEW DIRECTORY
    OF . . . LEEDS, WITH WAKEFIELD [etc.] . . . PART ONE OF
    THE . . . DIRECTORY OF THE YORKSHIRE CLOTHING DISTRICTS
    . . . [imprint as above]. 1853.
        6 + 3–4 + 9–408 ; adverts, 130.
        Price, with plan, 5s. 6d., non-subsc. 6s. 6d.
    Re-issue, with new title and index and without preface or
    the adds. on next page, of first part of above.
    A.R.W.

1854

806. DIRECTORY OF LEEDS, BRADFORD [etc.] . . . IN THE YORK-
SHIRE CLOTHING DISTRICTS . . . [imprint as 1853]. 1854.
8 + 13–788.
Price, subsc, with map & plan, 10s.
Re-issue of 1853 without the preface or the adds. which are
not incorporated, and with some places added.
I.H.R. Leeds U.L. (impf).

1855

807. MELVILLE & CO.'S DIRECTORY & GAZETTEER OF . . .
KINGSTON-UPON-HULL, BEVERLEY [and other places] . . .
HULL : WM. KIRK, PRINTER . . . LOWGATE. 1855.
4 + 204 ; adverts, c. 140 pp. [Ct. Cm. Tr. for Hull ; Gen.
for other places.]
$8\frac{1}{3} \times 5\frac{1}{4}''$. Red cloth.
Preface dated May 1855.
Hull.

808. [Another issue.] [Title as above but YORK added before
KINGSTON-UPON-HULL and no imprint.] 1855.
4 + 245. Re-issue of above with York added.
Price, non-subsc, with a map, 10s.
Preface dated November 1855.
York.

809. B. H. GILLBANKS & CO.'S VISITORS' & RESIDENTS' DIRECTORY
& GAZETTEER OF SCARBOROUGH, WHITBY [and other watering-
places on the Yorkshire coast] . . . HULL : WILLIAM KIRK,
PRINTER, 53 LOWGATE. 1855.
4 + 80 ; adverts, 64. [Ct. Tr. for larger, Gen. for smaller
places.]
$8\frac{1}{8} \times 5\frac{1}{8}''$. Red cloth.
Preface dated September 1855.
Scarborough. A.R.W.

BEVERLEY

(*See* Hull directories.)

BRADFORD

1845

810. IBBETSON'S DIRECTORY OF . . . BRADFORD . . . BRADFORD :
PRINTED & PUBLISHED BY J. IBBETSON, BRIDGE STREET.
1845.
2 + xviii + 160 ; adverts, 32, 4. [Gen. Tr.]
$7 \times 4''$.
Guildhall. Halifax. Manchester. A.R.W.

1850

811. IBBETSON'S GENERAL & CLASSIFIED DIRECTORY . . . OF BRADFORD . . . BRADFORD: PRINTED & PUBLISHED BY JAMES IBBETSON . . . 1850.

4 + xvi + 284 ; adverts, 20 ; plan. [Gen. Tr.]

7 × 4″. Price, 5s. 6d. cloth, 6s. 6d. leather, non-subsc. 1s. extra.

Preface dated January 1850.

I.H.R.

DEWSBURY

(*See* HUDDERSFIELD, 1850.)

HALIFAX

1845

812. WALKER'S DIRECTORY OF . . . HALIFAX . . . HALIFAX: J. U. WALKER, GUARDIAN OFFICE, GEORGE STREET. 1845.

4 + 188 ; adverts, 20. [Gen. Tr; also Gen. for neighbouring villages.]

7 × 4⅛″. Roan.

Preface, dated 7 April 1845, says this is the first directory of Halifax.

B.M. Halifax.

1850

813. DIRECTORY OF HALIFAX, HUDDERSFIELD, HOLMFIRTH & ADJACENT VILLAGES. 1850. BRADFORD: PRINTED BY DANIEL BURTON, 16 IVEGATE.

2 + 118 + 26 ; adverts, 10. [Gen ; Tr. also for Halifax & Huddersfield.]

7 × 4⅛″. Roan.

B.M. (10358.bbb.53). Halifax.

HUDDERSFIELD

The Huddersfield directory in *The Commercial Directory For 1818-19-20* (No. 31 above) was reprinted, with title *Our Ancestors, or, Huddersfield Sixty-two Years Ago*, by T. W. Taylor, King St., Huddersfield, in 1880, price 1d. There is a copy of this reprint in the Huddersfield Public Library.

1845

814. WILLIAMS'S DIRECTORY OF . . . HUDDERSFIELD . . . LONDON: PRINTED FOR J. WILLIAMS. SOLD BY F. G. LANCASHIRE, 17 MARKET PLACE ; & W. DEWHURST, 38 NEW

STREET, HUDDERSFIELD. 1845. [Printer, J. Rider, 14
Bartholomew Close, London.]
(adverts), 28 + 8 + 102. [Gen. Tr. for Huddersfield;
Gen. for adjacent villages.]
7¼ × 4⅛″. Roan.
Huddersfield. I.H.R.

1850

See HALIFAX, 1850.

815. CHARLTON & CO.'S DIRECTORY OF HUDDERSFIELD, LEEDS,
DEWSBURY & THE ADJACENT VILLAGES. 1850. LEEDS:
PRINTED FOR THE PROPRIETORS BY D. I. ROEBUCK, 14 BANK
STREET . . .
(adverts), 22 + 4 + 118 + 520; adverts, 18; plan of
Leeds. [Gen. St. for Huddersfield; Tr. for Huddersfield
& district; same arrangement for Leeds & for Dewsbury.]
7⅛ × 4″.
Preface dated February 1850. The Leeds section is dated
1849 and is a re-issue, without the adds., of Charlton &
Archdeacon's directory of Leeds, 1849–50 (*see* LEEDS, 1849).
Huddersfield.

HULL

1791

816. BATTLE'S HULL DIRECTORY FOR . . . 1791 . . . TO WHICH
IS ADDED A DIRECTORY FOR BEVERLEY . . . HULL: PRINTED
BY J. & W. RAWSON FOR THE EDITOR & SOLD BY HIM AT
HIS HOUSE IN MANOR ALLEY.
88 pp. [Gen.]
7 × 4″.
Dedication dated 19 July 1791. Robert Gray Battle
describes himself in successive directories as editor, bookseller, newspaper distributor and, from 1814, as ink and
blacking manufacturer. He advertised the quality of his
ink by signing his name in it on the label of his directories.
A competitor describes him in 1803 as a hawker. This
directory was used for the Hull and Beverley sections of
The Universal British Directory. The Beverley section,
which includes some of the 1792 additions (*see* below), was
published in Part 24, which appeared in 1792 (No. 13).
The Hull section is in Part 39, which was not published
until late in 1793 (No. 15). *See also* p. 18 above.
B.M. (T.882/3). Hull.

1792

817. BATTLE'S APPENDIX TO THE HULL & BEVERLEY DIRECTORY
FOR . . . 1792 . . . HULL: PRINTED BY D. INNES & A.
GRAY FOR THE EDITOR . . .
134 pp.; adverts, 2. [Adds.]
7 × 4″.

The title is ambiguous but it is the Appendix which is ' for 1792 '. There was no edition of the directory for that year. The 1791 directory, with the Appendix, was reprinted by M. C. Peck & Son in 1885. I.H.R. has a copy of the reprint.

Hull (bound with the 1791 directory, which lacks title and iii–viii).

1803

818. BATTLE'S ORIGINAL HULL DIRECTORY FOR . . . 1803 . . . COWLEY, PRINTER, HULL, CORNER OF BOWLALLEY LANE, LOWGATE . . .

　142 ; adverts, 143–4. [Gen.]
　　$6\frac{3}{8} \times 3\frac{3}{4}''$.
　Preface dated 30 June 1803.
　Hull.

819. THE MERCHANT'S & TRADESMAN'S DIRECTORY FOR . . . KINGSTON-UPON-HULL . . . PRINTED & SOLD BY T. CLAYTON AT THE GENERAL PRINTING OFFICE, 26 CHURCH LANE. HULL . . . 1803.

　4 + 72. [Gen.]
　　$6\frac{1}{2} \times 3\frac{5}{8}''$. Price 1s. 6d.
　Preface dated 4 July 1803. The publisher makes a determined attack on Battle, saying in the preface that he has not himself taken twelve years to compile his materials. Battle's address is given as Fiendly Square, with the following curious footnote : ' The above place was known as Fearnley's Entry prior to Mr B.'s residence in it . . .' There are more names in Battle's directory but not all of those in Clayton's.
　Chetham. Hull (without title, bound with Battle, 1803).

1806

820. BATTLE'S HULL DIRECTORY FOR . . . 1806–7 . . . HULL : PRINTED BY W. RAWSON, LOWGATE. SOLD BY R. G. BATTLE, 16 PARADISE PLACE.

　xii + 144. [Gen.]
　　$6\frac{1}{2} \times 3\frac{7}{8}''$.
　Preface dated 1 September 1806.
　Guildhall. Hull. A.R.W.

1810

821. BATTLE'S HULL DIRECTORY FOR . . . 1810–11 . . . HULL : PRINTED BY M. W. CARROLL, ROCKINGHAM OFFICE, BOWL-ALLEY LANE . . .

　xii + 160. [Cm.]
　　$6\frac{1}{2} \times 3\frac{7}{8}''$.
　Preface dated 1 September 1810.
　Hull. A.R.W.

1814

822. BATTLE'S HULL & BEVERLEY DIRECTORY FOR . . . 1814–15
. . . HULL : PRINTED BY WILLIAM RAWSON, LOWGATE . . .
184 pp. [Gen.]
$6\frac{7}{8} \times 3\frac{7}{8}''$. Printed label. Price 4s. 6d.
The Hull list is headed 1814 and the Beverley list, 1815.
The label is an advertisement of Battle's inks.
B.M. Guildhall. Hull. A.R.W.

1818

823. BATTLE'S NEW DIRECTORY FOR KINGSTON-UPON-HULL . . .
SIXTH EDITION . . . HULL : PRINTED BY TOPPING &
RAWSON, LOWGATE . . .
xii + 156. [Gen.]
$6\frac{5}{8} \times 4\frac{1}{8}''$. Boards, printed label. Price 4s.
Dated 1818 from the name of the mayor.
Hull. A.R.W.

1821

824. [Title as above but] SEVENTH EDITION . . . PRINTED BY
THOMAS TOPPING, 47 LOWGATE . . .
xii + 156. [Gen.]
$6\frac{5}{8} \times 4\frac{1}{8}''$. Roan, printed label. Price 5s.
Preface dated October 1821. 'For 1822' on label.
Hull. I.H.R. A.R.W.

1826

825. THE DIRECTORY, GUIDE & ANNALS OF KINGSTON-UPON-HULL
. . . [with] NEIGHBOURING TOWNS & VILLAGES IN LINCOLN-
SHIRE & YORKSHIRE . . . BY WILLIAM WHITE & CO.
EDITED BY WILLIAM PARSON. LEEDS : PRINTED BY
EDWARD BAINES . . . 1826.
lxxxiv + 278. [Gen ; Tr. also for Hull.]
$6\frac{7}{8} \times 4''$. Price, 5s. 6d. sheep, 6s. 6d. calf, non-subsc.
8s. 6d. calf.
Also issued with Lincolnshire, 1826, q.v.
B.M. Chetham. Hull.

1835

826. A NEW TRIENNIAL DIRECTORY & GUIDE OF KINGSTON-UPON-
HULL . . . COMPILED BY JOHN CRAGGS, JUN. HULL :
PRINTED FOR JOHN CRAGGS, SILVER STREET, BY GEORGE
LEE, ROCKINGHAM OFFICE, BOWLALLEY LANE . . . 1835.
iv + 69 + iii + 176 (including 4 pp. numbered 163*) ;
notice pasted inside front cover, errata pasted inside back
cover, plan, 5 adverts interspersed. [Gen.]
$7 \times 4''$. Green cloth.

Preface dated 8 October 1835. The book was re-issued, with a new title page and without directory, in 1836.
Guildhall. Hull. A.R.W.

1838

See YORKSHIRE, 1837–1838.

827. THE DIRECTORY OF KINGSTON-UPON-HULL. HULL : PRINTED & PUBLISHED BY JOSEPH NOBLE . . . 23 MARKET PLACE. 1838.
　　xvi + 248. [Gen. Tr.]
　　$7\frac{3}{8} \times 4''$. Boards, label.
Guildhall. Hull.

1839

828. THE DIRECTORY OF . . . KINGSTON-UPON-HULL . . . BY WILLIAM PURDON. HULL : PRINTED BY WILLIAM PURDON, 49 MARKET PLACE . . . 1839.
　　2 + xx + 16 + 270 ; adverts, 8 & interspersed ; plan, 4 plates. [Tr. Gen.]
　　$6\frac{7}{8} \times 4\frac{1}{8}''$.
Hull. I.H.R. A.R.W.

1842

829. STEPHENSON'S DIRECTORY OF KINGSTON-UPON-HULL & ITS ENVIRONS . . . HULL : WILLIAM STEPHENSON . . . 51 LOWGATE.
　　(adverts), 2, 92 + 306 ; plan. [Gen. St. Tr.]
　　$8\frac{1}{8} \times 3\frac{1}{2}''$. Calf, black label.
Preface dated 11 October 1842.
Guildhall. Hull. A.R.W.

1848

830. [Title as above but] 1848.
　　(adverts), 68 + 398 ; addenda slip between 312/3. [Gen. St. Tr.]
　　$8\frac{1}{4} \times 3\frac{1}{8}''$. Calf, gilt.
Preface dated January 1848.
Bod. B.M. Hull. A.R.W. (with slip).

1851

831. FREEBODY'S DIRECTORY OF KINGSTON-UPON-HULL . . . HULL : PRINTED BY J. PULLEYN, 20 SILVER STREET.
　　(adverts), 100 + vi + 440. [Gen. Tr. St.]
　　$7\frac{1}{4} \times 4\frac{1}{8}''$.
Hull.

LEEDS

1797

832. A History of . . . Leeds. Compiled from Various Authors. To which are added a History of Kirkstall Abbey & a Leeds Directory. Leeds : Printed & Sold by all the Booksellers.

190 + 34 + 64 ; adverts, 2 ; map, 2 plates. [Pr. Gen.]
5⅝ × 3¼″.

Attributed to Griffith Wright and printed by Thomas Wright, proprietors of the *Leeds Intelligencer*. The histories were also published together, without the directory and with a different title. The directory (64 pp., with title The Leeds Directory for 1797) is said to have been first published separately but, as the sale was small, to have later been sold bound up with the histories, as above.
Leeds (P.L. & U.L.).

1798

833. Re-issue of the directory section of above, with 7 altered to 8 on title and 8 to 9 in the preface, both in ink. Pp. 3–4 are new, with the mayor (John Beckett instead of Henry Hall), aldermen and council brought up to date. A few names have been added in print to the directory, *e.g.* on p. 13. This edition was reprinted in 1893, with an introduction. The statement about the change in the names of the mayor on p. iv of this introduction is a confusion, as may be seen by comparing it with the text.
Guildhall. I.H.R. Leeds. B.M. (reprint).

1800

834. A Directory for . . . Leeds . . . Leeds : Printed by Binns & Brown . . . 1800.

2 + 88. [Gen.]
5⅞ × 3⅝″. Price 1s. 6d.

John Binns and George Brown owned the *Leeds Mercury* from 1794 until 1801, when it was bought by Edward Baines.
Leeds. A.R.W.

1807

835. A New & Complete Directory for . . . Leeds . . . Leeds : Printed by George Wilson, near the Old Church. 1807.

4 + 80. [Gen.]
6¾ × 4⅛″. Boards, label. Price 1s. 6d.
Leeds.

1809

836. THE LEEDS DIRECTORY FOR 1809 . . . LEEDS : PRINTED
FOR THE COMPILER & FOR M. ROBINSON & CO. . . . COM-
MERCIAL STREET . . . [Printer, E. Baines. Leeds.]
    108 + 36 ; errata slip. [Gen. Merchants.]
    $6\frac{3}{8} \times 3\frac{1}{8}''$. Price 2s. 6d.
In the 1807 directory there is an entry for M. Robinson,
bookseller and librarian to the Old Library, Kirkgate.
Gen. Soc. Leeds. A.R.W.

1817

837. DIRECTORY, GENERAL & COMMERCIAL OF . . . LEEDS FOR
1817 . . . LEEDS : PRINTED BY EDWARD BAINES AT THE
MERCURY OFFICE.
    4 + 220 ; adds. slip opp. p. 97 ; map. [Gen. Tr. Country
manufacturers.]
    $6\frac{3}{4} \times 4\frac{1}{8}''$. Price 4s. 6d. sewed, 5s. bound.
Preface dated 1 October 1817. The first of William
Parson's Leeds directories. He is said in the preface to
have been employed on it for some months, assisted by a
resident of the town, and to have visited the houses and
all trade establishments in the town and in the villages
within the borough. The directory covers the gentry and
better class merchants and traders.
B.M. Guildhall. Halifax. Leeds (P.L. & U.L.). A.R.W.

1826

838. GENERAL & COMMERCIAL DIRECTORY OF . . . LEEDS,
INCLUDING THE OUTTOWNSHIPS . . . AND . . . PRINCIPAL
NEIGHBOURING VILLAGES . . . COMPILED UNDER THE DIREC-
TION OF WILLIAM PARSON . . . CORRECTED TO 1ST OF MAY,
1826 . . . PRINTED & PUBLISHED AT THE MERCURY OFFICE
BY EDWARD BAINES. 1826.
    4 + 280 + xcii ; plan. [Gen.; Tr. St. also for Leeds.]
    $6\frac{3}{4} + 3\frac{7}{8}''$. Boards.
Gen. Soc. (lacking pp. lxxxvii–cxii). I.H.R. Leeds (P.L.
& U.L.). Manchester. A.R.W.

839. [Another issue] . . . CORRECTED TO 1ST DECEMBER,
1826 . . .
    With pp. 281–312, more village directories, added.
    Price 7s. 6d. sheep, 8s. 6d. calf.
The heading on p. 281 refers to 'republished editions' in
which the additional villages are 'incorporated', presumably in their alphabetical order among the other villages.
No copy of such an edition has been found.
A.R.W.

1827

839a. Re-issue of the 1826 May edition, with an Appendix, 16 pp.,
dated April 1827.
Leeds.

1834

840. GENERAL & COMMERCIAL DIRECTORY OF . . . LEEDS; IN-
CLUDING THE OUT-TOWNSHIPS . . . & . . . PRINCIPAL NEIGH-
BOURING VILLAGES . . . LEEDS: BAINES & NEWSOME, 149
BRIGGATE. 1834.
> 444; adverts, 445–52; plan. [Gen. Tr; St. also for
> Leeds.]
> $7\frac{1}{8} \times 4\frac{1}{8}''$.
Published later than September 1834 (*see* p. 419).
Guildhall. I.H.R. Leeds (P.L. & U.L.).

1839

841. A GENERAL & COMMERCIAL DIRECTORY OF . . . LEEDS, IN-
CLUDING THE OUT-TOWNSHIPS & NEIGHBOURING VILLAGES
COMPILED UNDER THE SUPERINTENDENCE OF THOMAS HAIGH
. . . [imprint as above]. 1839.
> viii + 424; adverts, 28; plan. [Gen. Tr. St.]
> $7\frac{1}{8} \times 4\frac{1}{4}''$.
Thomas Haigh was a schoolmaster. He also wrote several
works on Latin grammar and two Latin dictionaries.
B.M. (10360.cc.35). Leeds (P.L. & U.L.). Manchester.
A.R.W.

1845

842. WILLIAMS'S DIRECTORY OF . . . LEEDS . . . LEEDS: PRINTED
BY EDWARD BAINES & SONS FOR J. WILLIAMS, SEN. . . . 1845.
> (adverts), 2, 84 + x + 426; plan. [Gen; Tr. St. also for
> Leeds.]
> $7 \times 4\frac{1}{4}''$. Red stamped leather.
Dedication dated 18 December 1845.
Guildhall. Leeds (P.L. & U.L.). Manchester. A.R.W.

1847

843. CHARLTON'S DIRECTORY OF . . . LEEDS. 1847. LEEDS:
PRINTED BY C. A. WILSON & CO. FOR R. J. CHARLTON &
SOLD BY THEM IN SHERWOOD'S YARD, BRIGGATE.
> (adverts), 96 + viii + 504. [Gen; St. Tr. also for Leeds.]
> $7\frac{1}{4} \times 4\frac{1}{4}''$. Leather, gilt. Price 5s., non-subsc. 6s. 6d.
Preface dated 26 April 1847.
Leeds (P.L. & U.L.).

1849

844. CHARLTON & ARCHDEACON'S DIRECTORY OF LEEDS, 1849–50.
LEEDS : PRINTED & PUBLISHED FOR THE PROPRIETORS BY
T. W. GREEN & CO, COMMERCIAL STREET . . .
(adverts), 4, 118 + x + 520. [Gen ; Tr. St. also for
Leeds.]
7 × 4".
Preface dated 29 May 1849. Re-issued in Charlton & Co.'s
directory of Huddersfield, etc. for 1850, *q.v.*
Leeds. Manchester. A.R.W.

1851

845. SLADE & .ROEBUCK'S DIRECTORY OF THE BOROUGH & NEIGH-
BOURHOOD OF LEEDS. 1851. LEEDS : WILLIAM SLADE,
JUN. 7 BOND STREET & D. I. ROEBUCK, 14 BANK STREET . . .
(adverts), 94 + vi + 556. [Gen ; St. Tr. also for Leeds.]
$7\frac{1}{8}$ × $4\frac{1}{8}$". Mauve wrappers, with contents table on first
wrapper. Price 6s., non-subsc. 7s.
Preface dated 9 June 1851.
B.M. Leeds.

MIDDLESBOROUGH

(*See* NORTHUMBERLAND, 1851.)

SADDLEWORTH

(*See* CHESHIRE, 1845, also issued in LANCASHIRE, 1845. *Also*
LANCASHIRE (Whellan), 1852, 53, 54.)

SCARBOROUGH

1846

846. A NEW GENERAL DIRECTORY OF . . . SCARBOROUGH . . .
SCARBORO' : PRINTED & PUBLISHED BY T. STORRY, RECORD
OFFICE, 49 NEWBORO' STREET & 1 WITHOUT BAR.
52 ; adverts, 20. [Misc. Tr.]
7 × $3\frac{7}{8}$". Buff wrappers.
The alphabetical list includes fishermen and boat-builders.
Dated from the name of the mayor.
Scarborough. A.R.W.

SELBY

1800

847. THE HISTORY OF SELBY . . . BY JAMES MOUNTAIN . . .
YORK : PRINTED FOR THE AUTHOR BY EDWARD PECK, LOWER
OUSEGATE. 1800.
4 + x + 162 + 2 + 40 + 24 ; plate, plan. [Gen. for Selby
& Cawood.]
$6\frac{3}{4}$ × 4".

Preface dated July 1800. James Mountain is entered as a clockmaker. He made the drawing for the frontispiece. Bod. B.M. (291.d.17). Gen. Soc. York.

SHEFFIELD

The facsimile reprint of the 1787 directory of Sheffield, edited by S. O. Addy (1889), contains an account of early Sheffield directories and of their compilers. There are copies of this reprint in the Sheffield P.L., in the Guildhall and in I.H.R. Most of the Sheffield directories have interesting reproductions of cutlers' marks.

1774

848. SKETCHLEY'S SHEFFIELD DIRECTORY; INCLUDING THE . . . VILLAGES IN THE NEIGHBOURHOOD . . . BRISTOL, PRINTED FOR THE AUTHOR & SOLD BY MR. WILKIE, ST PAULS CHURCH YARD, LONDON . . .
   iv + 12 + 108 + 2. [Tr. Cm. London merchants.]
   $5\frac{1}{2} \times 3\frac{1}{4}''$.
Dated 1774 from the names of officials. This is by Samuel Sketchley in conjunction with T. Sketchley of Hull. Both of them were auctioneers. For an account of the Sketchley family, *see* BIRMINGHAM, 1763. The editor, probably T. Sketchley, applied personally for names but was not able to include everyone. *See also* p. 8.
Sheffield.

1787

849. A DIRECTORY OF SHEFFIELD; INCLUDING THE MANUFACTURERS OF THE ADJACENT VILLAGES . . . SHEFFIELD: COMPILED & PRINTED BY GALES & MARTIN; AND SOLD BY G. G. J. & J. ROBINSON, PATERNOSTER ROW, LONDON. 1787.
   iv + 87 + 80–86 (2 pp. numbered 48 and no 79); plate. [Gen. Manufacturers.]
   $6\frac{3}{4} \times 4\frac{1}{4}''$.
Gales & Martin founded a newspaper called *The Sheffield Register*, in this same year. Joseph Gales was a printer, bookseller, auctioneer and insurance agent. He was later in danger of trial for sedition and fled to America, where he published an edition of the debates of Congress, 1789–91, in 1834 and *A Sketch of General Zachary Taylor* in 1848. David Martin was an engraver, not to be confused with David Martin, portrait painter and engraver (1763–98). He also went to America, where he died insane. (*See* Addy, *op. cit.*, and J. Holland & J. Everitt, *Memoirs of James Montgomery*, 1854.) This directory was reprinted in 1889 (*see* note at beginning of Sheffield section).
B.M. Sheffield. A.R.W.

1797

850. A DIRECTORY OF SHEFFIELD INCLUDING . . . ADJACENT
VILLAGES . . . SHEFFIELD : PRINTED BY J. MONTGOMERY, IN
THE HARTSHEAD, FOR JOHN ROBINSON, SPRING STREET. 1797.
4 + 188 ; map. [Cm. Manufacturers.]
$6\frac{7}{8} \times 4\frac{1}{4}''$.
The preface is signed John Robinson. The firm of G. G. J.
& J. Robinson of London, who were concerned in the 1787
directory, had gone bankrupt some time before this date.
John Robinson seems to have set up again in Sheffield.
James Montgomery is the well-known revolutionary poet.
He edited a paper called *The Sheffield Iris* and was twice
prosecuted for sedition. (*See* Holland & Everitt, *op. cit.*)
The account of Sheffield is by the Rev. Edward Goodwin
and is dated 21 January 1797. It also appears, with some
differences, in *The Universal British Directory*, in Part 56,
which seems to have been published during the summer
of 1796 (*see* No. 18 above). The directory of Sheffield in
this Part of *U.B.D.* has considerably fewer names than
Robinson's directory.
Bod. B.M. Sheffield.

1817

851. SHEFFIELD GENERAL DIRECTORY . . . BY W. BROWNELL
. . . PRINTED FOR THE COMPILER BY W. TODD . . . 1817.
viii + 132. [Cm. Manufacturers.]
$6\frac{7}{8} \times 4\frac{1}{4}''$.
Brownell was secretary to the Sheffield Fire Office. He says
in the preface that unavoidable delays have given precedence
to another directory (probably *The Commercial Directory
for 1816–17*, No. 30 above) which, he implies, only includes
such names as the compiler thought important, whereas he,
Brownell, believing that a guide to unimportant people is
obviously more necessary than one to the well-known, has
published a larger list of names and occupations than any
Sheffield directory has included before. This list is ' the
result of a personal attendance on all the parties contained
therein and not the copy of any other that the regulations
of the town may require '. He has refused to insert copper-
plate cards or other devices, as appearing to favour certain
tradesmen against others, and has rejected a brief history
as irrelevant to the purposes of a directory.
B.M. Guildhall. Sheffield.

1821

852. SHEFFIELD GENERAL & COMMERCIAL DIRECTORY . . . COM-
PILED BY R. GELL & R. BENNETT. SHEFFIELD. PRINTED
AT THE INDEPENDENT OFFICE BY H. A. BACON . . . 1821.
4 + 176. [Gen. Tr.]
$7\frac{1}{2} \times 4\frac{1}{4}''$. Blue boards. Price 4s. 6d.

Gell had collaborated with T. Bradshaw in a directory of
Gloucestershire the year before.
Sheffield.

1825

853. A New General & Commercial Directory of Sheffield
& its Vicinity . . . Compiled by R. Gell. Manchester :
Printed at the Albion Press by D. Varey . . . June,
1825.
    214 ; adverts interspersed. [Gen ; Tr. also for Sheffield.]
    6¾ × 3⅞″. Price 4s.
Guildhall. Sheffield. A.R.W.

1828

854. The Sheffield Directory & Guide . . . Sheffield :
Printed & Published by John Blackwell, Iris Office,
High Street. 1828.
    lxxxii + 204 ; adverts interspersed. [Gen ; Tr. also for
Sheffield.]
    7 × 4¼″.
B.M. (lacks 67–74). Sheffield. A.R.W.

1833

855. History & General Directory of . . . Sheffield . . .
and all the Villages . . . within . . . Ten Miles . . .
by William White . . . Sheffield : Printed by Robert
Leader, Independent Office . . . 1833.
    2 + xii + 431 ; adverts, 21. [Tr. with Gen. for Sheffield &
Misc. for villages.]
    7 × 3⅝″. Price, subsc. 5s. 6d. sheep, 6s. 6d. calf, map 1s.
Preface dated 8 April 1833. Pp. 1–144 (the history without
the directories) were also published separately, with the
same preface and title, *History, Guide & Description of
. . . Sheffield* (1833).
Guildhall. Halifax. Sheffield. A.R.W.

1837. *See* Yorkshire, 1837–38.
1839. *See* Birmingham (Robson), 1839.

1841

856. White's General Directory of . . . Sheffield, with
Rotherham & [places within 6 miles] . . . Sheffield :
Printed by Robert Leader . . . for William White
. . . 1841.
    vi + 372 ; adverts, 20 ; adds. slip ; plan. [Gen. St. Tr.
for Sheffield ; Misc. Tr. for other places.]
    7 × 3⅝″. Price, subsc. with plan, 5s. 6d.
With adds. up to June 1841. Includes some places in
Derbyshire.
Guildhall. Sheffield. A.R.W.

857. The Sheffield & Rotherham Directory . . . by Henry A. & Thomas Rogers. Sheffield : Printed . . . by J. H. Greaves, Angel Street. 1841.
> 296 ; adverts, 24, 6. [Gen. with Tr. for Rotherham, St. Tr. for Sheffield.]
>> 7¼ × 4½".
>
> H. & T. Rogers were collectors of rents and debts and insurance agents.
Gen. Soc. Sheffield. A.R.W.

1845

858. General Directory of . . . Sheffield, with Rotherham, Chesterfield [and places within 12 miles] . . . by William White . . . Printed by Robert Leader . . . 1845.
> 408 ; adverts, 72. [Tr. with Gen. for Sheffield, Misc. for other places.]
>> 7 × 4¼". Black calf. Price 5s. 6d., non-subsc. 6s. 6d., map 1s.
B.M. Guildhall. Sheffield. A.R.W.

1849

859. [Title as 1845.] 1849.
> 404 + 501–544 ; adverts, 544–8, 100 ; plate. [Tr. etc. as above ; St. also for Sheffield.]
>> 7⅛ × 4¼". Red calf. Price, subsc. 6s. 6d. bound, map & plan 1s. each.
>
> Note on p. 6 dated 10 July 1849. Pp. 501–48 (containing the Sheffield street directory) are printed by W. Ford, York Street. All copies seen have the gap in pagination.
Guildhall. Sheffield. A.R.W.

1852. *See* Yorkshire, 1852.

1854

860. Post Office Directory of Sheffield with the Neighbouring Towns & Villages. London : Printed & Published by Kelly & Co . . . Old Boswell Court, Temple Bar. 1854.
> viii + 205 ; adverts, 206–48. [Ct. Cm ; St. also for Sheffield and Tr. for whole district.]
>> 10 × 6½". Red cloth. Price 7s. 6d.
>
> Preface dated August 1854.
B.M. Sheffield.

TODMORDEN

(*See* Lancashire, 1845 and (Whellan), 1852, 53, 54.)

YARM

(*See* NORTHUMBERLAND, 1851, 1855.)

YORK

1787

861. THE YORK GUIDE . . . TO WHICH IS ADDED AN ALPHABETICAL
DIRECTORY . . . YORK. PRINTED & SOLD BY A. WARD . . .
1787.
    4 + 32 + 2 + 33–54 ; plan, 3 plates. [Cm.]
    $7\frac{1}{4} \times 4\frac{1}{4}''$. Price 1s. 6d.
Bod. (2 copies, one impf). Chetham. York.

1843

862. CITY OF YORK DIRECTORY . . . ALSO INCLUDING VILLAGES
. . . HULL : PRINTED BY W. H. SMITH, 203 QUEEN STREET.
1843.
    4 + 9–148 ; adverts, 70. [Ct. Gen. Tr.]
    $6\frac{3}{4} \times 4\frac{1}{8}''$. Cloth or leather.
The preface is in the name of Messrs. Williams & Co, whose
name also appears on the leather binding.
A.R.W.

WELSH DIRECTORIES

1848–1850

E. Hunt & Co.'s directories of places in South Wales and Monmouthshire are divided into three groups which were issued and reissued in various combinations with various parts of their Bristol and Gloucester directories. The three groups are as follows : *A*, Towns in Monmouthshire and Glamorgan, 180 pp. *B*, Towns mostly in Monmouthshire, Cardiganshire and Brecon, with Gloucester, 164 pp. *C*, Cardigan and towns mostly in Carmarthenshire and Pembrokeshire, 168 pp. These groups are not easily identified from the title pages, on which the towns named for each group vary in different issues. The number of slightly different combinations of these groups with various parts of other Hunt directories is considerable and there are evidently some of which no copy has been found, so it has seemed less confusing to give a list of copies examined, with an indication of their contents, than to attempt a detailed description of each issue, which would probably not correspond with other copies which may be in existence but which have not been located.

In the following list the groups of Welsh towns are indicated by *A*, *B*, or *C*, as above. *A* was first published in 1848, the other two in 1849. The Bristol directories are extracts from Hunt's *Bristol*, 1848, with some additions in 1850. There was probably an edition for Bristol alone in 1850 but no copy has been traced.

863. HUNT & CO.'S . . . BRISTOL, NEWPORT & WELCH TOWNS DIRECTORY . . . JANUARY, 1848, PRINTED FOR E. HUNT & CO. BY B. W. GARDINER . . . LONDON. Parts of Bristol, 1848 + *A*, 180 pp.
Cardiff. Newport. A.R.W.

March 1849 *see* GLOUCESTERSHIRE, 1849.

864. HUNT & CO.'S DIRECTORY & TOPOGRAPHY FOR GLOUCESTER & BRISTOL [& Welsh towns]. JUNE, 1849. *B*, 164 pp. + *A*, 180 pp. + parts of Bristol, 1848.
Newport. N.L.W.

865. [As above, with other Welsh towns] JULY, 1849. Parts of Gloucester, 1849 & of Bristol, 1848 + *C*, 168 pp. + *A*, 180 pp.
Bangor. Guildhall.

866. . . . FOR CARDIGAN [etc.] AND BRISTOL . . . 1850. *C*, 168 pp. + Bristol (Ct. Cm.).
N.L.W.

867. [As above for] BRISTOL . . . AXBRIDGE [with other towns in Somerset and towns in Wales]. 1850. Preface dated January 1850. Bristol, 1848 with additions, including a street directory + towns in Somerset as in No. 622 + C, 168 pp.
Bristol. N.L.W.

1852. *See* BRISTOL, 1852.

There are no separate county directories for Wales and the towns below are arranged in alphabetical order irrespective of their county.

ABERYSTWITH

1816

868. THE ABERYSTWITH GUIDE . . . ABERYSTWITH, PRINTED BY SAMUEL WILLIAMS IN BRIDGE STREET. 1816.
2 + v–viii + 130. [Gen.]
$6\frac{1}{8} \times 3\frac{5}{8}''$. Stiff printed wrappers. Price 3s.
Samuel Williams was an elder of the Calvinist-Methodist church. He would only print what he thought religious or edifying. (*See* I. Jones, *History of Printing in Wales* (1925), pp. 202–4.)
Bod. B.M. (10369.aaa.24).

CARDIFF

1796

869. A COMPLETE DIRECTORY & GUIDE TO . . . CARDIFF . . . PRINTED FOR & SOLD BY J. BIRD, ADJOINING THE CASTLE GATE. CARDIFF. 1796.
2 + 24. [Ct. Cm.] ·
$6\frac{1}{4} \times 3\frac{3}{4}''$.
John Bird set up a printing press in Cardiff in 1791. In 1792 he supplied information about Cardiff and Caerphilly to John Wilkes, the editor of *The Universal British Directory* and it seems probable that, like other assistants of Wilkes, he was supplied with an offprint of the Cardiff section of the *U.B.D.* for publication under his own name, but if so, no copy has survived. The contents of his 1796 directory were used, with slight omissions and re-arrangements, for the second edition of Vol. II of the *U.B.D.* (No. 14). He became alderman and bailiff of Cardiff and in 1802 he was appointed postmaster, which position he held till his death in 1840. Other members of his family were also printers in Cardiff. (*See* Jones, *op. cit.*, pp. 92 ff.)
Cardiff.

1813

870. A COMPLETE DIRECTORY & GUIDE TO . . . CARDIFF &
CAERPHILLY . . . CARDIFF : PRINTED & SOLD BY THOMAS
RIDD, HIGH STREET . . . 1813.
  40 pp. [Ct. Pr. Cm. for Cardiff ; Gen. for Caerphilly.]
  $6\frac{5}{8} \times 4''$.
Cardiff.

1829

871. THE CARDIFF GUIDE & DIRECTORY . . . CARDIFF : PRINTED
BY AND FOR W. BIRD . . . 1829.
  2 + 80 ; 2 plates. [Ct. Pr. Cm. for Cardiff & Llandaff ;
  Gen. for Caerphilly.]
  $8\frac{1}{2} \times 5\frac{1}{8}''$. Stiff wrappers, label. Price 2s.
William Bird was John Bird's nephew and his assistant at
the post office, where he also had a printing press. (*See*
Jones, *loc. cit.*)
Cardiff.

1855

872. EWEN'S GUIDE & DIRECTORY FOR . . . CARDIFF . . . FOR
. . . 1855. COMPILED BY JAMES EWEN . . . & PUBLISHED
BY HIM AT 65 UNION STREET, CARDIFF . . . PRINTED BY
W. JONES, DUKE STREET.
  iv + 194 ; adverts, 30. [St. Gen. Tr. for Cardiff ; Gen. for
  Llandaff & suburbs.]
  $4\frac{3}{4} \times 2\frac{3}{4}''$. Blue cloth.
Preface dated 6 January 1855. Ewen was an accountant
and insurance agent. A note at the head of the contents
table says that John Street is omitted from its proper place
and inserted on p. 81 in a few copies.
Cardiff (with John St. on p. 81).

873. WAKEFORD'S CARDIFF DIRECTORY . . . EMBRACING LLANDAFF
[etc] . . . CARDIFF : PRINTED & PUBLISHED BY CHARLES
WAKEFORD . . . 1855.
  x + 3*–25* + 3–92 ; adverts 93–4, 40. [Gen. St. Tr.]
  $7 \times 4\frac{1}{4}''$. Purple cloth.
Preface dated 31 January 1855. The directory contains
chiefly business information. A complete list of householders was not attempted.
Bod. Cardiff. A.R.W.

LLANIDLOES

(*See* LEAMINGTON 1846.)

NEWTOWN

(*See* LEAMINGTON 1846.)

SWANSEA

1802

874. THE SWANSEA GUIDE . . . SWANSEA : PRINTED BY Z. B.
MORRIS & SOLD AT OAKEY'S & EVANS'S LIBRARIES.   1802.
4 + 198 ;   plate.   [Pr. Cm.]
 5½ × 3⅜".
Zecharias Bevan Morris was sent to prison in 1806 for
stealing thirty reams of paper.   He afterwards moved to
Carmarthen.   (*See* Jones *op. cit.*, p. 151.)
Bod.   Cardiff.

1830

875. MATHEWS'S SWANSEA DIRECTORY FOR . . . 1830 . . . SWAN-
SEA : PRINTED & SOLD BY THE EDITOR, M. MATHEWS, 71
HIGH STREET . . . 1830.
72 pp.   [Pr. Gen.]
 7⅛ × 4¼".   Yellow printed wrappers.   Price 1s. 6d.
A.R.W.

WELSHPOOL

(*See* LEAMINGTON, 1846.)

WREXHAM

(*See* CHESHIRE, 1789, 1846 (also printed in LEAMINGTON, 1846).)

ADDENDA

1805

876. THE BRIGHTON & LEWES GUIDE . . . BY J. V. BUTTON OF
THE CLASSICAL & COMMERCIAL ACADEMY, LEWES . . . LEWES:
PRINTED & PUBLISHED BY J. BAXTER . . . & CROSBY & CO.
. . . LONDON. 1805.
   vi + 80 ; 3 plates, map. [St. Pr for Brighton and Lewes.]
      $6\frac{1}{2} \times 4''$.
   B.M. (10351.c.47/1).

c. 1845

877. W. H. MASON'S FASHIONABLE HANDBOOK FOR VISITORS TO
BRIGHTON . . . SECOND EDITION. PUBLISHED BY W. H.
MASON . . . 81 KING'S ROAD, BRIGHTON : AND E. BURN
. . . 23 NORTH STREET. [Printer, B. Clarke, Silver Street,
London.]
   ii + ii + 74 ; 6 plates. [Tr.]
      $6\frac{1}{2} \times 4''$. Stiff printed wrappers.
   N.d. but c. 1845. The first edition (no copy found) also
   probably contains a directory.
   B.M. (2 copies, 10351.c.47/6, 10358.aa.35/4).

ROSS

c. 1825

878. COMPANION TO THE WYE TOUR. ARICONENSIA OR ARCHAE-
LOGICAL SKETCHES OF ROSS . . . SECOND EDITION. BY
THOMAS DUDLEY FOSBROKE . . . ROSS : PRINTED BY & FOR
W. FARROR, SOLD BY . . . T. FARROR, MONMOUTH.
   x + 196 ; plate. [Pr. Tr.]
   N.d. but later than the 1821 census. The directory was
   no doubt added by Farror. Fosbroke was vicar of Walford,
   Herefordshire, and a distinguished antiquary.
   Guildhall.

INDEX OF AUTHORS, PUBLISHERS AND PRINTERS

This index shows the connection between the persons named and the directories for which they were variously responsible. Reference should also be made to the General Index for other information about them, which occurs in divers places about the book. Names marked * are those of people whose only connection with a directory appears to be that of having printed it for someone else. When a person has been concerned with directories both as a publisher and also only as a printer, as, for instance, Edward Baines, the directories with which they are only connected in the latter capacity are marked *.

*Adams, Jun.	Leicester, 1794
Adams, O.	*See* Sketchley, J. & Adams
*Adlard & Palmer	Norwich, 1852
*Akenhead, D.	Newcastle-on-Tyne, 1790
Allbut, J. & Son	Staffordshire, 1802
Allbut, T.	Staffordshire, 1822
Alsop, Wm.	Southport, 1832
*Andrews, J.	National, 1784 (No. 3)
*Angus, M.	Newcastle-on-Tyne, 1795
*Angus, Thos.	Newcastle-on-Tyne, 1778, 1787
Archdeacon, Wm.	Surrey, 1851. *See also* Charlton, R. J. & Archdeacon
*Ashton, Wm.	National, 1781 (No. 1)

*Bacon, H. A.	Sheffield, 1821
*Bacon, R. M.	Norwich, 1803
Bagshaw, Samuel	Derbyshire, 1846; Kent, 1847; Cheshire, 1850; Shropshire, 1851
Bailey, Wm.	National, 1781, 1783, 1784, 1785, 1787 (Nos. 1–5); Bristol, 1787; Liverpool, 1787
*Bailey, Wm. & Thomson, Henry	Lancashire, 1854
Baily & Jones	Cirencester, 1847
Baines, Edward	Yorkshire, 1822; Lancashire, 1824; *Leeds, 1809, 1817, 1826, 1827; *Hull, 1826; *Lincolnshire, 1826; *Durhamshire, 1827; *Cumberland, 1829; *Yorkshire, 1830
Baines, Ed. & Newsome	Leeds, 1834, 1839
*Baines, Ed. & Sons	Leeds, 1845.
Baker	*See* Victor & Baker
Baker, J.	Kent, 1807
Baldwin & Cradock	West Bromwich, 1836
Baldwin, R.	Manchester, 1772
Balshaw, Chas.	Altrincham, 1855
Bancks, Gerard	Manchester, 1800, 1802
*Barbet, S.	Channel Isles, 1833
Barfoot, Peter & Wilkes, John	National, 1790–8 (Nos. 8–19)
*Barling	*See* Benson & Barling
Bathew, Thos.	Derby, 1823
*Battenbury, L. E. G.	Plymouth, 1847
Battle, Robert G.	Hull, 1791, 1792, 1803, 1806, 1810, 1814, 1818, 1821

GENERAL INDEX

For references to individuals, this index supplements the *Index of Authors, Publishers and Printers*, which should be consulted also. It should be remembered that, as well as under the main headings given below, any county or town may be included in the national directories, pp. 30–67, and any town in the county directories. For these, the notes on classification and cross-references on pp. 27–8 should be consulted. The figures in this index are those of the pages on which the reference will be found.

Aberystwith, directory of, 223
Abingdon, directory of, 160
Advertising, 1–4, 13, 189
Allen, Ralph, 6
Altrincham, directory of, 73
Amsterdam, directories of, 4
Archdeacon, Wm., 17
Ashton-under-Lyne, directory of, 72

Bailey, Wm., 6, 8, 30
Baines, Ed., 14, 65, 66
Banbury, directories of, 22, 160, 161
Barfoot, Peter, 32, 33
Bath, directories of, 13, 21, 164–8, 196
Battle, R. G., 8
Bedfordshire, directory of, 68
Berkshire, directories of, 68, 69
Berwick-on-Tweed, directories of, 15, 88, 153
Beverley, *see under* Hull directories
Bingham, directory of, 157
Bird, John, 34
Birkenhead, directories of, 73
Birmingham, directories of, 5, 7, 13, 182–92
Blackburn, directories of, 117, 121, 170
Blackpool, directory of, 141
Blégny, N., 2
Bolton, directories of, 118, 121
Bowtell & Co., 59
Boyle's *Court Guide*, 11
Bradford, directories of, 267, 268
Bradshaw, George, 66, 134
Bradshaw, Thos., 65, 66
Brampton, directory of, 78
Brighton, directories of, 176–9, 226
Bristol, directories of, 91–7
Bromley, directory of, 114
Buckinghamshire, directories of, 70
Burton-on-Trent, directories of, 80
Bury, directory of, 121
Buxton, directory of, 80

Caerphilly, directory of, 224
Cambridge, directories of, 17, 106
Cambridgeshire, directory of, 70
Cardiff, directories of, 223, 224
Carlisle, directories of, 78, 79, 152
Cartmel, directory of, 77
Cassey, 23
Champante & Whitrow, 33, 34, 92, 164
Channel Islands, directories of, 102, 106–8
Chatham, directories of, 114, 116
Cheltenham, directories of, 97–101
Cheshire, directories of, 71–3, 120
Chester, directories of, 73–5
Chichester, directory of, 179
Chorley, directories of, 122, 140–1
Cirencester, directory of, 101
Commercial travelling, 9
Cope, Sir Walter, 3
Cornwall, directories of, 75, 76
Cottle, Joseph, 92
Cottrill, Isaac, 14
Coventry, directory of, 192
Cricklade, directory of, 101
Critchett, B., 12
Croydon, directories of, 174, 175
Cumberland, directories of, 76, 77

Deal, directory of, 115
Defoe, Daniel, 6, 7
Derby, directories of, 80, 81
Derbyshire, directories of, 79, 80
Devonshire, directories of, 81, 82
Dewsbury, directory of, 209
Dorking, directory of, 175
Dorsetshire, directories of, 87
Dover, directory of, 115
Drake, E. S., 23, 67
Dublin, directories of, 5, 12, 129
Durham, directories of, 89
Durham County, directories of, 88, 151, 152

239